POETRY FM

CONTEMPORARY
NORTH AMERICAN POETRY
SERIES
Alan Golding, Lynn Keller,
and *Adalaide Morris,*
series editors

POETRY FM

American Poetry and Radio Counterculture

LISA HOLLENBACH

UNIVERSITY OF IOWA PRESS, IOWA CITY

University of Iowa Press, Iowa City 52242
Copyright © 2023 by the University of Iowa Press
uipress.uiowa.edu
Printed in the United States of America

Text design by Richard Hendel

No part of this book may be reproduced or used in any form
or by any means without permission in writing from the publisher.
All reasonable steps have been taken to contact copyright holders of material
used in this book. The publisher would be pleased to make suitable
arrangements with any whom it has not been possible to reach.

Printed on acid-free paper

Quoted excerpts from *The Heads of the Town Up to the Aether*,
The Holy Grail, and *Language* from *My Vocabulary Did This to Me:
The Collected Poetry of Jack Spicer* © 2008 by the Estate of Jack Spicer.
Published by Wesleyan University Press. Used by permission.

A previous version of chapter 3 first appeared in
Modernism/Modernity Print Plus, Volume 3, Cycle 2, July 12, 2018.
Copyright © 2018 The Johns Hopkins University Press.

Library of Congress Cataloging-in-Publication Data
Names: Hollenbach, Lisa, author.
Title: Poetry FM: American Poetry and Radio
Counterculture / by Lisa Hollenbach.
Description: Iowa City: University of Iowa Press, 2023. |
Series: Contemporary North American Poetry Series |
Includes bibliographical references and index.
Identifiers: LCCN 2022040207 (print) | LCCN 2022040208 (ebook) |
ISBN 9781609388911 (paperback) | ISBN 9781609388928 (ebook)
Subjects: LCSH: Radio and literature—United States—History—20th century. |
American poetry—20th century—History and criticism. | Pacifica
Radio—History. | KPFA (Radio station: Berkeley, Calif.)—History. | WBAI
(Radio station: New York, N.Y.)—History. | Radio programs—United States—
20th century. | Counterculture—United States—History—20th century.
Classification: LCC PN1991.8.P6 H65 2023 (print) |
LCC PN1991.8.P6 (ebook) | DDC 791.440973—dc23/eng/20221114
LC record available at https://lccn.loc.gov/2022040207
LC ebook record available at https://lccn.loc.gov/2022040208

CONTENTS

Acknowledgments *vii*

Abbreviations *xi*

INTRODUCTION
American Poetry and the FM Revolution *1*

CHAPTER 1
Poets and Pacifists: The Origins of Pacifica Radio *26*

CHAPTER 2
KPFA and the San Francisco Renaissance *57*

CHAPTER 3
"The Poet Is a Counterpunching Radio" *89*

CHAPTER 4
WBAI and the Lower East Side Scene *123*

CHAPTER 5
The Poetics of Feminist Radio *155*

Notes *189*

Bibliography *225*

Index *243*

ACKNOWLEDGMENTS

I would not have been able to write this book without the support of many mentors, colleagues, students, interlocutors, friends, and family members, or without continuous sources of institutional support and funding. There are many to whom I owe a debt of gratitude, and those I acknowledge here can only be a partial accounting.

I am especially grateful to Lynn Keller, who has seen this project from conception to completion, and whose encouragement as an advisor, editor, and friend has been of incalculable value to me. The rest of my PhD advisory committee at the University of Wisconsin–Madison—Russ Castronovo, Michele Hilmes, Cherene Sherrard-Johnson, and Timothy Yu—offered crucial guidance for the dissertation out of which this book grew and various forms of support in subsequent years. Thanks to the following friends and writing group colleagues who generously read and provided feedback on chapter drafts: Andrew Belton, Cailey Hall, Katherine Hallemeier, Rafael Hernandez, Alyssa Hunziker, Jeff Menne, Sandy Peterson, Chelsea Silva, Rebecca Couch Steffy, Graig Uhlin, and Lindsay Wilhelm. My writing coach and friend, Michelle Niemann, deserves special mention; her expertise, feedback, and conversation informed much of this book and was a lifeline for me during the most isolating years of the pandemic. Others who contributed in various ways to my thinking and writing of this project include Mathieu Aubin, Dominique Bourg Hacker, Leslie Bow, Joel Calahan, Jamie Christopher Callison, Julie Cyzewski, Julia Dauer, Michael Davidson, Steve Evans, Harris Feinsod, Jonathan Gaboury, Edgar Garcia, Grant Jenkins, Damien Keane, Whitney Kerutis, Kimberly Lamm, Emily Madsen, Timothy Murphy, Chris Mustazza, Andrew Rippeon, Susan Rosenbaum, Karis Shearer, Jennifer Lynn Stoever, Jessica Teague, Lauren Tilton, Martin Wallen, and Shilyh Warren.

The research for this book draws extensively from archival sources, and I would not have been able to access them without the help of many library professionals or funding support. I am especially grateful to current and former staff at the Pacifica Radio Archives who gave generously of their time, their office space, their resources, and their knowledge during and after my research visit, including Brian DeShazor, Mark Torres, Jolene Beiser, Shawn Dellis, Joseph Gallucci, Holly Rose McGee, and Edgar Toledo. In addition, the following librarians, archivists, and curators helped me to access collections related to this project: Lynda Claassen and Rob Melton at the Archive for New Poetry at the University of California, San Diego; Amy Wong and Cesar Reyes at the Charles E. Young Research Library at the University of California, Los Angeles (UCLA); Steve Dickison at The Poetry Center and American Poetry Archives at San Francisco State University; Tamara Jones at the Ward M. Canaday Center for Special Collections at the University of Toledo; Susan Barribeau at the University of Wisconsin–Madison Libraries; and various staff members at the Bancroft Library of the University of California, Berkeley, and at the Beinecke Library at Yale University, the William Andrews Clark Memorial Library at UCLA, the Columbia University Rare Book & Manuscript Library, the George Washington University Special Collections, the Special Collections in Mass Media and Culture at the University of Maryland Libraries in College Park, and the Wisconsin Historical Society Archives. Thanks also to the Silberman family (George, Cathy, Reuvie, Haniya, Reuben, and Laura) for their generous hospitality during one of my research trips.

I was able to visit many of these collections thanks to a 2013 to 2014 Mellon Fellowship for Dissertation Research in Original Sources from the Council on Library and Information Resources, which made it possible for me to devote a full year to archival research at a crucial early stage in this project. Additional research travel and financial support was provided by the College of Arts and Sciences and the Department of English at Oklahoma State University. The completion of my dissertation was supported by a Mellon-Wisconsin Summer Dissertation Fellowship and UW–Madison Chancellor's Dissertation fellowship.

I am fortunate to have had the opportunity to present parts of this book at conferences and institutes, including the American Comparative Literature Association Annual Meeting, the Futures of American Studies Institute, the Louisville Conference on Literature and Culture since 1900, and the Modern Language Association Annual Convention. The conversations generated by a seminar that Jamie Christopher Callison and I organized on the topic "Listening to the Modernist Audio Archive" for the 2019 Modernist Studies Association Conference especially informed my thinking about digital audio archives. Part of chapter 3 was previously published as "Broadcasting 'Howl'" by *Modernism/Modernity Print Plus* in 2018, and I am grateful to Debra Rae Cohen and the anonymous readers for their generous feedback and for the opportunity to publish a multimedia version of this article. An earlier version of part of chapter 5 is forthcoming as a chapter titled "In the Air: Broadcasting the Poetry of the U.S. Women's Liberation Movement" in *The Oxford Handbook of Radio Studies*, edited by Michele Hilmes and Andrew J. Bottomley.

My interests in post-1945 poetry have been deeply informed by the Contemporary North American Poetry series, and I am humbled to be included as an author in this series alongside so many scholars whose work I admire. Thank you to the series editors Dee Morris, Alan Golding, and Lynn Keller for continuous support and guidance, and to Debra Rae Cohen and the anonymous reader for offering such generous and generative feedback on the manuscript. It is an honor to have one's work read with such attention and care. At the University of Iowa Press, I am grateful to Meredith Stabel for helping to steer this book to publication; thanks also to Karin Horler for her editorial acumen and Sarah Osment for creating the index.

Finally, my family has given me a foundation of love and support for which I am ever grateful; thank you to my parents, Cindy Hollenbach and Mike Hollenbach, my brothers Andrew Hollenbach and Spencer Hollenbach, my sister-in-law Molly Rooney, and my parents-in-law Laurence and Nanette Freedman. To Lewis Freedman, my life and my love, "for every page he reads there is a ghostly page [he] recovers from his own life."[1]

ABBREVIATIONS

AWMHC
American Women Making History and Culture: 1963–1982 Collection, Pacifica Radio Archives and the Internet Archive

BA
Paul Blackburn Audio Collection, Archive for New Poetry, University of California, San Diego

BP
Paul Blackburn Papers, Archive for New Poetry, University of California, San Diego

MV
Jack Spicer, *My Vocabulary Did This to Me: The Collected Poetry of Jack Spicer*

PF
Pacifica Radio Archives Digitized Folio Collection, Internet Archive

PM
Pacifica Foundation Records, National Public Broadcasting Archives, University of Maryland Libraries, College Park

PRA
Pacifica Radio Archives, North Hollywood, California

PW
Pacifica Foundation Records, Wisconsin Historical Society Archives, Madison

RC
Kenneth Rexroth Papers, Charles E. Young Research Library, University of California, Los Angeles

UC
Untide Press Records, Bancroft Library, University of California, Berkeley

INTRODUCTION
AMERICAN POETRY AND THE FM REVOLUTION

On a warm, sunny Saturday in Berkeley, California, in May 1977, an audience of nearly 4,000 gathered at the open-air Greek Theatre on the University of California campus for a poetry festival. The event was billed as a fundraiser for local public radio station KPFA-FM, which had promoted it as a celebration "of three generations of Bay Area poets, both men and women, of diverse lives and cultures" who would gather for "the biggest poetry reading staged in the Bay Area since the Vietnam era, and perhaps the biggest ever."[1] As the crowd filed into the amphitheater, Allen Ginsberg took the stage with Peter Orlovsky and Robert Bly to lead a collective chant of the mantra *ah*—to purify speech, Ginsberg explained, before guiding the audience in a collective meditation exercise. After attuning the audience's speech, bodies, minds, and senses, Ginsberg ceded the microphone to KPFA station manager Jo Anne Wallace and master of ceremonies Fred Cody of Cody's Books, who officially kicked off the day of poetry, music, and protest.[2] In addition to Ginsberg, Orlovsky, and Bly, the festival lineup included Alta, Victor Hernández Cruz, Ed Dorn, Jessica Hagedorn, Jana Harris, Bobbie Louise Hawkins, David Henderson, Joanne Kyger, Lewis MacAdams, Michael McClure, Simon J. Ortiz, Ishmael Reed, and Alan Soldofsky.

Through hours of performances, the KPFA Poetry Festival celebrated the San Francisco Bay Area's reputation as a countercultural center for an oral, public, and politically committed poetry. Ginsberg, whose "long awaited return ... to Berkeley" headlined publicity for the event, presided as the festival's queer patriarch in a snow-white suit, his appearance positing a historical continuity between the day's performers and the San Francisco Renaissance of the 1950s and 1960s.[3] Several of the poets incorporated music or song into their performances, like Jessica Hagedorn, who performed with her backup band the West Coast Gangster Choir. Several others employed theatrical or dramatic elements, like Bly, who donned masks and mingled with the crowd. And many of the poets read political and protest poetry, like the explicitly feminist poems read by Hagedorn, Jana Harris, and Alta, which garnered enthusiastic applause and cheers from the audience. Collectively, the festival performances communicated a commitment to live public performance as a privileged if not primary medium for poetry and a belief that the transmission of a poem from the present, embodied voice of the poet to the equally present, embodied ears of a receptive audience carried the potential for a transformative communal experience. Lending a classical gravitas to it all was the University of California's Greek Theatre—the symbolism of its imposing stone structure appearing as a motif in an independent film documentary that was made of the event, *Festival of Bards*, which captured some of the day's dynamic performances as well as scenes of its youthful audience lounging on the stone benches, on each other, and in the sun-soaked grass.[4]

KPFA also recorded the readings for radio broadcast, giving over four hours of its program schedule later that summer to airing the festival's celebration of contemporary West Coast poetry in performance. Indeed, KPFA, as it accurately noted in its promotion of the festival, had "long been an important medium for the presentation of the works of contemporary poets."[5] Established in Berkeley in 1949, KPFA was the inaugural station of the Pacifica Radio network—the first listener-supported noncommercial radio broadcaster in the United States—and its founders, a group of Bay Area war resisters, radio professionals, and poets led by the pacifist Lewis Hill, envisioned the broadcasting of poetry as central to their experiment in independent FM radio, making poetry a cornerstone of KPFA's programming from the beginning. When Pacifica Radio expanded in the 1960s and 1970s, acquiring independently operated stations in Los Angeles (KPFK), New York (WBAI), Houston (KPFT), and Washington, DC (WPFW), KPFA provided the blueprint through which each of these stations made contemporary poetry part of their programming, contributing in turn to the oral emphasis of post-1945 American poetry and the alternative sound of early FM radio.

KPFA's role in the 1977 festival thus amounted to more than a co-organizer, beneficiary, and broadcaster. Over nearly three decades, the station had played an instrumental role in cultivating the festival's nexus of Bay Area poetry, spoken word performance, liberation politics, university culture, and alternative media. The flow of influence between Pacifica Radio and the San Francisco poetry community also moved both ways, to the extent that the influential public broadcasting institution could be considered part of the legacy of the San Francisco Renaissance. By the late 1970s, KPFA was deeply embedded in the Bay Area literary community, and nearly all of the writers who performed at the KPFA Poetry Festival had previously appeared on the local public radio station's airwaves for readings and interviews; a few, including David Henderson and Ishmael Reed, had even produced programming for KPFA or hosted their own radio shows—as many poets, from Jack Spicer to Kenneth Rexroth to Susan Howe to Lorenzo Thomas, had at KPFA and other Pacifica stations.[6]

This book is about the public radio institution at the center of this scene of embodied poetic performance, literary community, and left politics. By this, I mean that it is about Pacifica Radio: about how Pacifica Radio became one of the most significant yet least acknowledged outlets for and archives of contemporary poetry performance, and about how poets, in turn, influenced the aesthetics and countercultural ethos of one of the most influential public broadcasting networks in the United States. More generally, though, this is a book about how the once-dominant mass medium of radio became an underground medium for and complex figure in post-1945 American poetry. Contrary to dominant narratives about the death of radio in the television age, I argue that the transformation of the U.S. broadcasting industry after World War II (WWII) opened a window of opportunity for experimentation on the FM band that poets seized, reconfiguring the relationship between poetry and radio, and reimagining their respective and overlapping publics.

That poets would turn to radio as a medium for the spoken word in the post-WWII decades makes a certain kind of intuitive sense, given the revitalization of oral poetics in experimental American poetry of this period. In 1960, the publication of Donald Allen's canonizing anthology *The New American Poetry, 1945–1960* announced a new avant-garde in American poetry that was defined by the embrace of oral and speech-based poetics, open forms, and romantic ideals of immanence and spontaneity among poets who rejected Eliotic modernism and the New Critical academic establishment as well as the quietism of postwar American consumer and political culture. The oral emphasis of the "new" poetry was in many ways print-mediated, at least initially, but it also gave rise to the cultural phenomenon of the public poetry reading. Though popular poet-performers like Langston Hughes and Carl Sandburg had commanded large audiences on the U.S. lecture circuit long before the Beats made reading poetry in public hip, the poetry readings of the post-WWII era created new social, institutional, and political contexts for poetry that were often embedded in local avant-garde arts communities, publicized through alternative media, and, especially in the 1960s, linked to New Left protest movements. As Raphael Allison writes in his study of "the sixties poetry reading," these readings contributed to a counterculture "deeply invested in . . . the authenticity that a live voice produced," called up in the iconic figures of "a radical protestor declaiming a university administration, a civil rights leader addressing massive crowds, a lone singer with a guitar."[7]

The affective and political power attributed to the authenticity of the live voice within the sixties' counterculture was accompanied by a similar investment in the authenticity of the listening experience, or the belief that listening constituted a more richly sensorial, participatory, intersubjective, and democratic mode of public engagement in contrast with the co-opted visual regimes of commercial television and print. While the aurality of the counterculture was especially invested in collective experiences of public listening manifest at protests, political assemblies, concerts, festivals, and poetry readings, the participatory meaning ascribed to listening could also carry over to more obviously technologically mediated experiences of listening to recorded and broadcast sound. As Robert Cantwell argues of the sixties folk revival, the counterculture's "real milieu was extra- or subtelevisual," projecting a rich "aural imagination" against the "spectocracy" of postwar culture.[8] In poetry, poets' experimentation with new postwar sound technologies like the tape recorder and the 33⅓ long-playing (LP) record helped to create what Michael Davidson identifies as "the tapevoice of contemporary poetics": a poetic voice not only disseminated in auditory media but fully embedded in—and ambivalent about—the technological mediation of presence.[9]

Radio was also essential to the "aural imagination" of sixties culture, including, as we will see, sixties poetry. Yet, while literary scholars have been keenly attuned in recent years to the various and specific ways that post-1945 poetry is entangled with new media technologies from the tape recorder and the record to the typewriter, the mimeograph machine, and the networked computer, poetry's intermedial relationship with radio during this same period has received comparatively little attention.[10] This is despite the fact that literary radio studies, or the study of the intersections between literary and radio culture, has been a growing subfield

INTRODUCTION

of interdisciplinary research in modernist studies since the late 1990s.[11] The neglect of radio in this period by literary scholars—and, until recently, by media historians—can be at least partly explained, though, by the ambiguous position that radio has occupied in the media ecology of the United States since the 1950s.[12] The rapid popularization of television in the 1950s radically transformed the broadcasting industry, and as most of the major broadcast networks shifted their focus to the new medium, taking their talent and advertisers with them, the so-called golden age of radio was superseded by what would become known as the format era, and the radio dramas, variety shows, live concerts, and literary programming of the former largely gave way to prerecorded music.[13] Ever since, radio's place in the national imaginary has been unstable, evident in the contradictory ways that radio still appears in American public discourse as both dead and resurgent, dominant and marginal.

One consequence of the transformation of the broadcasting industry after WWII was, simply put, the end of poetry broadcasting on commercial radio. In the 1930s and early 1940s, it was not uncommon to hear poetry on network radio, as poetry programs like Ted Malone's *Between the Bookends* and Norman Corwin's *Words without Music* as well as verse radio dramas by poets like Archibald MacLeish and Edna St. Vincent Millay reached a national listenership.[14] Indeed, as Mike Chasar argues, the immensely popular and long-running CBS program *Between the Bookends*, which gave significant airtime to poems written or selected by listeners, "helped to sell the idea of corporate radio itself" in the years when the American system of privatized commercial radio had not yet been fully codified by projecting a national public steeped in a shared verse culture that was seemingly "facilitated if not engendered by *corporate* radio ... which in its coast-to-coast reach, links the needs of the individual, even isolated listener to a national community of listeners."[15] Chasar characterizes this demotic literary radio imaginary as "modern and American but antimodernist," which perhaps explains why many modernist poets, including those who wrote for or appeared on radio, were critical of the American system especially as compared to national public broadcasting systems like the British Broadcasting Corporation (BBC) and the Canadian Broadcasting Corporation (CBC). In 1930, Harriet Monroe lamented what she saw as the deleterious effects of commercial radio on poetry and its reception, asserting that in the U.S., unlike in England, "the poets of quality and standing are not being broadcast, while numerous impossibles are reading their maudlin verses to invisible audiences of millions."[16]

Harriet Monroe's highbrow critique of American radio's literary taste, however, would have seemed irrelevant in the post-WWII period. While some AM radio stations did continue to give snippets of airtime to poetry in the late 1940s and early 1950s, literary programming of this kind would become increasingly rare in commercial radio. WMEX-AM in Boston, for example, which broadcast Cid Corman's *This Is Poetry* program weekly from 1949 to 1951, switched in 1957 to a full-time Top 40 rock 'n' roll station. For some listeners and writers, the end of the network era signaled the wholesale takeover of radio by the "mu-sick," to borrow Charles Olson's formulation, of an expanded consumer culture.[17] Lytle Shaw argues that the embrace of both audiotape and speech-based forms by experimental poets in this period constituted a rejection not only of academic poetry or Cold War culture but of "dominant American media—radio above all."[18] This is the context in which Allen Ginsberg, recording on his portable tape recorder the pop songs, news bulletins, weather reports, and ads spewing from his car radio in *The Fall of America: Poems of These States, 1965–1971* (1972), pitched his poetic mantra against the radio vortex of consumerism and war that circulated across the nation.

This critical view of radio, however, has had the effect of oversimplifying radio's ubiquitous presence in American life and literature long after the end of the "golden age" of network radio. After all, most poets writing in the post-WWII period (like most Americans then and now) were radio listeners, and their experiences of radio listening informed their poetry in ways that are more specific, varied, and contradictory than one monolithic understanding of radio would allow. Ginsberg's *Fall of America* might read differently, for example, if more cars in the 1960s had been outfitted with FM radio receivers.[19] FM radio, which became generally available for licensing in the U.S. in 1945, was the other major force of change for the broadcasting industry alongside television, though its growth was much slower. AM remained the dominant radio service until the late 1970s, which means that for three decades FM radio stations made little profit but attracted significant experimentation. This experimentation generated alternatives to the commercial mainstream in American radio, giving rise to the FM revolution. Though the FM revolution usually refers in common usage to the brief eruption in the late 1960s of freeform underground or progressive rock radio, I use the term more expansively to describe the longer period of FM radio's development from the late 1940s to the late 1970s, over which a wider range of alternative forms of both noncommercial and commercial radio flourished (including local, public, community, and freeform radio).

Ginsberg was an enthusiastic listener to and contributor to early FM radio and, like many writers, he was quick to recognize the opportunity that local FM stations offered for broadcasting an oppositional and oral poetry—as he did in his first radio appearance in 1956, when he recorded a reading of "Howl" for Pacifica Radio station KPFA. Of course, federal restrictions on broadcast speech still limited what one could say on air, while prohibitive social barriers and discriminatory practices limited who could gain access even to local FM radio stations. But it is in part due to writers like Ginsberg, who contested these limits, that FM radio became a terrain of cultural and political struggle in this period. And because FM stations were generally less controlled by advertiser and corporate interests than their AM counterparts, and therefore more responsive to community demands, they also became important outlets for the protest and liberation movements of the 1960s and 1970s—movements in which poetry and its performance played a vital role. Thus, while poets in general were largely banished from mainstream commercial radio, more experimental and radical poetic voices began to be heard "on the lower frequencies" (to echo Ralph Ellison's invisible man) of the FM underground.[20]

Poetry FM listens back to this period of radio history to show how American poetry was shaped by and shaped in turn this expansive FM revolution. Like the cultural history of FM radio, the literary history of American poetry from the late 1940s to the 1980s is defined by waves of opposition to the literary and critical establishment by poets and movements who likewise embraced artistic experimentation, alternative networks of distribution, and local community. In contrast to the national and transnational imaginaries of modernist literary and radio culture, the narrowcasting, so to speak, of both FM radio and avant-garde poetry in this period rewards a localized approach to their study, one that accounts for the specific intermedial relationships that manifest in different places and times, and for specific literary communities and radio stations. In this study, I focus on just two radio stations in the Pacifica Radio network—KPFA-FM in Berkeley and WBAI-FM in New York—to develop a local and institutionally grounded analysis of poets' involvement with FM radio as both producers and listeners. While Pacifica Radio has since its founding

INTRODUCTION

taken a capacious approach to poetry programming, broadcasting poetry by historical as well as contemporary writers, poetry in translation, and poetry by unpublished writers, my case studies focus on poets who played important roles at these stations and/or who embraced oral poetics and radio and sonic tropes in their work. These especially include poets associated with the New American Poetry—William Everson, Kenneth Rexroth, Jack Spicer, Allen Ginsberg, Paul Blackburn, and Amiri Baraka, among others—who first brought the oral poetics of the "new" poetry to Pacifica Radio's experiment in listener-sponsored radio. But I also focus on poets who contested the silencing of Black, queer, and women's voices in both American radio and American poetry by bringing onto Pacifica Radio stations and into their poetry alternative aural imaginaries—poets like A. B. Spellman, Audre Lorde, Pat Parker, Susan Howe, and Bernadette Mayer (as well as Baraka, Ginsberg, and Spicer).

This is not, then, simply the story of an oral poetry finding an auditory medium. As we will see, many of the writers and radio producers who brought poetry on to Pacific Radio—beginning with Pacifica's founder, Lewis Hill—expressed profound ambivalence about the technics and poetics of reception, about poetry and its mediated publics, and about the phonocentric claims of their era. To describe the many contradictions of this relationship between post-1945 poetry and radio, I borrow a line from Jack Spicer's *Language* (1965): "The poet is a counterpunching radio."[21] Spicer's mixed metaphor for a strange poetics of mediumship, in which medium and message, poet and poem, spar like a pair of boxers, characterizes for me many of the poets of this study, whose engagement with radio in their writing and their lives was linked to their contradictory relationships to hegemonic culture and media as well as the unresolved contradictions of their own poetics. But the image of the "counterpunching radio" also seems to me a useful way of describing radio itself during this period of crisis and change, when multiple forms of resistance to dominant aesthetic and commercial models of radio arose within the broadcasting industry itself, of which Pacifica Radio's pacifist experiment in listener-sponsored radio is just one example. To give a sense, then, of the wider context in which poets' involvement with Pacifica took place, in the next section I sketch some of the "counterpunching" media, cultural, and *literary* histories of American FM radio.

INTRODUCTION

"Turn On, Tune In, Drop Out"

The story of how FM radio became, for a time, a countercultural outlet is the story of how technological, regulatory, and cultural changes opened (and then closed) a window of experimentation on the airwaves after WWII—one that promised to change not only *what* Americans heard on the radio but *how* they listened and the very sensory experience of listening itself. Radio inventors in the early 1900s had experimented with both amplitude modulation (AM) and frequency modulation (FM) radiotelephony, but AM radio became the dominant form of mass broadcasting after 1920, enabling radio's global rise as a communication and entertainment medium. AM radio's susceptibility to static interference and electrical noise, however, combined with increasing congestion on the newly regulated spectrum, encouraged investment in FM radio research by North American corporations like RCA.[22] The invention of wideband, high-fidelity FM radio is generally attributed to the American radio engineer Edwin Howard Armstrong, who filed two patents for his FM radio technology in 1933. In public demonstrations of his system to radio professionals in New York, Armstrong impressed his audiences by broadcasting sounds that would be inaudible or distorted over AM: paper being crumpled, water pouring, recordings of quiet piano solos and brassy marches, and all against a background of "velvety silence with a presence that was something new in auditory experience."[23] The early association of FM with high-fidelity sound—and with new auditory experiences—would continue throughout much of the century, eventually linking FM in the post-WWII period to other listener-oriented hi-fi technologies like stereo.

But while a small number of broadcasters obtained experimental FM licenses in the 1930s, it wasn't until 1945 that the Federal Communications Commission (FCC) allowed for the expansion of FM radio. Many factors had contributed to FM radio's stalled development, including a patent battle between Armstrong and RCA, resistance from the major commercial radio networks to the creation of a new broadcast system, a wartime freeze on new licenses, and a series of protracted FCC hearings about the potential for frequency competition between FM radio and the other major 1930s invention in broadcasting: television. In 1945, the FCC finally resolved the spectrum allocation issue by moving the FM frequency band further up the dial (to 88–106 MHZ), which, to the frustration of FM broadcasters, required the production of new FM receivers and reissuing of licenses. Nevertheless, a wave of new FM stations came onto the airwaves in the late 1940s, including KPFA-FM in Berkeley, established by the nonprofit Pacifica Foundation in 1949. As I discuss in chapter 1, Pacifica Radio's founders, like many early FM adopters, saw in the opening of the FM band an opportunity to create a less commercial, more independent, more local, and higher-quality radio system. Widespread predictions that FM would quickly overtake AM as the dominant radio service, however, did not come to pass, as the development of FM continued to stall in the 1950s. Congress's decision to allow the broadcasting of duplicate content on both AM and FM stations, combined with a slowdown in the production and import of FM receivers, suppressed growth. Many of the independent FM stations that survived in the 1950s did so by adopting classical music ("beautiful music") formats that appealed to educated, upper-class consumers, hi-fi audiophiles, and classical music enthusiasts willing to invest in an FM receiver.[24] As a result, FM radio took on the connotations of an elite, luxury service.

KPFA also broadcast its fair share of classical music in the 1950s, but the station's survival was due to another FM radio trend: the expansion of public radio. Though the American system of privatized commercial broadcasting had been codified with the Communications Act of 1934, advocates for public broadcasting laid the groundwork in the 1930s and 1940s for what would become a federal investment in FM public radio after WWII.[25] This federal investment was manifest in new FCC policies, such as the allocation of the 88–92 MHZ frequency range to educational broadcasters, and was supported by private grant funding from the Rockefeller and Ford Foundations that, in the context of the WWII and early Cold War years, reflected a strategic cooperation between government and private institutions to create an infrastructure for public broadcasting in the U.S. and abroad.[26] It is in large part through noncommercial and educational FM radio stations that poets were able to find a back door onto the nation's airwaves, especially since these stations (as well as some nominally commercial "beautiful music" FM stations) often saw the broadcasting of literature as an important component of "quality" cultural programming.

Meanwhile, the immediate popularity of television among U.S. consumers had far outpaced industry expectations, and as the major networks and advertisers began to funnel more and more of their dollars and talent to TV, the economics and sound of commercial AM radio changed radically too. Seemingly overnight, the national listening public dissolved, and in its place emerged more local and increasingly segmented radio markets. So, too, was the family radio set displaced from its symbolic hearth in the American home as the inexpensive, portable transistor radio made radio listening more individualized and more mobile. And as listeners tuned in at the park and the beach, in their bedrooms, cars, and workplaces, on public transit and in the street, what they heard, increasingly, was recorded music. In comparison to original programming, prerecorded popular music was low-cost and appealed to the burgeoning youth market, reaping easy profits for the commercial radio, recorded music, and advertising industries. The 1950s is thus enshrined in American popular memory as the decade when teenagers gained control of the radio dial: the decade when rock 'n' roll, the Top 40 countdown, and the disc jockey as cultural tastemaker and celebrity personality were born.[27]

The origins of fifties rock radio, however, lie in the emergence a decade earlier of so-called Black-appeal radio stations and formats, which remapped radio's color line after decades of activism by African American listeners, performers, and writers against the industry's discriminatory practices and racist representations. As Amiri Baraka observed in *Blues People*, "By the forties, after the war had completely wiped out the remaining 'race' record categories, the radio became the biggest disseminator of blues music."[28] Though "Black-appeal" stations were still overwhelmingly white-owned, African American disc jockeys at these stations brought rhythm and blues and jazz music to cities around the country. The subsequent crossover appeal of Black music to young white audiences opened a new chapter in a long history of "love and theft" that would come to be heard not only in the musical appropriation of white rock 'n' roll performers but in the racial ventriloquy of white disc jockeys like Alan Freed.[29] In the context of the burgeoning civil rights movement, this dynamic made radio, as Susan Douglas argues, "*the* media outlet where cultural and industrial battles over how much influence black culture was going to have on white culture were staged and fought."[30]

My point is that in the 1950s, even popular commercial AM radio began to take on a subversive ethos in the white-dominated American media sphere, which conjured images of a young generation of rebellious, oversexed, drug-addled, race-mixing teens hooked to cheap transistor radios. Or "bleatniks," as a 1961 *Time* magazine article mockingly dubbed this "new order of restless Americans."[31] Linked to the sensationalized image of the beatnik, then, was the transistor radio with its ceaseless blare of popular music, DJ chatter, station jingles, and ads. Restless sounds for a restless generation, especially as the technology of the transistor radio also made car radios more ubiquitous:

> We were suddenly driving along the blue waters of the Gulf, and at the same time a momentous mad thing began on the radio; it was the Chicken Jazz'n Gumbo disk-jockey show from New Orleans, all mad jazz records, colored records, with the disk jockey saying, "Don't worry 'bout *nothing!*"[32]

It is true that for the Beats, as Jack Kerouac put it, "The radio was always on" (*On the Road*, 249). As Beat writers channeled the new sounds of postwar radio and especially Black radio into their work, they modeled radio listening as a practice of countercultural rebellion and self-fashioning. In Kerouac's *On the Road*, for example, the Neal Cassady character Dean Moriarty listens to radio like it's a physical performance: twisting the dial, drumming the dashboard, shouting over booming brass, conversing with a sports announcer's play-by-play. Dean's consumption of radio falls outside the binary of passive and active listening; it is continuous and disjunctive, distracted and enthralled, private and social, and violent and tender, all at once. When they hit on a jazz program, Dean also acts as a mediator between the music and his acolytes, instructing Sal Paradise and others how to interpret and internalize what they hear: "'listen will you to this old tenorman blow his top'—he shot up the radio volume till the car shuddered—'and listen to him till the story and put down true relaxation and knowledge'" (*On the Road*, 135). Kerouac may have wished he was "a jazz poet, / blowing a long blues in an afternoon jam / session," but the hero of his fiction appears more like a disc jockey, the Benzedrine speed yet seductive intimacy of his talk cutting from one thought, one moment, one bop record to the next, hell, even "[h]is laugh was . . . exactly like the laugh of a radio maniac, only faster."[33]

If, as Tom McEnaney argues, "in the radio age, writing . . . became a practice of listening: a specific audile technique that sought to influence radio listening practices in turn," then the Beats contributed to a reinvention of radio listening at a time when "the radio age" seemed to be coming to an end.[34] A few years after the publication of *On the Road*, the disc jockey as cultural icon also underwent a spectacular fall from grace after a series of payola scandals in 1959–1960 exposed widespread pay-to-play practices in the industry. The media scandals and subsequent congressional hearings, driven as much by the racist backlash to rock music as the cause of anti-corruption, particularly targeted rock 'n' roll DJs like Alan Freed whose careers were ruined by the scandal. In the wake, radio management seized the opportunity to regain control over the nation's airwaves (and profit flows) from DJs by adopting new Top 40 preprogrammed music formats built around rotations of *Billboard* hit singles. Top 40 formats made commercial AM radio more standardized and homogenous, though as media historian William Barlow observes, it also "had the unintended effect of curtailing . . . racial ventriloquy on the nation's airwaves."[35]

Black radio, moreover, expanded in the format era, and R&B and soul format AM radio stations were vital news and music outlets for the Black liberation struggle in the 1960s, though the largely white-owned stations were also subject to critique in ways that register in Black poetry of the sixties. David Henderson's poem "Keep on Pushing (Harlem Riots / Summer / 1964)," for example, which takes its title from The Impressions' hit that topped the *Billboard* charts in the summer of 1964, reflects critically on the role that New York station WWRL-AM, "[t]he most soulful station in the nation," played in the Harlem uprising.[36] Henderson skewers the paternalism of the station, which sends a commentator "(eight to one he's white, representing management)" on the air to preach calm, "tell[ing] us . . . violence only hurts (and he emphasizes hurts) the causes of freedom and dignity," without acknowledging that the cause of the spontaneous uprising is the "hurt" to "the causes of freedom and dignity" wrought by anti-Black racism, police violence, and economic disenfranchisement. More ambivalent is Henderson's representation in the same poem of WWRL's most popular African American DJ—Douglas "Jocko" Henderson—who "hustles wine" and reads ads for aspirin on his late-night program, "his tongue baroque-sinister" as he delivers commercial messages that also seem aimed at quelling resistance but are perhaps spoken with a forked tongue ("Keep on Pushing," 243, 244). WWRL listeners tuned in for the music, though, and as the sounds of the riot transmit "in the air   death static / over everything," the music is also what cuts through this "death static" with "soul"; at the end of the poem, Henderson follows Jocko's adspeak with Curtis Mayfield's chorus, back on rotation: "Keep on a' pushin' / Someway somehow / I know we can make it / with just a little bit of soul" (243, 244).[37]

The onset of the format era in commercial AM radio also spurred the

(13)

search for FM alternatives. The outlook for FM radio's growth as an independent radio service had started to improve in the late fifties and early sixties with the importation of more affordable FM receivers and the FCC's decision to finally limit AM/FM duplication. Though FM radio was still largely the province of "beautiful music," the stirrings of what would become known as freeform radio began to be heard "in the nocturnal experimentation at fledgling commercial FM stations and in the eclecticism found at some of their commercial-free counterparts in the lower portion of the megahertz band."[38] Pacifica Radio was one of the earliest incubators of freeform, and programs like John Leonard's *Nightsounds* (KPFA) and Bob Fass's *Radio Unnameable* (WBAI) filled late-night hours in the early 1960s with experimental collages of music, sound, comedy, unscripted talk, and—importantly for my interests—poetry. Indeed, the emergence of freeform radio at and beyond Pacifica owed something to the experimental poets who trafficked in and out of KPFA and WBAI in these years, and who helped to cultivate a more experimental sound and countercultural ethos on the network that proved influential on the FM revolution.

The FM revolution in underground radio, also known as progressive rock radio, erupted out of these early experiments in freeform. DJs like William "Rosko" Mercer and Scott Muni at noncommercial stations WOR-FM and WNEW-FM (New York), and Larry Miller and Tom Donahue at commercial station KMPX-FM (San Francisco), adapted freeform to rock music broadcasting oriented around long album cuts by bands like The Doors and Jefferson Airplane, DJ-improvised set lists, few commercials, and absolutely no jingles, promotions, or gimmicks—the self-styled antithesis, in other words, to AM Top 40. Adopting a slow, laid-back (i.e., stoned) announcing style, these DJs also took advantage of FM's relative marginality to push the boundaries of what was considered acceptable speech in radio, especially in relation to drugs, sex, and politics. The approach quickly spread, and by 1968, there were more than sixty full-time commercial underground stations and many more underground and freeform programs broadcasting in FM around the country.[39] The appeal of underground radio for its predominantly white male producers and listeners was not only that it offered a musical alternative to the hit parade but that, in shifting the object of high-fidelity listening from classical to rock music, it promised an auditory revolution implicitly linked to social and political revolution. Yet, even as underground DJs created an acoustic space to imagine alternative forms of masculinity, they continued to reify musical appreciation and expertise as the domain of elite white masculinity.[40]

For its listeners, underground radio made "tuning in" to FM radio seem like a defiant "dropping out" of mainstream American culture. Timothy Leary's famous slogan—"turn on, tune in, drop out"—was not about radio per se, though it was in a certain sense about television, which Leary often rhetorically figured as the icon of consumer culture from which, in his view, more young people were detaching with the aid of mind-opening psychedelic drugs. In a 1967 conversation with Allen Ginsberg, Gary Snyder, and Alan Watts that was recorded by the Haight-Ashbury newspaper *The San Francisco Oracle* and broadcast by Pacifica station KPFA, Leary looked ahead to a future in which "thousands of groups will just look around the fake prop television set American society, and just open one of those doors . . . lead[ing] you *out* into the Garden of Eden, which is this planet."[41] This legendary conversation, which took place on Watts's converted ferry boat in Sausalito a few months after Leary had proclaimed his slogan to the crowd at the Human Be-In at Golden Gate Park, centered on the meaning of the controversial last phrase of Leary's slogan, with the four gurus agreeing that "dropping out" represented the first not last step in a revolutionary movement toward the creation of what they envisioned, in primitivizing terms, as a tribalist utopia. But their anti-technological consensus—tempered only by Ginsberg ("where are people going to buy their Uher tape recorder machines?")—was countered by their respective commitments to an alternative media ecology in which they, the *Oracle*, and KPFA were all embedded.[42] Leary, for example, who often cited the Beats' savvy use of media as inspiration, elsewhere celebrated the fact that the Human Be-In had been organized entirely by "the Underground Press and progressive, free-form radio stations."[43] And when KPFA broadcast the tape of "the houseboat summit" in June, in the midst of the Summer of Love, it contributed to a movement it had helped to cultivate over more than a decade of broadcasting voices from the counterculture, including Ginsberg, Snyder, and Watts, the last of whom was known to Bay Area listeners as the former host of a long-running weekly KPFA commentary program on Buddhism and Eastern philosophy, *Way Beyond the West*.

The popularity of underground radio among a hippie subculture, however, is ironically what finally persuaded station owners and advertisers that FM radio could be profitable. They were helped along by a new generation of radio programming consultants, including Lee Abrams, a young consultant from Chicago, who invented a new commercial music format to capitalize on the underground market: album-oriented rock (AOR).[44] Though many in the underground radio world decried the tightly controlled, market-researched, commercially motivated playlists of AOR as a diluted imitation of freeform radio's defiantly "anti-format" sound, they could not stem the tide of change. Not only did nearly all commercial freeform stations convert to AOR formats in the early 1970s, but the success of AOR paved the way for the wider formatization and automation of FM radio, as an expanded slate of commercial music formats were adopted by commercial FM stations to segment the adult radio market, including Top 40, classical, soul, country, middle-of-the-road, and disco.[45] To many, the format crossover from AM to FM signaled the end of the FM revolution, and by the end of the decade, even diehard underground stations like KMET in Los Angeles had begun to supplement DJs' freeform intuition with market research, "eliminat[ing] the possibility," as DJ Jim Ladd dismissively put it, "that one of the jocks would be playing an hour of jazz or poetry readings at three in the afternoon."[46]

One could still hear an hour of poetry (or jazz) on Pacifica Radio stations and other noncommercial and educational FM broadcasters, though, even as the 1970s also brought about a sea change in American public radio. In 1967, President Lyndon B. Johnson had signed into law the Public Broadcasting Act "to encourage the growth and development of public radio and television broadcasting" through the establishment of the private nonprofit Corporation for Public Broadcasting (CPB).[47] The law codified what media reformists had long sought: a federally supported public broadcasting system. And through CPB grants, the number of public radio stations did grow substantially, especially after National Public Radio (NPR) was incorporated in 1970. From the start, however, the relationship between NPR and other noncommercial and educational broadcasters was complicated and even antagonistic in some cases, as the latter had to negotiate their relationship to this new centralized, state-funded system. Some stations and networks, like Pacifica Radio, decided not to apply for CPB funds or join NPR in order to preserve their independence; many other smaller broadcasters simply could not meet the eligibility requirements for CPB funding and membership, which favored larger, more established stations.[48]

The de facto creation of a subgroup of non-NPR nonprofit stations helped to crystallize the burgeoning community radio movement, which constituted another wave in the counterpunching history of alternative FM radio, and the last that contextualizes this study. In the most general terms, community radio is a civic model or even ideal of radio in which stations are owned, operated by, and/or in service to a local community. In the U.S., the community radio movement represented a collective flowering of several FM radio trends that emerged across the 1960s and 1970s and that coalesced around the formation of the National Federation of Community Broadcasters in 1975.[49] One branch, grafted from the Pacifica model of listener-supported radio, was cultivated by early freeform radio innovator Lorenzo Milam, who, after getting his start at KPFA in Berkeley, founded the listener-supported station KRAB-FM in Seattle in 1962. Using KRAB as a blueprint, Milam and his supporters went on to found many more noncommercial freeform stations around the country that shared programming as part of the "KRAB nebula."[50] Another branch was the expansion of college FM radio; though not all college stations adopt a community radio or freeform model, their numbers grew substantially in this period.[51] A third, multilingual branch of the community radio movement is represented by the establishment of the first Native American and Chicano radio stations in the 1970s.[52] These stations, many of which broadcast in rural areas, developed in tandem with the American Indian and Chicano movements as well as in solidarity with Indigenous and postcolonial community radio activism around the world.[53] Several Black community radio stations were also established in this period, and feminist broadcasters and collectives at freeform, college, and Chicano stations brought a flourishing of feminist and lesbian programming to the community airwaves.[54] Pacifica Radio influenced the community radio movement, but, as I discuss in chapter 5, it was also transformed by it, as local activists, poets, and listeners pushed Pacifica stations to diversify their staff and radically reimagine their programming in the 1970s. More generally, including community radio in the history of the FM revolution reveals the broad range of alternatives to both commercial radio and NPR that emerged in this period.

Like the mimeograph revolution to which it is closely connected, the U.S. community radio movement in the 1970s and 1980s promoted ephemerality, localism, access, and limited circulation, while dismantling rigid divisions between genres, gatekeeping around professionalism and amateurism, and the boundaries between art, politics, and everyday life.

But while the significance of the mimeograph for the fostering and dissemination of post-1960 avant-garde and social movement poetry is well known among literary scholars, we know less about how community radio stations contributed to their sounding. There is evidence, though, that the community radio movement created many more broadcasting outlets for poets. Since this history is so little known or studied, I'll note just a few non-Pacifica examples, though a full recovery lies outside my scope. KRAB in Seattle regularly broadcast poetry during its twenty-two years on the air, and some of the recorded programs have been preserved and digitized.[55] At KRAB nebula station KDNA-FM in St. Louis, poet Michael Castro and Jan Garden Castro started *River Styx Poets* (1969–1972), a monthly poetry and music program whose guests included poet Ajulé Rutlin and writer and actor Malinké Elliott of the Black Artists' Group (BAG).[56] In the 1970s, the Feminist Radio Network in Washington, DC, distributed cultural and public affairs programming to community and college stations around the country, including literary programs with poets such as Judy Grahn, Marilyn Hacker, and Sonia Sanchez. At the University of New Mexico station KUNM-FM in Albuquerque, Chicano poet and activist Cecilio García Camarillo started *Espejos de Aztlán* in 1980, a long-running bilingual cultural and public affairs program that included poetry as well as interviews, music, drama, and commentary. And from the early 1980s to the 2000s, Nathaniel Mackey hosted a weekly jazz and world music show, *Tanganyika Strut*, on community station KUSP-FM in Santa Cruz, which, in his own words, "diverg[ed] from a prepackaged sense of what appropriate content for a radio program is" by creating a "cross-cultural mix" that aligned with his poetics.[57] These examples point to a notably diverse but as yet largely unexplored history of broadcast poetry on community radio.

Finally, I would be remiss if I did not credit NPR for the role it has played in bringing poetry to radio listeners, particularly as the reach of its nationally syndicated programs to millions of listeners—a reach most locally produced community and college programs neither achieve nor aspire to—is the largest contemporary poets have been able to attain via radio since the network era of the 1930s and 1940s. In its early years, NPR saw the broadcasting of literature as an important part of its educational and public service mission, and a few early syndicated programs like *Voices in the Wind*, *Poems to a Listener*, and *Word Jazz* regularly broadcast poetry and interviews with poets. Over the years, however, NPR has trended toward a greater emphasis on news and public affairs over cultural programming,

INTRODUCTION

with a few notable exceptions, like Garrison Keillor's *The Writer's Almanac* and Terry Gross's *Fresh Air*, that still occasionally bring poets onto the air.[58]

The overlapping forms of alternative radio that flourished on the FM band in the 1960s and 1970s—freeform, underground, public, college, and community radio—all continue to the present day. But in the 1980s, the era that had given rise to experimentation on the FM band began to come to an end. At the start of the decade, FM radio broadcasters could finally claim a larger share of the U.S. market than their AM counterparts; by the 1990s, the FM takeover of American radio was complete.[59] As FM radio became more profitable, competition for FM licenses pushed out smaller, local broadcasters while format stations crowded the dial. Public broadcasters faced new challenges, too, as the election of President Ronald Reagan ushered in a period of deregulation and disinvestment in public media. NPR still expanded in the 1980s and 1990s, but its growth did not stem the overall decline in locally produced radio. Pockets of resistance to the new radio mainstream persisted in the growth of unlicensed low-power FM radio stations and, on the other side of the dial, in the emergence of conservative talk radio on the newly depopulated AM band. But the broader trend toward deregulation and conglomeration was enshrined into law with the Telecommunications Act of 1996, which effectively automated license renewal and ended most limits on the number of stations a company could own, enabling large corporations like Clear Channel and Infinity to take control of wide swaths of the nation's airwaves. The impact of this law is still evident in American terrestrial radio today, though new forms of radio (satellite radio, internet radio, podcasting) have continued to belie assumptions about radio's obsolescence, generating new and ongoing waves of experimentation and resistance, and new and ongoing intersections between radio and literary culture.[60]

As of this writing, all five Pacifica Radio stations are still on the air, though their future is ever and increasingly precarious. The reasons for the network's struggle since the 1990s with a declining listenership and subscriber base, unsustainable debt burden, dysfunctional management structure, and constant infighting are hotly debated and ultimately beyond the scope of my inquiry here.[61] In choosing Pacifica Radio stations KPFA and WBAI as the primary institutional sites for my case studies, I aim instead to draw attention to an exemplary but undervalued aspect of Pacifica's history and legacy: its role as an important media outlet for contemporary poetry. Though, as I've noted, there were other FM radio stations that broadcast poetry during this period, it would be difficult to find a network that has been as committed to literary programming, or attracted as much participation from poets, as Pacifica. This is true of all of Pacifica's stations, though my focus in this study will be on its flagships in Berkeley and New York, each of which has a long history of exchange with poets in these bicoastal literary centers. Pacifica is exemplary in other ways, too, from its embeddedness in social movement history, to the major role it has played in First Amendment battles over the regulation of broadcast speech, to its large independent archive, which houses an estimated 100,000 recordings from over seventy years of broadcasting. Indeed, my decision to focus on Pacifica is due in part to the existence of the Pacifica Radio Archives, which, though underresourced, constitutes one of the most significant radio collections in the U.S. Its thousands of unique literary recordings, a fraction of which have been digitized and made publicly accessible online, constitute a major audio record of post-1945 poetry. One of my aims in this study is therefore to show how the Pacifica Radio Archives—and community and public radio archives in general—offer a rich resource for literary study, and how literary critical approaches can, in turn, inform radio studies and bring attention to neglected cultural histories and genres of radio.

Radiophonic Poetics

To inquire after the relationship between post-1945 American poetry and FM radio is necessarily to undertake a study of oral poetics. But in many ways, *Poetry FM* is as much a study of aural poetics as it is of oral poetics, or, perhaps more accurately, of the inextricability of these two near-homophones and the feedback loop they mark between a poetics of speech or voice and a poetics of listening or writing; between composition, performance, and reception; between poet and audience; and between poetry's aural attunements and other sonic cultural imaginaries. The call to attend to aurality as well as orality in the study of modern and contemporary poetry is not a new one. Charles Bernstein, in his field-defining introduction to *Close Listening: Poetry and the Performed Word* (1998), argued that his own "insistence on aurality" as an approach to studying poetry readings "averts the identification of orality with speech" by "emphasiz[ing] the sounding of the *writing*" over "the presence of the poet" "to invoke a performative sense of 'phonotext' or audiotext" that he suggests "might better be spelled *a/orality*."[62] Other critics have

INTRODUCTION

considered the role that sound media technologies have played in creating what Michael Davidson describes as contemporary poetry's "divided character of orality," in which poetic voice is constructed simultaneously as embodied presence and as always already having been technologically inscribed, reified, and heard.[63] I argue, however, that there is a specifically *radiophonic* character to the aurality of twentieth-century poetry that, on the one hand, reflects poets' actual material engagements with radio as both producers and listeners and, on the other hand, signifies a conception of poetry itself as a medium for the encryption, transmission, and broadcasting (or narrowcasting) of linguistic meaning and phonic materiality.

This conception of poetry *as* radio—represented most directly in Jack Spicer's analogy of the poet to a radio receiver, but resonant, too, in the poetry of Allen Ginsberg, Amiri Baraka, and Susan Howe, among others—involves a poetic refiguration of phonographic logics of sound storage and playback as well as wireless logics of intermediality, networking, transmission, and dissemination. Just as radio represents not one media technology but rather an assemblage (the content of which is also, as Marshall McLuhan famously argued, other media), what I describe as the radiophonic poetics of post-1945 poetry involves an understanding of poetic aurality as generated not by the monodirectional relay of poet-poem-audience but through a contingent, changing network of relations that are linguistic, textual, technological, bodily, and social.[64] The radiophonic poetics of contemporary poetry also has methodological implications for those of us engaged with its audio archives, requiring that we go beyond "close listening" to critically examine the matrix of technologies, institutions, practices, and discourses in which listening takes place, and through which listeners construct the sounds of the past.[65]

The chapters of this book follow a roughly chronological narrative of poets' involvement with Pacifica Radio stations KPFA in Berkeley and WBAI in New York from the late 1940s through the 1970s. The first three chapters focus on the interwoven histories of the San Francisco Renaissance and KPFA. Chapter 1 begins by tracing their shared genealogy back to the WWII-era radical pacifist movement and to the group of pacifists and poets in San Francisco who, after the war, founded Pacifica Radio and launched a noncommercial FM radio station in Berkeley that made contemporary poetry a cornerstone of its programming. Pacifica Radio was the brainchild of Lewis Hill, a poet and conscientious objector (CO) who during the war served in a CO service camp in Coleville, California, and lobbied on behalf of COs for the ACLU. These wartime experiences, as well as a part-time job as a radio announcer, inspired Hill's idea for how radio could be used, not in the service of profits or militaristic propaganda, but to intervene in a global communication crisis to promote "a pacific world in our time."[66] In this chapter, I argue that Hill's vision for what became Pacifica Radio was also influenced by his engagement in debates about how to create a pacifist culture, specifically as these debates emerged around the formation of a CO artist and print collective at a camp in Waldport, Oregon, that was led by the poet William Everson. Hill and Everson corresponded during the war, and Hill published poetry in and read Waldport publications; after the war, both men moved to San Francisco, where they joined other former COs from Waldport and a wider network of pacifist activists, artists, and writers in creating the infrastructure of independent presses, bookstores, galleries, theaters, reading groups, and an FM radio station that fostered the San Francisco Renaissance and helped make the Bay Area a center for alternative culture and alternative media. KPFA first went on the air in 1949, and its early emphasis on literary programming under Hill's leadership was informed by his pacifist poetics and critique of mass culture. Through an analysis of a series of experimental radio programs on modern poetry that Hill produced in the mid-1950s, I show how Hill sought new methods for bringing poetry on the radio in order to educate an idealized, individualized listener—an "audience of one"—in an implicitly pacifist mode of listening attuned to the subtleties of human language, assured of the sanctity of the individual, and committed to free expression and association.

Much of the early literary programming on KPFA was print-oriented, reflecting a liberal belief in print culture as the foundation of a participatory democratic public sphere that broadcast media should emulate, not supplant, and echoing New Critical views about the primacy of the printed poem over oral or recorded forms. In the late 1940s and 1950s, however, San Francisco poets were beginning to contest these beliefs by taking poetry off the page, out of the university classroom, and onto the airwaves of their local noncommercial radio station. In the second chapter, "KPFA and the San Francisco Renaissance," I turn to the local poets who initiated the mutually influential relationship between KPFA and the experimental poetry community in San Francisco. Richard Moore, who was involved in founding KPFA and was one of its first staff members, was especially instrumental in connecting the station to the local poetry scene, including by inviting Kenneth Rexroth to host a book review program that lasted for more than twenty years on the air. Many San Francisco poets appeared on KPFA as guests or program hosts in the 1950s, including Jack Spicer, Robert Duncan, William Everson, Josephine Miles, Helen Adam, Philip Lamantia, Allen Ginsberg, and Lawrence Ferlinghetti, among others. These poets recognized in KPFA a unique radio outlet that enabled them to disseminate an oral poetry, publicize their work to a local audience, stay attuned to local literary happenings, and hear their own voices echoed back over the radio as representatives of a distinctly West Coast avant-garde. In turn, they transformed KPFA into a freewheeling, experimental, free speech organ for the emerging counterculture. To explore the origins of this connection, I focus on two radio programs hosted by poets in KPFA's early years: a live folk music program hosted by Jack Spicer, which aired during the station's first year on the air, and Rexroth's *Books*. Though these programs differed significantly, and neither was devoted to broadcasting poetry, I argue that each contributed to the mythos of the San Francisco Renaissance and to a broader reimagining of local, noncommercial FM radio as a subversive and even coterie form of media.

While chapter 2 is about poets' involvement with KPFA as radio producers, the next chapter examines the significance of radio as a "counterpunching" trope in the queer poetics of Spicer and Ginsberg. Though Spicer and Ginsberg are often positioned in histories of the San Francisco Renaissance as aesthetically and socially at odds, I argue that both poets queer radio in their work in ways that resonate against a contemporaneous media discourse about sexuality and censorship. I begin with the story of KPFA's broadcasting of Ginsberg's "Howl" in the mid-1950s as a flashpoint in literary, media, and LGBTQ+ history that anticipated KPFA's shift in the early 1960s toward a more overt defense of free speech in radio and alignment with progressive social movements. Listening to the poem "Howl" as a radio text, however, reveals the extent to which censorship, surveillance, and silence are inscribed at the heart of Ginsberg's visionary, telepathic poetics. In Spicer's poetry, radio is a governing motif and a metaphor for his theory of poetic dictation, in which the poet acts as a receiver for the transmissions of messages from an alien beyond. Spicer developed his anti-expressivist theory of dictation in part through his critique of the Beat media machine and Ginsberg specifically. But by tracing the radio motif as it appears first in Spicer's poetry and then his late lectures, I analyze how Spicer transforms, or rather deforms, the image of the poet-as-radio to imagine a poetics of interference that undermines dictation by creating a static field for queer desire to circulate through language and across time, space, and material bodies.

The fourth and fifth chapters turn from the West to the East Coast to examine New York poets' involvement with radio station WBAI in the 1960s and 1970s during the rise of freeform and community FM radio. Pacifica Radio acquired WBAI in 1960, and the station—Pacifica's first outside the state of California—quickly became the network's flagship, known for its independent coverage of the Vietnam War and antiwar, student, and civil rights movements as well as its innovations in freeform radio. Chapter 4, "WBAI and the Lower East Side Scene," is about the mutual exchange that developed between WBAI and the Lower East Side poetry community of the early 1960s that first coalesced around a few coffeehouse reading series that preceded the founding of the Poetry Project at St. Mark's Church in 1966. Though WBAI's original studios were in midtown, the independent FM radio station quickly became connected to the downtown scene as poets and jazz artists came onto the airwaves. Through this, WBAI contributed to the oral and aural poetics of the Lower East Side poetry community and the New American Poetry, and extended Pacifica Radio's commitment to fostering local poetry communities and airing experimental, boundary-pushing literature. This chapter focuses especially on the radio work and radiophonic poetics of Paul Blackburn and Amiri Baraka, both of whom played central roles in the downtown poetry community. Blackburn saw radio as a participatory medium and approached it—as an avid FM radio listener and producer of his own WBAI radio show—as an extension of his audiotape practices, oral poetics, and narrowcasting of literary community. Baraka, on the other hand, whose 1965 appearance on Blackburn's radio show allegedly resulted in the show's cancellation for obscenity, had a more ambivalent relationship to the white-dominated medium of radio as a listener and (increasingly in the mid-1960s) as a media figure. Pacifica Radio played an important role in broadcasting the media event of his oft-mythologized transformation from LeRoi Jones, East Side bohemian poet, to Amiri Baraka, leader of the Black Arts movement, and in this chapter, I examine a few of Baraka's early radio broadcasts on WBAI as they relate to the figure of radio in his early work and the aurality of his poetry.

INTRODUCTION

Baraka's appearances on WBAI and other Pacifica Radio stations in the 1960s also contributed to the broader struggle at the network to diversify its programming and staff and live up to its progressive ideals—a struggle that reached its peak in the 1970s with the formation of women's and "Third World" programming collectives and departments at Pacifica stations. In chapter 5, "The Poetics of Feminist Radio," I draw on a recently digitized collection of recordings from Pacifica Radio's broadcasting of the women's movement—and close analysis of recordings and poems of Audre Lorde, Pat Parker, Adrienne Rich, Susan Howe, and Bernadette Mayer, among others—to examine the role that poets and poetry broadcasting played in the groundbreaking emergence of feminist and lesbian feminist radio at WBAI and other Pacifica stations. The fact that poetry was ubiquitous in 1970s feminist programming represented not only an extension of Pacifica's commitment to poetry but the centrality of poetry in the women's movement. Radio, and community FM radio in particular, was an important part of the feminist communications network, in part because of radio's ability to extend the oral poetics and auditory culture of the movement. But as Pacifica stations amplified the voices of diverse women poets engaged across different feminist discourses and aesthetic traditions, these poets and the broadcasts themselves raised complex questions about listening as a feminist and poetic practice; about the meaning of community in the context of radio, literature, and second-wave feminisms; and about the future of the radio archive.

1

POETS AND PACIFISTS
THE ORIGINS OF PACIFICA RADIO

The story of poets' involvement with Pacifica Radio begins not with the establishment of the Pacifica Foundation in 1946 but earlier, in the din of war, when millions of Americans tuned their radio sets to hear news and sounds of the front, and a small group of war resisters sought to amplify their pacifist message. The mutual genealogy of Pacifica Radio and the San Francisco Renaissance traces back to the Civilian Public Service (CPS) camps on the West Coast where conscientious objectors like Pacifica's founder Lewis Hill and the poet William Everson were conscripted to alternative service during WWII, and which fostered the emergence of a more radical, but also more marginalized, pacifist movement in the United States. It was at a CPS camp in California that Hill first dreamed of a different kind of radio station beholden to neither advertisers nor the state that would realize the medium's potential as an organ for peace. Radicalized, like many COs, by his experience in the camps, Hill developed his idea in relation to debates within the radical pacifist movement about how to counter the drum of war not only through nonviolent resistance but by creating forms of community and art that could foster a peace culture. Everson, too, was radicalized by his experience as a CO in WWII, and he sought to put some of these ideas into practice at a CPS artists' camp in Waldport, Oregon, that became the locus of a remarkable amount of artistic production and small-press publishing during the war. Everson and Hill first became acquainted around the establishment of the "Fine Arts group" at Waldport, which Hill supported from afar, including by publishing his own poetry in one of its literary magazines. Both men also believed that poets and poetry could play an important role in the revitalization of a pacifist culture, though the question of what a pacifist poetry would or should be fueled debate at Waldport and beyond. After the war, Hill and Everson joined the influx of former COs and pacifist anarchists to the San Francisco Bay Area, where they helped to lay the groundwork for the city's emergence as a center for experimental poetry, social activism, and alternative media in the 1950s and 1960s.

This history provides important context for understanding the formative relationship between the San Francisco Renaissance and Pacifica Radio, and the background of a West Coast counterculture that would trace some of its roots to those war resisters whose art, politics, and forms of sociality starkly opposed hegemonic wartime and postwar American society. In what follows, I draw first on the experiences, writings, and correspondence of Hill and Everson during the war years to investigate how Hill's views on poetry and media were shaped by the radical pacifist movement and the pacifist poetics of the Waldport Fine Arts group. I then turn to the founding of Pacifica Radio and KPFA-FM to examine how these views—as well as Hill's critique of the American system of commercial radio—influenced KPFA's early noncommercial mission, programming, and aesthetics after it went on the air in 1949. Poetry was a cornerstone of KPFA's early programming, and its founders sought to make the station an outlet for poets and literary experimentation. Hill, moreover, considered the broadcasting of modern poetry to be an essential part of educating radio audiences in the specific and implicitly pacifist practices of individualized, participatory listening that he believed were necessary to intervene in a communication crisis that was becoming only more dire with the onset of the Cold War. This chapter thus establishes the pacifist origins and pacifist poetics of Pacifica Radio under the leadership of Hill, from the mid-1940s until his death in 1957, as the ground on which San Francisco Renaissance poets—whose involvement with KPFA I take up in the next two chapters—negotiated their relationship to the noncommercial FM radio station as performers, producers, and listeners.

The Art of Radical Pacifism

Unlike most registered conscientious objectors in the United States during WWII, Lewis Hill came to war objection not through religious affiliation but through a secular moral commitment rooted in his participation in the pacifist movement. Born in Kansas City in 1919 and raised there and in Tulsa, Oklahoma, in a wealthy and politically influential family, Hill attended high school at a military academy that inspired his lifelong hatred of militarism.[1] Determined to escape his family's values and sphere of influence, he attended university at Stanford, where he studied philosophy and poetry, the latter with the poet-critic Yvor Winters, and became involved in the pacifist movement. Pacifism had a degree of mainstream acceptance among the U.S. public in the 1930s, as institutions like the Fellowship of Reconciliation and the War Resisters League attracted significant membership. Yet as that acceptance waned with the rise of fascism in Europe and the onset of the war, Hill remained committed to the pacifist cause. After the Japanese attack on Pearl Harbor, he registered as a CO and was drafted to alternative service at CPS camp no. 37 in Coleville, California, where he served from June 1942 until his release in October 1943 on 4-F status for a worsening spinal arthritis condition. While at the Coleville camp, Hill shared with fellow CO Roy Finch his vision of a radio station that would be "like a living room," where people would communicate genuinely with one another about vital, contentious issues, their dialogue carrying out over the wireless to a wider public.[2] After his release, he moved to Washington, DC, where he worked for the duration of the war as a lobbyist for the ACLU's National Committee on Conscientious Objectors (NCCO) and as a part-time radio announcer for a commercial AM radio station. In 1946, he moved to San Francisco to pursue his own dream for an independent, pacifist radio station.

William Everson's path to pacifism was similarly unanchored, at least initially, to a denominational set of beliefs. Though the poet would later convert to Catholicism and join the Dominican order as a lay monk, taking the name Brother Antoninus, his principled stance of war objection was first influenced by the pantheism he found in Robinson Jeffers's poetry.[3] Everson was born in Sacramento in 1912 and spent much of his early adulthood in the San Joaquin Valley, where he worked in farms and canneries before leaving to join the Civilian Conservation Corps. In 1938, he married Edwa Poulson, bought land to start a vineyard, and started his career as a poet, publishing three books between 1935 and 1942. In 1943, after registering as a CO, he was conscripted to CPS camp no. 56 in Waldport, Oregon, known as Camp Angel, where he served until 1945; he spent time at other camps before his release in July 1946. COs at the Waldport camp were tasked with forestry work, but while there, Everson also founded Untide Press, led the establishment of the Fine Arts group, and composed most of his long autobiographical poem about the war, "Chronicle of Division." Everson published the first section of the poem under the title *The Waldport Poems* through Untide Press in 1944; the complete five-part poem appeared in *The Residual Years* (1948), published by New Directions. Like Hill, he moved to San Francisco after the war, and became an influential voice in the San Francisco Renaissance.

The system of CPS camps that structured Hill's and Everson's experience of war resistance was unique to WWII.[4] Prior to the U.S. entry into the war, a delegation of the historic peace churches of the Brethren, Friends (Quakers), and Mennonites negotiated with President Roosevelt and Congress a new accommodation for COs who refused military service on religious, philosophical, or political grounds in an effort to forestall the harsh prison sentences given to war resisters during World War I. Under the Selective Training and Service Act of 1940, CPS camps, modeled after and often located in former Civilian Conservation Corps camps, were established to provide forms of alternative service for COs in "work of national importance." An unprecedented number of men applied for 4-E CO status during WWII, the majority citing membership in one of the peace churches, and while many served in noncombatant roles in the military, nearly 12,000 were sent to CPS camps.[5] The historic peace churches managed and financed the 151 camps, and the federal government provided camp space, supplies, and work tasks that ranged from park maintenance and agricultural labor to work in mental hospitals. Although many COs were initially proud to serve in this capacity, some came to feel that their labor for CPS was more "make-work" than "work of national importance," engineered to separate and isolate them from the general population without regard for their skills or their safety, and without wages or benefits for their families.[6]

Little united the nation's COs beyond the act of war refusal, a stance taken for divergent reasons by men from diverse religious, economic, and geographic backgrounds. As Everson writes in "Chronicle of Division," the only "binding belief" linking the men in the camps was "cruxed on rejection: / *Thou shalt not kill.*"[7] Experience in the isolated and intense community of the camps, however, led to another shared rejection: CPS itself, which to some COs represented an unethical and hypocritical compromise between the peace churches and the U.S. military. At notorious camps like those in Germfask, Michigan, and Minersville, California, COs protested conscription, racial segregation, and labor conditions through radical acts of resistance that included hunger strikes, work stoppages, walkouts, and theatrical protests. Other COs deserted the camps, taking advantage, in Everson's words, of "the vast temptation and the obscure threat" of the camp's gate, "Broad for departure, / To pass if we choose" (*Residual Years*, 14). COs who protested or deserted the camps often faced punishment, criminal charges, or imprisonment, but their tactics spread quickly. Everson participated in strikes and demonstrations at Waldport in protest against conscription and the dangerous labor conditions of the forestry camp. And Hill, as part of his work for the NCCO, advocated on behalf of striking war resisters at camps and prisons, though he also came to question the efficacy of their tactics for sparking a broader pacifist movement.[8]

Radicalized COs, together with other war resisters in federal prisons who had been denied 4-E status or who refused the draft altogether, sought to put into practice a pacifism that signified more than a personal or denominational objection to war: "a way of life," as A. J. Muste put it, and "an economic and social movement" committed not only to the refusal of violence but to social justice and political change through spiritual transformation, direct action, and civil disobedience.[9] Though radical pacifist views were extremely unpopular during the war, they would have far-reaching influence in the decades that followed, as the civil rights, antiwar, antinuclear, and student movements could trace many of their leaders (such as Bayard Rustin and Dave Dellinger), institutions (such as the Congress of Racial Equality), ideologies, and nonviolent tactics of resistance to the camps and prisons of WWII radical pacifism. Roy Kepler, an early KPFA staff member and the founder of Kepler's Books in Palo Alto, spent part of his conscripted years at both the Germfask and Minersville camps; he would later recall that his "own experience was one of entering the camp in a state of euphoria.... The biggest single mistake the government made was introducing us to each other.... They helped build the pacifist network."[10] After the war, Hill would rely on this pacifist network to fund and establish Pacifica Radio; in turn, KPFA would become a rare broadcasting outlet for radical and secular pacifists like Muste, Dellinger, and Rustin to communicate the principles of nonviolent social protest.

The belief that radical pacifism entailed more than an objection to or even dramatic acts of protest against war—that it demanded a complete spiritual and philosophical transformation of the individual and society—inspired the birth of a cultural wing of the movement, whose nascent beginnings centered around the formation of the Waldport CO artists' group. Everson may not have felt Kepler's "euphoria" when he stepped off the bus in Waldport in January 1943, but he was initially hopeful about what might be accomplished there. In "Chronicle of Division," Everson recalls how, upon arriving at Waldport, he "marvel[ed]" to find himself in the presence of so many other COs: "This he had dreamed, / In his glimmering visions, / Projecting the shape of some nebulous life" (*Residual Years*, 14). Indeed, in earlier poems like "Now in These Days," Everson had addressed an imagined community of fellow war resisters, a masculine "we," "Who, outside the narrows of nationalism and its iron pride, / Reject the compulsion" and find strength in "know[ing] we have not been alone" (117, 118). The camps owed their existence to conscription and war, but they still held out the faint utopian promise of concretizing in place this fraternal community of war resisters. Though "Chronicle of Division" depicts the poet's rapid disillusionment with this promise—in part because it enforced a separation of men from women that in the poem is seen to lead to the dissolution of the poet's marriage and his spiritual crisis—the "nebulous life" of pacifist community did initially take form for Everson with the establishment of Untide Press and the formation of the Fine Arts group.[11]

A few of the COs at Waldport had already started a little mimeograph of satiric writing and poetry they titled *Untide* (after the official camp newsletter *Tide*) before Everson's arrival, and once there, Everson collaborated with its editors to put out a fine letterpress volume of his early pacifist poems, *X War Elegies* (1943). Encouraged by the success of the slim volume, Untide Press went on to publish more letterpress books by Everson, Glenn Coffield, Kenneth Patchen, and the Canadian poet and anarchist George Woodcock. In addition to bringing outside attention to pacifist poets, these books also circulated in a network of CO periodicals and small presses that helped to link the isolated camps with one another. In 1943, Everson corresponded with Kemper Nomland and Kermit Sheets, editors of *Illiterati*, a little magazine published out of a nearby CPS camp in Cascade Locks, Oregon, about his idea for an arts initiative that would bring the many CO artists dispersed across the camps to one location. Skeptical at first that "a formalized project" could be organized in the camps, Everson proposed instead "simply a free anarchical association" of artists, "like our Untide and your Illiterati groups."[12] Everson was no doubt aware of the irony of his proposal to form an anarchist community in the context of a conscripted labor camp, but he still imagined that such an experiment, conceptualized as "a creative living and arts camp,"[13] could "form the seed, the nucleus that may after the war, when we can make ourselves heard," instigate a movement, one that would demonstrate the fundamental "tie-in between aesthetic creativity and pacifism."[14] Everson posited that such an experiment could represent as strong a protest against conscription as strikes or walkouts, but with the potential to be sustained after the war and with a wider public impact.

In 1944, Brethren leadership approved the establishment of a Fine Arts group or "school" at Waldport with Everson as its first director, an official status that granted some resources and, most importantly, the ability to recruit transfers from other camps.[15] While members of the Fine Arts group never constituted even half of the total CO population at Camp Angel, and while fifty-hour work weeks laboring on behalf of the Forestry Service remained obligatory for most of its members, Waldport's artists made the most of the limited time, resources, and sunlight on the desolate coast.[16] Small press publishing continued to be a major focus, especially after Nomland and Sheets brought *Illiterati* to Waldport and Martin Ponch arrived with his magazine *The Compass*, but Fine Arts members also gave musical recitals, taught art and craft classes to other COs, exhibited art, and formed a collective theater group that wrote and performed original dramatic works.[17] In addition to poets and printers, Waldport's notable Fine Arts members included book designer Adrian Wilson, painter Morris Graves, violinist Broadus Erle, and artist and sculptor Clayton James. There were also women who, though not conscripted to military or alternative service, voluntarily participated in the artistic, administrative, and social activities of Fine Arts (such as pacifist Manche Langley, who volunteered as the Fine Arts secretary); their presence was controversial, however, among both the conservatively religious COs of the camp and neighboring communities wary of the war resisters in their midst.

In 1944, as part of his outreach to CO artists who might be interested in transferring to Waldport, Everson wrote to Lewis Hill, who he knew only as a young poet who had submitted a few poems for publication in *Illiterati*. Everson's letter took some time to reach Hill, detouring first through the Coleville camp where Hill had served before his discharge. In Hill's eventual letter of reply, he informed Everson of his new position with the NCCO, "exploring," in his words, "the ineptitude of American pacifism."[18] Hill knew of "the Waldport colony," and wrote of his admiration for

Untide Press and Everson's poetry, praising *X War Elegies* as "the ranking achievement of CPS and an ample definition of your leadership in the literary phase of war objection." But, Hill explained, he would not be able to join their initiative:

> During my last days in CPS—indeed during most of those days—I wrestled like everyone else with the problem of remaining or not, or at least of relating my presence in CPS to some integer of integrity. Before my discharge—it was a great surprise—I had concluded that one must either walk out cleanly or find a cove in some tributary such as yours. I had decided to follow the former course, and doubt if I could have accepted your generous suggestion at that juncture. But you're attempting a fine thing, I believe, and I wish there were some way I could participate in it more than is possible.

Hill's thwarted resolution to "walk out cleanly," or to desert the camp in protest against all forms of conscription, reflected the radicalization of his pacifist views, but his assessment of the Waldport Fine Arts group as merely "a cove in some tributary" of CPS was also indicative of his growing disillusionment with how marginalized, and therefore easily contained, the pacifist movement had become. Pacifists, Hill had become increasingly convinced, needed better, more modern ways of communicating to the broader public; as he asserted later, it was long past time to reject "the puerile notion of creating an awareness of crisis by entering the community from the outside at the top of one's lungs, with a crummy propaganda sheet."[19] Hill's critique of the pacifist movement's outmoded methods of communication furthered his resolve to license an independent radio station that could serve as a blueprint for other pacifist counterinstitutions that would attract cultural producers. With such ambitions in mind, it's no wonder that Hill initially saw the Waldport Fine Arts group—an official CPS project under the authority of Brethren leaders—as a minor "cove in some tributary."

Everson, too, later described Waldport as a place "where people, penned out of their lives, fashion another, a kind of minor civilization."[20] But Everson first envisioned the Fine Arts group neither as confined to nor accepting of CPS conscription but as a "seed" that, after the war, might inspire actual anarcho-pacifist artist communities, presses, and counterinstitutions that would grow a cultural movement—not unlike, in other words, Hill's vision for a pacifist radio station. Even during the war, Waldport's network extended beyond COs in the camps, and Untide Press, *Illiterati*, and *The Compass* ranked alongside *Circle* and *Ark* as important early publishers of West Coast writing in the 1940s, establishing a regional tradition of small press publishing and literary experimentation that would thrive in the 1950s and 1960s. And Hill did go on to participate in the Waldport experiment from afar—by continuing his correspondence with Everson, by reading and publishing in Untide publications, and, later, by recruiting former CO artists from Waldport and its network to help establish Pacifica Radio.[21] In fact, the Fine Arts group at Waldport, and the debates that it inspired about pacifist culture and art, helped to shape Hill's vision of how radio could promote pacifism as much through the broadcasting of poetry, drama, and music as through roundtable discussions and independent news and public affairs.

But what distinguished a poem, a work of art, or a radio station as pacifist? In debating this question, Everson and other members of the Fine Arts group would eventually settle on a curiously depoliticized aesthetic that focused on the spiritual transformation of the individual rather than societal transformation. After the Fine Arts group became official at Waldport, Everson published a mission statement that echoed his earlier correspondence with Sheets and Nomland in claiming an "inherent sympathy between the purposes of pacifism and the purposes of art" and arguing that CO artists could have a "wide influence" on an American society starved for authentic, universal, humanist art.[22] Pacifist artists, he explained, need not concern themselves only with antiwar content. If artistic creation participated in, by imitating, the creative, organic, spiritual forces of life, then it necessarily communicated humanist and pacifist values of the sanctity of life, the inviolable rights of the individual, and the indivisibility and interdependence of all living things. Antiwar statements, Everson suggested, were therefore redundant or even counterproductive, as preserving artistic freedom must mean above all avoiding the encroachment of a preformed ideological content—even if that ideological content was pacifism itself.

This view was a typical one among WWII CO poets, whose views on art and politics were shaped as much by the literary historical context of the 1930s and 1940s as by their war resistance. As Philip Metres argues, pacifist poets of Everson's generation shared a "characteristic resistance to issue-oriented poetry in favor of a peace culture," in part because they associated "issue-oriented poetry" with the socialist poetry of the interwar period.[23] This resistance was not simply due to an anarcho-pacifist antipathy to communism; Everson, for example, had cited Mexican communist art of the 1930s as a model for the Waldport artists in a letter to Nomland, contrasting "the vitality of conviction" among Mexican communist painters with what he saw as the failure of the American Left to create a lasting art.[24] In his own poetry, Everson attempted to navigate what Metres describes as "a third way between 'engaged' poetry and the apolitical poetry trumpeted by the New Critics," seeking "an art that refuses to be propaganda yet still emerges from an ideological position."[25] In his role as an editor for Untide Press, though, resistance to explicitly political art often took priority, even leading Everson to distance himself from some of his earlier work.[26] Objecting to Kenneth Patchen's original title for a volume of poetry to be published by Untide, "Poems Against War," Everson cited the "declamatory cover" of his own *X War Elegies* as a negative example of an overt "propaganda point of view" that went against the press's publicly staked position of artistic integrity over political purpose.[27] The cover and book design for Patchen's volume, retitled *An Astonished Eye Looks Out of the Air* (1945), would later inspire Lawrence Ferlinghetti's City Lights Books Pocket Poets series, giving vivid illustration to Waldport's influence on the small presses that gave rise to the San Francisco Renaissance. The link between Untide Press and City Lights Books, however, could also be seen as forecasting the fraught debates about committed and autonomous poetry, participation and disaffiliation, marginalization and mass public appeal, that would return with renewed waves of intensity in the Vietnam War era—and that would find their way onto Pacifica Radio stations.[28]

Other editors at Waldport expressed views similar to Everson's. Kemper Nomland, in a 1944 letter to Robert Duncan soliciting poems for *Illiterati*, enclosed a press statement describing the periodical as "a magazine of directed pattern in creative expression" that, though published by COs in a CPS camp, "is not exclusively pacifist in material, nor in contributors, although it will be predominantly so." *Illiterati*'s mission, it explained, was guided not by the editors' committed pacifism but by a shared belief "that all organisms form an interconnected whole, and that separation is possible only on the mental or verbal level."[29] *Illiterati* did sometimes adopt a more overtly radical antiwar rhetoric; the title page of its summer 1945 issue, for example, is emblazoned with the statement: "THE ILLITERATI PROPOSES: CREATION, EXPERIMENT, AND REVOLUTION TO BUILD A

CHAPTER 1

WARLESS, FREE SOCIETY; SUSPECTS: TRADITION AS A STANDARD AND ECLECTICISM AS A TECHNIQUE; REJECTS: WAR AND ANY OTHER FORM OF COERCION BY PHYSICAL VIOLENCE IN HUMAN ASSOCIATIONS."[30] However, the poems and art published in the issue—by Everson, Hill, Nomland, Patchen, Woodcock, and Henry Miller, among others—are unified neither around this theme nor in their style.

Hill's contribution to the issue, a poem titled "Of a Woman Screaming in the Street," suggests that he shared the expansive view of pacifist aesthetics advocated at Waldport. The poem presents a surreal scene of abstract horror, in which an unnamed woman's screams ring out across a desolate town square. The townspeople, whose collective point of view is represented by the first-person plural speaker, "only hear her" but "[n]one of us asks what is she saying." In the last stanza, the poem forecasts a terrible fate for the woman at the hands of an unspecified *they*: "They will knock the beam from her exploded eye, / Put gas in her throat, unlock her teeth, / While we sit under amber lamps / With thoughts that roll around the orb to sleep."[31] The imagery of bodily dismemberment, gas, complicit bystanders, and (elsewhere in the poem) explosions evokes the horrors of WWII and the Holocaust. But unlike other explicitly antiwar poems published in the same issue of the *Illiterati*—like Patchen's "The Stars Go to Sleep So Peacefully," in which "Truth rots in a bloody ditch; / And love is impaled on a million bayonets"[32]—Hill's poem makes a more general provocation to the reader to resist conformity and awaken an individual sense of responsibility to act against violence. Poetically, in terms of its imagery, diction, and metrically varied stanza form, the poem also situates itself within the kind of modernist lineage signaled by the issue's cover and artwork.

Given the emphasis in WWII radical pacifism on direct action, it may seem ironic that Waldport artists would suppress direct rhetoric in their efforts to establish a cultural wing for the movement. But we should see both as rooted in an overarching emphasis on individualism. For the architects of the American radical pacifist movement, as historian James Tracy explains, "the inviolable constitutive unit of society was the individual," making their pacifism "a thoroughly American radicalism" that owed as much to Thoreau as to Gandhi.[33] Hill and Everson were both critical of the radical pacifist movement's reliance on isolated, individual acts of symbolic resistance in the absence of a wider movement, but they also both believed that the creation of a pacific world—and the possibility of a truly free, anarchic society built on free association—must begin as a revolution in individual consciousness.

Everson's own poem about his experience in the CO camps, however, raises doubts about whether such a revolution in the self is possible without a broader societal revolution.[34] In part 1 of "Chronicle of Division," first published by Untide Press as *The Waldport Poems*, Everson shows how the pervasive authoritarian structure of the camps—and, by extension, the militarized state—isolates the individual and destroys the poet's "glimmering visions" of pacifist community (*Residual Years*, 14). The long poem represents this conflict in various ways, but in its first instances it appears as a problem of communication that is, importantly for my inquiry here, represented as a corruption of the act of listening. Early in Everson's poem, the speaker assumes that his difficulty in finding the community he seeks with the other COs is the result of insurmountable ideological differences between them:

> The pacifist speaks,
> Face to face with his own kind,
> And seeks to fashion a common course
> That all may mark.
> But whatever he offers,
> Finds already framed in another's thought
> A divergent approach.
>
> (15)

Bringing his soapbox into the Oregon forest, "the pacifist" finds that while his fellow COs share a rejection to war, their common dissenting stance does not result in a corresponding consensus on "a common course" of action. The next stanza, however, indicates that the failure to "fashion a common course" may have as much to do with surveillance by camp authorities as with ideological disagreement among the COs. While "the pacifist" holds forth, another figure sits back: "Apart on his rock, / The forester sucks his sufficient quid, / And never hears" (15–16). The forester is not a CO but a member of the Forestry Service who is there to oversee their labor and, the poem indicates, to eavesdrop on them. When the pacifist ends his speech—"[w]hen the rebel lays down his irksome axe at last"—the forester who "never hears" the meaning of what has been said but only the fact of its dissension, "[h]as only to scrawl the offending name" to seal the "rebel's" fate (16). The act of listening—necessary for the peaceful resolution of conflict—is weaponized by the camp's administration into a mechanism not of understanding but of control, rendering any hope of real community among the COs impossible.

The idea that communication is impossible in the context of an unfree society, and that listening as well as speech could be corrupted by authoritarianism, was also a belief deeply held by Hill, and it contributed to Hill's own sense of disillusionment with the failures of CPS—as well as with the American system of commercial radio. But while, as Metres argues in reference to Everson, "the larger trajectory in CPS life" may have been "from initial utopian promise to discontent and gradual dissolution," if we follow the movements and commitments of WWII radical pacifists into the late 1940s and beyond, we find not disengagement but an effort to engage on different terms on the grounds of an American society only nominally postwar.[35] Many former COs that had served in West Coast CPS camps, including many of the artists from Waldport, moved to San Francisco, where they shored up the city's reputation as a stronghold for dissenting politics, experimental arts and community, and alternative media. *Illiterati* editor Kermit Sheets, for example, went on to co-found the San Francisco Interplayers theater group and (with James Broughton) Centaur Press, which published Robert Duncan's *Medieval Scenes* (1950), among other works. And Everson became an active figure in the Bay Area poetry community, even after he entered the Dominican order, earning him the nickname "the Beat friar."

Indeed, it's hard to imagine how a pacifist radio station could have survived the hostile political and media climate of the immediate postwar years without this Bay Area community of former COs and pacifist artists. In 1946, with his work for the NCCO over, Hill and his wife, Joy Cole Hill, moved to San Francisco to make his dream for Pacifica Radio a reality. "Peace," as Everson ironically puts it at the end of "Chronicle of Division," may have been "[b]reached in the air over Nagasaki" (*Residual Years*, 55), but the birth of the atomic age amid escalating tensions between the U.S. and the Soviet Union, the continuation of conscription, and racial, social, and political conflict raised new exigent crises for the pacifist cause. But how to make the pacifist's voice heard in a postwar society celebrating victory in "the good war"? The rhetoric of the war had succeeded in painting pacifists as morally suspect outsiders, while the peace movement's failure to respond coherently to the rise of Nazism became only starker after the full revelation of the Holocaust. The future of radical pacifism,

Hill believed, would require a more compelling, holistic, and aesthetic imagination of a "pacific world," and a broadcast signal to transmit it.

Pacifica Radio and the "Audience of One"

In a 1952 lecture delivered to the Mental Health Society of Northern California and broadcast over Pacifica Radio station KPFA, Lewis Hill diagnosed postwar American society as suffering from an acute communication crisis. "In the vast suburbs of the dominant middle class," he opined, "where the individual and the electrical appliance alike are plugged into a socket of uniformity," each person lives as if trapped in a "private room."[36] This culture of bourgeois conformism had led, in his view, to "a general breakdown in the rules and customs of communication that might otherwise effectively link one private room with another," rendering citizens helpless to respond to an undefined "threat" that Hill depicted as rapidly approaching their door—a threat that promised "to destroy everything we possess or every hope of possession, and extinguish the individual identity completely." Like the titular character in Hill's poem "Of a Woman Screaming in the Street," the implication is that you can scream if you'd like, but there will be no one to respond; the sound will only reverberate against the walls of your "private room."

The alienation of the modern suburbanite, Hill went on, can be analogized to "the plight of the radio announcer, who like the rest of us, has his private room." The radio announcer, he explained, faces the meaningless task of "daily entering a studio, opening his mouth before a microphone, and simulating the use of his own faculties in a communication of values he does not believe or possess" ("Private Room," 2). Mechanized into a transmitter for the advertiser or the state propaganda office, the announcer—like the military conscript (a connection Hill made explicit)—must suppress individual conscience and self-expression to the extent that the very act of speaking becomes a form of silencing. In Hill's view, nothing illustrated this better than a test commonly given to applicants for radio announcing jobs that required reading aloud a text of "skillfully constructed gibberish," rendered in standard English but without "rational meaning," revealing in the process the basic truth of the mockery that commercial radio made of communication (2). "An ethical correction of this situation would require," Hill asserted, "either that the announcer quit his job, or that, when using the microphone, he communicate his own values out of his own interest and necessity" (6).

Hill spoke from experience. During the final years of the war, he had worked, in addition to his job with the ACLU, as a part-time news announcer and writer for the *Washington Post* radio station WINX-AM. He quit abruptly in May 1945, after refusing to read on the air a story about the notorious Japanese American internment camp at Tule Lake that he considered to be propagandistic.[37] Hill's idea for Pacifica Radio emerged, as we've seen, out of his embedded critique of the radical pacifist movement, but it was equally shaped by his critique of the radio industry's complicity in the war. As Susan J. Douglas observes, "World War II was a radio war" that brought the dramatic sounds of rallies, political speeches, and, for the first time, battlefields into Americans' homes.[38] For many, radio offered a narrative of national consensus under trusted leadership in a time of uncertainty and fear. But for war resisters like Hill and Everson, radio was a clear enemy of peace. "The world wars on," Everson writes in "Chronicle of Division," "But the abstract voice that spills from the box / Cannot bring it clear" (*Residual Years*, 22). Radio's dominance as a mass medium in the 1930s and 1940s gave it profound influence on American public opinion, and the radio-savvy Roosevelt administration had been quick to recruit it for the war effort. The broadcast networks, fearful of threatened antitrust regulation or even a complete government takeover (as had happened during World War I), were eager to comply. Supported by the new federal Office of War Information, which directly disseminated information and programming to the networks, and constrained by the FCC's 1941 decision to effectively ban editorializing in broadcasting, the radio industry helped to build a national consensus on military conscription and intervention prior to and during the U.S. involvement in the war. Hill's critique of radio went much further, though; in his view, the history of mass broadcasting in the U.S. and Europe had so far primarily served to stifle dissent, block public debate necessary for a functioning democracy, and facilitate the spread of propaganda on an unprecedented scale.

Hill's belief that radio was both the cause of and a potential cure for a global crisis in communication was typical in the era when *communication* took on new connotations as a cultural buzzword and object of institutional study. The rise of communication theory in the late 1940s was driven in part by fears that mass media—radio in particular—had created a "mass society" of alienated individuals no longer fully capable of speaking or listening to one another, eroding the necessary conditions for democracy and the public sphere. As early as 1938, Theodor W.

Adorno had argued that the commercial standardization of music, to which radio contributed, led to the "reduction of people to silence, the dying out of speech as an expression, the inability to communicate at all."[39] And like Hill, Adorno also associated radio with the "private room" of the atomized bourgeois subject, claiming, in an unfinished study based on research he conducted for the Princeton Radio Research Project, that the subsumption of radio into the private realm made it an essentially authoritarian medium. "When a private person in a private room is subjected to a public utility mediated by a loudspeaker," Adorno writes, "his response takes on aspects of a response to an authoritarian voice even if the content of that voice or the speaker to whom the individual is listening has no authoritarian features whatsoever."[40] For Adorno, radio's fundamental deception lies in its acousmatic veiling of the source of the broadcast, which enables radio voices to sound as if they derived from the listener's private property or, since it amounts to the same thing in a capitalist society, the listener's private mind: "the more [the listener] gets the impression that his own cupboard, his own phonograph, his own bedroom speaks to him in a personal way, devoid of the intermediary stages of the printed word; the more perfectly he is ready to accept wholesale whatever he hears."[41] Adorno argued that the authoritarian structure of radio could not be overcome, but Hill and the other founders of Pacifica Radio believed that it could be—despite or even because of what Hill described as the medium's "peculiar intimacy," its "nightly solicitude to your own internal organs."[42]

In the summer of 1946, Hill officially incorporated the Pacifica Foundation in San Francisco as a nonprofit with the mission, as he defined it in a fundraising prospectus, to establish "new channels of education" to support "the cause of peace."[43] Of the four incorporators named alongside Hill—H. Don Kirschner, Homer Sisson, William Triest, and John Waldron—all had connections to the pacifist movement except Waldron, a prominent radio producer, whose name lent Pacifica credibility as a media institution.[44] These men were primarily signatories and advisors, though; the Berkeley-based group who actively worked alongside Hill to secure the funding, license, and talent to launch Pacifica's first radio station included E. John Lewis, a former CO; Edward Meece, a former CO who became the station engineer; pacifist composer Americo Chiarito and his wife, Gertrude Chiarito, who became the station's first music director and accountant, respectively; and then-married couple Richard Moore, a poet and dancer, and Eleanor McKinney, a radio producer. Moore and McKinney would be especially instrumental in recruiting poets to KPFA, and McKinney's radio experience was invaluable at a station that attracted more committed pacifists than radio professionals.

The Pacifica Foundation first proposed to establish an AM radio station in Richmond, California: an ethnically diverse, working-class, and rapidly growing community five miles north of Berkeley. The FCC, however, under pressure from local NBC and CBS affiliates concerned about signal interference, declined Pacifica's application. With no viable AM channels left in the area, Hill and the other founders quickly shifted their efforts to establishing an FM station in Berkeley. It was a promising and precarious moment to start a noncommercial FM radio station: the FCC had finally reopened licensing for FM broadcasters and had created new low-wattage licenses and a designated frequency range for educational and noncommercial broadcasters. The 1948 fundraising prospectus for KPFA was right, moreover, to assert that "it has been an accepted fact for some time that FM radio is destined to replace AM as the chief method of aural broadcasting," though it would take much longer to do so than Hill and the other founders could have imagined, belying their optimistic claim that "independent stations can bank on a sound economic future."[45] The change in station location also had significant implications for Hill's pacifist project. The decision was practical: Berkeley was one of the few communities in the area with enough households with FM receivers to make launching an FM station feasible, and the university city promised a wellspring of local talent and expertise from which to develop programming. But while Berkeley may have seemed a better fit for Pacifica's founders (McKinney states that starting KPFA "was like creating a place where we could be with people like ourselves"), media historian Matthew Lasar points out that the move risked making KPFA subject to the kind of "ivory-towerism" that Hill—and Pacifica's first prospectus—had objected to in the pacifist movement.[46] To borrow Hill's phrase from his letter to Everson about the Waldport artist group, KPFA would often appear in its early years like "a cove in some tributary" of American radio, but this position of marginality in U.S. media was also what facilitated the mutually influential relationship between KPFA and the San Francisco Renaissance.

On the afternoon of April 15, 1949, on a low-wattage transmitter and license, KPFA made its first official broadcast with a brief announcement by Hill and the first installment of a folk music program produced by Richard Moore.[47] Over the next sixteen months, during a trial period they termed "KPFA Interim," the fledgling FM station broadcast a daily program of classical and folk music, drama and literature, children's programming, cultural commentaries, and public affairs programs. Broadcast roundtable discussions sought to create dialogue between differing viewpoints, particularly on subjects of pressing interest to the station's founders, such as "How Can War with Russia Be Prevented?"; "Should the University of California Faculty Sign the Loyalty Oath?"; and "The Dilemma of America's Racial Antagonisms" (on which Bayard Rustin appeared as a panelist). Literary programming included a series for local book clubs developed in cooperation with the Great Books Foundation and a Friday evening poetry reading series that sometimes broadcast new spoken word LP recordings in their entirety. Local poets appeared on various programs in this first year, often through a connection to Moore. Robert Duncan joined an early roundtable to discuss "Ezra Pound, Poetry and Politics" with George Leite, editor of *Circle*; Muriel Rukeyser appeared on a program about the Sacco-Vanzetti case; the writer and ethnographer Jaime de Angulo hosted a children's program, *Indian Tales*, derived from Indigenous stories he had collected in his research with Pit River tribal communities; and Jack Spicer joined Moore's *Folk Music Series* to host a weekly show on American ballads.[48] Mounting debts forced KPFA off the air in August 1950, but a successful listener-led subscription drive put the station back on the air with a more powerful transmitter the next summer.

KPFA's listener-subscription funding model was based on Hill's theory that some listeners could be persuaded to pay for a free signal if they felt the noncommercial station's programming was superior to commercial offerings, and that a listener-supported station could fully fund its operations if just 2 percent of the available radio audience subscribed.[49] While voluntary listener-sponsorship is now a common source of revenue for public radio and television—because of the influence of Pacifica Radio—it was a radical, untested, and perhaps foolhardy theory when KPFA adopted it, and it remained more a theory than a practical solution at first. In 1952, Hill secured Pacifica's first major grant from the Ford Foundation Fund for Adult Education, and grants from the Ford and Rockefeller Foundations would sustain the station through the worst of FM's drought years in the 1950s.[50]

A strong ethos of anti-commercialism informed not only the economics of KPFA but every aspect of its sound. If commercial radio avoided controversy in pursuit of a bland "objectivity," KPFA would seek to air minority opinions, debates on controversial issues, and literature that challenged social mores and popular tastes. If commercial radio played a narrow musical repertoire of popular crooners, big band jazz, "light" classical standards, and (as the decade went on) rock 'n' roll record singles, KPFA would make use of FM's superior sound quality to broadcast "serious" classical and opera music, folk music with an ethnographic aura, educated musical commentary, and live sessions with local musicians. And it wasn't just through its programming that KPFA broke with the conventions of commercial radio; in Eleanor McKinney's words:

> There were no fanfares, no themes, no organ strings. Duration of programs was designed to fulfill natural content—not to be chopped off in regular segments by the stop watch. So that programs could begin at scheduled times, the spaces between the flexible endings were filled with bits of prose or poetry, or simply by silence when the mood or impact would have been jarred by a sudden shift to another subject.[51]

The "bits of prose or poetry" read by announcers between programs might include work by writers such as Marianne Moore, Jonathan Swift, or Henry David Thoreau or selections from periodicals like the theosophical *Manas*. Practices like these certainly marked KPFA as a new kind of radio station, but they also looked back to the early, experimental days of radio when local announcers would sometimes read poems between programs or suspend broadcasting (as KPFA did) during the dinner hour.[52] And while KPFA's anti-commercialism was linked to the pacifist beliefs of its founders, as at Waldport, the station initially seemed resistant to airing explicitly political cultural programming—an aesthetic that poets, including antiwar poets, would later overturn at the network.

KPFA also published a biweekly program guide for subscribers, the *Folio*, which Hill hoped to one day develop into a more substantial, literary publication along the lines of the BBC magazine *The Listener* (but with more of the independent, small press feel of a little magazine like *Illiterati*).[53] In its early years, the *KPFA Program Folio* featured, in addition to program listings, short cover essays anonymously penned by Hill and other staff that laid out the station's anti-commercial principles, including its commitment to free expression.[54] A *Folio* essay from 1951, for example, states, "As in ordinary conversation, actual communication can take place only when the persons involved speak as themselves."[55] Such rhetorical appeals to "ordinary conversation" echoed a persistent political and media discourse that "idealize[s] notions of the face-to-face dialogic encounter" as the mode of communication to which all public speech should aspire.[56] But they also chimed with the pacifist individualism that informed Hill's insistence on both the responsibility of the "individual before a microphone," who must seek "to communicate to a single person," and the freedom of the listener.[57] In a report on KPFA's experiment with listener-sponsorship, Hill explained that KPFA conceived of the station's audience as "an individual, whose intention was to listen"—"the audience of one"—who "was assumed to have an alertness, an intelligence, an interest, and an attention-span" similar to the broadcasters themselves.[58] Yet just as announcers new to KPFA had to be coached, as McKinney recalled, "to speak like themselves—and not like an imitation of a dulcetly-sincere announcer being sincere," so too did the listener, in the view of Pacifica's founders, need instruction in the new practices of individualized radio listening that KPFA hoped to cultivate.[59]

The broadcasting of poetry was imagined to play a particularly important role in the education of the ear of this idealized "audience of one." A 1952 *Folio* essay titled "Briefly, on the Spoken Word . . ." opens by critiquing commercial radio's flattening of the diversity of spoken English to a few standardized styles: "one for news, one for the grrreeat [*sic*] composers, and, of course, one for the commercial" (fig. 1).[60] But the essay's primary concern is the nefarious effect that the "mechanical" speech of broadcast media has on "[o]ur heritage of the spoken word," which the writer worries "is fast leaving us":

> We can say that the public does not have "an ear for verse," but the fact is that one seldom hears verse spoken or read. And there is no reason to believe that the ear is no longer capable of receiving and distinguishing subtleties, shifts of tone and richnesses of sound in the spoken word or line. True, most of what we hear is "flat," it has the monotony of a code, but the instrument for hearing is there, and, given the experience, it will respond.

The implication here is that poets, as well as radio broadcasters, have contributed to the diminishment of spoken language by keeping poetry

KPFA

PROGRAM FOLIO

MARCH 23 • APRIL 5

94.1 MC   FM CHANNEL 231

Briefly, on the Spoken Word . . .

The beauty of a tale is in the telling, and the telling becomes beautiful because of the teller's skill and his aware relation to the tale. A separation enforced in the person between himself and what he says can produce only a mechanical mouthing of syllables, no matter how smoothly they tumble forth. One might expect that on the radio we would be reminded again and again of the inherent dignity, beauty and power of human speech. But apart from the "personality" of the stars, radio has narrowed rather than extended the modes and variety of common speech. A kind of semi-official style has been developed—one for news, one for the grrreeat composers, and, of course, one for the commercial. Our heritage of the spoken word, particularly in poetry, story telling and drama, is fast leaving us because we have so little to do with it. We can say that the public does not have "an ear for verse", but the fact is that one seldom hears verse spoken or read. And there is no reason to believe that the ear is no longer capable of receiving and distinguishing subtleties, shifts of tone and richnesses of sound in the spoken word or line. True, most of what we hear is "flat", it has the monotony of a code, but the instrument for hearing is there, and, given the experience, it will respond.

Obviously, with regard to speech, more than the ear is involved; but what is in question is not a series, in complex arrangement, of meaningless sounds. The important matter is that the enormous flexibility and power of speech be employed out of the speaker's direct and controlling relation to what he has to say — whether announcing a concert or telling a story. The beauty of the speech will come clear, and the listener will recognize it, so long as the speaker speaks as himself, and not as the parrot, who amuses us only because of his wide distance from the human.

Figure 1. "Briefly, on the Spoken Word . . . ." *KPFA Program Folio* 2, no. 26 (March 23–April 5, 1952), 1. Courtesy of the Pacifica Radio Archives.

bound to the page or reading it only in the "'flat'... monotony of a code." Radio can be an outlet for authentic spoken poetry, but only if poets—like the radio announcer in Hill's "Private Room" lecture—use it to communicate an individual truth to an individual reader in order to cultivate the "instrument for hearing."

Many San Francisco poets would have agreed. Jack Spicer, for example, argued in a 1949 essay that "[p]oetry demands a human voice to sing it and demands an audience to hear it."[61] In the early years, though, the station's literary programming was dominated by BBC dramas, readings from modernist poetry, lectures by university professors, and discussions of canonical "great books." Beyond simply putting more literature on the radio, though, Hill was interested in how radio's medium-specific capabilities might be used to cultivate an "ear for verse." In the summer of 1954, he applied for and received a grant of nearly $10,000 from the Rockefeller Foundation for precisely this purpose: to establish "a gross proof of something held in doubt—that new and effective ways of employing radio for the communication of poetry are possible."[62] The programs and documents that Hill produced for this project represent only a small part of his radio production work, but they offer insight into how he conceived of poetry broadcasting as serving pacifist ends in the context of McCarthyism and the Cold War. Before turning to the local poets who brought the oral and coterie poetics of the renaissance onto KPFA, I therefore want to use this last section to listen to a few archival recordings from this project, in which Hill centers the poetry reader—not the poem or the poet—in dramatic programs that represent the subjective, transformative, and aural experience of poetry through and as a "theater of the mind."[63]

"Experiment in the Broadcasting of Poetry"

This is an essay. A formal essay. And what is more it's a *literary* essay. All literary essays as you know are very difficult. But the present one is especially so, for it's about *poetry*, and what is more, *modern* poetry. All modern poetry, as you know, is somewhat obscure and boring. For my part I rather dislike poetry... these precious modern poets will make a fool of you, unless you give as good as you take. And for my part, I flatter myself that I'm way ahead of them.[64]

So begins *A Word by Wallace Stevens: An Essay for Radio*, one of the programs that Hill created in 1954 as part of his grant-funded "Experiment in the Broadcasting of Poetry," conducted on behalf of the National Association of Educational Broadcasters (NAEB), broadcast on KPFA in 1955, and preserved by the Pacifica Radio Archives.[65] The voice is Hill's, playing the role of a pompous literary critic, and the hour-long program that follows is neither an essay nor a lecture but a radio drama that centers on a fictional dialogue between a critic and an imagined reader about Wallace Stevens's "The Idea of Order at Key West." Addressing the radio listener directly, Hill explains in character that instead of "a long essay sprinkled with quotes and at the end a pious proposal that, launched into understanding, you now go read the poem yourself," he will concoct "a little fantasy," a "universal scene" of reading. The acoustic setting then shifts to the living room of an unnamed female reader addressed simply as "the Lady" (played by KPFA drama producer Virginia Maynard), who metronomically plods through the poem's iambs, despairs of ever making sense of its oblique references and unfamiliar diction, and gets continually distracted by a ringing telephone and a plate of chocolate creams—not to mention the condescending comments of the critic. Over the course of the program, the critic nevertheless succeeds in persuading her that an extended close reading of a single word in the poem—the word *mimic*—can "illumine Mr. Stevens's poem and much of his other work as well." The radio listener may be similarly persuaded by what amounts to a textbook New Critical reading of Stevens's poem, but the program's satiric tone rhetorically positions its listener at a distance from both the naive, feminized listener and the elitist, paternalistic critic, encouraging a sense of skepticism toward professional literary criticism if not, ultimately, its object of study: modern poetry.

A Word by Wallace Stevens, like several of the more innovative programs that Hill planned as part of this project, may appear strikingly unlike the ways we are used to encountering poetry in broadcast media today. None of the programs Hill designed feature the poet reading their own work; none engage actual critics or poets to speak as experts; none take a documentary approach to their literary subject; and none appear concerned with generating publicity for the poet. As Hill explained in his report to the Rockefeller Foundation, he structured his "experiment" around a quasi-scientific method of comparison between five discrete approaches to presenting poetry on the radio, all five of which he proposed to apply to the work of four poets: Wallace Stevens, Robert Lowell, Marianne Moore, and Richard Eberhart.[66] The first two approaches (the control groups, in essence) would be simple half-hour readings of selections of the writer's poetry by Hill, with the second allowing for some commentary between poems. The three remaining approaches, in contrast, would be more complex in content and execution. The third would present a scripted lecture, with "technical discussion of the poem" and "colloquial comment on the problems of the 'average reader.'" The fourth and fifth would incorporate elements of radio drama and focus on a single poem, with the fourth developing a "quasi-dramatic" representation of a reader's "wholly subjective" response to the poem, and the fifth offering a "mingling of discursive and theatrical methods."[67]

Notably, these last three approaches all focus to some extent on an imagined "average reader." In his grant report, Hill explained that his project aimed to "awaken interest in a peripheral audience" of nonacademic readers who would nonetheless be willing to give their "close attention" to a broadcast poetry program.[68] Obviously, this "peripheral audience" was not imagined to be large, and Hill echoed the rhetoric he used to characterize KPFA's intended listenership as a "minority audience" or "audience of one" who would listen freely and discriminatingly. That audience's interest in modern poetry, however, he took to be latent and resistant, so to engage their interest he sought—particularly in the more dramatic approaches—radio-specific, or *radiogenic*, approaches to broadcasting poetry.[69] As radio scholar Kate Lacey observes, discourses about the radiogenic, which go back to the invention of mass broadcasting, have often involved two related calls: first, "a call for a form of textual production" that "would explicitly problematize the acoustic reorganization of sensory experience and legitimize sound broadcasting as art," and second, "a call for forms of broadcasting that properly acknowledged and engaged radio's distant, dispersed and domesticated audiences—its listening publics."[70] Hill's dramatic programs participated in this discourse by drawing critical attention to the apparatus of radio and by directly addressing a specific radio audience. Moreover, Hill sought to use the resources of radio to show how poetry could transform an "average reader" into an intentional *listener*, the "audience of one." This transformation had a sense of urgency for Hill in the context of the Cold War, and some of the programs more or less explicitly concern the question of how a properly attuned and literate ear might respond to a fragmented society once again racing to the brink of war.

Let's return, then, to *A Word by Wallace Stevens*. In this program, which exemplifies Hill's fifth approach by "mingling... discursive and theatrical methods," the supposed resistance of the "average reader" to modern poetry is exaggerated, mocked, and gendered through the character of the Lady. Within the fiction of the radio drama, she is expressly conjured not as an individual but as a recognizable type, "not *a* lady, but *the* Lady," as the critic puts it, "a completely general and typical lady... with nothing whatever to distinguish [her] from innumerable male and female ladies in the same situation" (Hill, *Word*). The "situation," put broadly, is modernity, and the Lady represents the white, Christian, bourgeois modern subject of middlebrow tastes and conformist attitudes. In critiquing these middle-class attitudes as feminized and feminizing, Hill draws on sexist tropes common in both modernist literature and radio discourse, in which the figure of the passive female reader/listener stands for the supposedly emasculating, infantilizing effects of mass culture. These sexist tropes were still in prevalent use in the 1950s, though "the Lady," as the formality of her moniker suggests, is also intended here as an anachronism: a stereotype of Victorian mores who appears as though she has been lifted from one of Stevens's poems and dropped in a postwar suburban living room.

To understand Stevens's poem, the drama suggests, the Lady, our "exemplary reader," must confront her resistance to modern poetry, which the critic diagnoses as arising from a fear not of misunderstanding but of understanding too well. "Everything of the little you think you understand in poetry," says Hill in the arch voice of the critic, "sets out immediately into those 'realities' on the horizon where no suburbanite should ever travel" (Hill, *Word*). To avoid these realities, he argues, the suburbanite sees "the world as a little space" where "you can move just a little this way and just a little that way, but not very far in any direction, because there's a great hurricane of problems you'd rather not think about just out of sight." Here is Hill's "private room" again: a constructed space of false security, privacy, and containment menaced by abstract threats but closed to any genuine communication with the outside, where the modern bourgeois subject lives alienated, afraid, and unfree. But if the conjoined imagery of containment, conformity, and white suburbia implies a more direct critique of 1950s American society, the critic never makes it explicit, as he guides his protégé toward a New Critical reading of the poem. In fact, much of the radio drama is about the legitimacy of New Critical methods, as the critic seems as much concerned with explaining the hermeneutics of close reading and the intentional fallacy as he is with presenting an interpretation of Stevens's poem.

Ultimately, the critic's interpretation of "The Idea of Order at Key West" hinges on an analysis of the paradox raised in the poem: that humans can only perceive the world through our subjective faculties and thus make it in our image, and that we nonetheless can gain knowledge of an objective world that exists outside of us. The critic develops his reading through an analysis of the alliterative phrase "mimic motion" from the first stanza of the poem: "The water never formed to mind or voice, / Like a body wholly body, fluttering / Its empty sleeves; and yet its *mimic motion* / Made constant cry" (emphasis added).[71] The connotations of *mimic*, the critic explicates, etymologically carry a "faint flavor of ridicule," imbuing the phrase with irony that in turn conveys the poet's self-conscious distance from the simile in the preceding lines (Hill, *Word*). In this moment, we see the "the same consciousness observing and ordering the creation as one's own," which is the consciousness of Stevens himself, who—like the singer in the poem—is engaged in subjectively creating an ordered form out of chaos while simultaneously observing the separation of that form from an inaccessible yet objective real. The conceit of the poem, the critic explains to the Lady, rests on the fact that "the thing shaped and its shaper depend completely, equally, on one another."

The conceit of the radio drama, though, is that the character of the Lady has become in a sense the "she" of Stevens's poem, and in more ways than one: in reading and interpreting the poem, she participates in the loop of its making; at the same time, she is herself a work of artifice, a "fantasy" that stands in metaphorically for an abstract concept. As the critic explicates, the singer in Stevens's poem, like the Lady herself, "also is simply a type; she is the type of the human spirit immersed in creating a form" (Hill, *Word*). In Stevens's words, "She was the single artificer of the world / In which she sang. And when she sang, the sea, / Whatever self it had, became the self / That was her song, for she was the maker" ("Idea of Order," 129). In the final minutes of the program, the critic is displaced by his own "fantasy," drowned out by instrumental sound effects and the Lady's reverent musings on the poem she now reads with rapt attention. And as his voice and other sounds fade away, Maynard proceeds to read the poem aloud again in its entirety, her voice shedding the affectations we've come to associate with the character of the Lady as her pitch lowers and she reads slowly, melodiously, expertly. It sounds, then, as if Maynard has dropped the theatrical role to read in her own voice, as herself—reciting Stevens's words, but making them her own by giving them vocal form and investing them with personal meaning. The literal and affective shift in tone invites the listener to likewise hear the poem anew, attuned not only to the sound of the spoken words but to one's own interpreting and observing mind, engaged in the creative and critical act of listening.[72] The "average reader" is thus transformed from a type to an *individual* through specific critical practices of listening, reading, and interpretation. But by feminizing the "average reader," Hill codes these critical practices as implicitly masculine even when they are performed by a woman. As long as the "audience of one" in Hill's conception remained an abstract, universal subject, the address to the individual listener would always fail to imagine how different individuals might come to see themselves as participants in an intentional listening community, much less a society built on free association.

A Word by Wallace Stevens thus models an approach to close listening that is particular to radio yet informed by New Critical methods for reading modernist poetry. Earlier, the critic had suggested as much when he compared the "two-mindedness" conveyed in Steven's poem to the experience of radio listening:

> I say, it's almost like your own two-mindedness, sitting there near your loudspeaker, where, I flatter myself, your thought is wholly absorbed in the progress of this essay, as are I in my companion Mr. Stevens's poem. Yet, while your whole awareness is thus focused, you are surely conscious also that a mere lazy motion of one arm and two fingers at your radio determines whether my voice shall visit you or not. [Laughs] Are you not the maker of what you hear? I wager you'd be a bit disturbed if you really thought about that a while. (Hill, *Word*)

Appealing directly to the listener to see their act of radio listening as intentional and participatory rather than passive, the critic instructs the listener in a practice of "conscious" radio listening that corresponds to a central tenet of modernist poetics, in which the reader becomes a co-creator of the text by inhabiting a critical "two-mindedness." If, for Adorno, radio's disembodied voice created an "illusion of privacy" that hid its authoritarian structure in a way "devoid of the intermediary stages of the printed word," then perhaps a listener aware of their participation in the auditory illusion might restore a textuality to radio that could free it for undetermined, creative, noncoercive ends.[73] A 1954 essay in the *KPFA Program Folio* put it thusly: "As the disembodied voice can assert with awesome authority, it can also suggest, imply, evoke, start a mind in motion with a destination still to be discovered."[74] Or, in the voice of Hill's literary critic reflecting on the scene he has conjured, "Fantasy it is, but is not also this very sound, flowing from the loudspeaker in the middle of your home, a fantastic illusion?" (Hill, *Word*).

To conclude, I'd like to consider one of the other radio dramas that Hill produced as part of his "experiment" that offers a more direct pacifist critique of Cold War American society while departing in significant ways from New Critical hermeneutics. *Section of a Soliloquy: On a Poem by Robert Lowell* is the fifth in Hill's series of programs on Robert Lowell, and it represents an imagined reader's internal response to Lowell's poem "At the Indian Killer's Grave." It is worth observing from the outset that Hill's decision to feature Lowell already allowed for a pacifist interpretation in a way that his programs on Stevens did not. Lowell was imprisoned for his war refusal during WWII, and his status as a critically acclaimed and Pulitzer Prize–winning poet meant that he was in a position to bring the kind of respect and attention to the pacifist cause that Hill (and Everson) believed writers and artists could do. "At the Indian Killer's Grave" is not an explicitly antiwar poem, but it is informed by the Catholic beliefs that influenced Lowell's war resistance. Yet none of the programs that Hill planned for Lowell offer an explicitly pacifist reading of this poem, nor do they provide any context about the poet's biography, his war resistance, or the poem's critical reception. *Section of a Soliloquy* is moreover one of the stranger, and more entertaining, programs that Hill planned for his series. The half-hour psychodrama takes place entirely in the mind of a reader who has just read "At the Indian Killer's Grave" for the first time as he debates the relevance of the poem to his own life. The characters in this drama—which, according to Hill, are "based on vaudeville stereotypes" depicting "the 'rational soul' confronting its 'demoniacal principle'"—include two voices that represent these opposing sides of the reader's mind, played by Hill and KPFA staff member Charles Levy, respectively, and a narrator, played by Richard Moore.[75] For the sake of clarity, I'll refer to Hill's character as "the brain" and Levy's character as "the antagonist."

The reader in this drama is imagined to be, like Lowell, a descendant of an elite Boston family. After a brief introduction by Moore, the drama begins with Hill in the personified voice of the reader's brain, mulling over the poem he has just read and comically reflecting on his own identity as a brain: "Real fancy Boston brain, that's what I mean. Me and the old mother tissue.... All that ripe mother membrane folded around and tucked in everywhere."[76] Levy, who acts throughout the program as the other side of the reader's split psyche—its critical apparatus and psychic antagonist, quick to mock the brain's psychoanalytic obsessions with mother and with sex—soon interrupts his ramblings by presenting a stack of "files." The initial files prompt the brain to "warm up" by reciting memorized lines by T. S. Eliot, E. E. Cummings, Hart Crane, and George Herbert, but the antagonist soon forces the brain to confront a set of repressed personal files about a previous suicide attempt. The brain initially resists what Moore, as the narrator, characterizes as "the transfer of anxiety" from the reader's own trauma onto Lowell's poem, but the antagonist persists by dragging out a new set of files about the supposed "triumphs" of their Puritan colonial ancestors over Native Americans. At this point, the relationship between the dialogue and the content of "At the Indian Killer's Grave" becomes apparent, and Levy's character even explicates allusions in the poem to King Philip's War, the Wampanoag chief Metacom, and the biblical word *raca*.

One might expect that *Section of a Soliloquy* would then continue to develop a close reading of Lowell's poem, but instead, the program shifts back to the question of the poem's relevance, not only to a fictional reader (who appears to stand in for Lowell) but to the contemporary 1950s political situation in the U.S. The character of the brain is horrified, after his initial resistance, to realize that his ancestors were perpetrators of genocide, but he refuses to accept any guilt, insisting that "those were days of superstition" and "I can't help what they did." Levy's antagonist, however, draws the link between the past and present by baiting Hill's character into voicing an anticommunist paranoia:

HILL: My good man, it is rather the spies among us, agents of an alien power, conspiring to destroy our way of life, and seize our hallowed country, sir.
LEVY: Now you've got it! Hold that.
HILL: It is these whose evil designs serve a foreign tyrant that should be wiped out!
LEVY: Preach to me, tubby, attaboy!

HILL: The masses of this fair land, whom destiny has appointed to freedom, must scourge the traitors, march on the dark strongholds of tyranny, and strike them down! An enemy of freedom is lower than a beast, sir! Exterminate them, and free the earth!

LEVY (LAUGHING): Indians all over the place!

By connecting Puritan colonial violence to the anticommunist crusades of the 1950s—for the radio in 1954, no less—Hill critiques the violent, genocidal, and imperial dimensions of U.S. Cold War domestic and foreign policy. In the fiction of the drama, though, Moore's narrator dismisses the whole internal dialogue as nothing more than the reader's subjective attempt "to become the poet, as though the poem were about to be written by the reader," which, he asserts, is ultimately "absurd, and has nothing to do with the poem as the poet actually conceived it." Yet, Moore states at the end of the program that "what is lacking" in the reader's response is not critical distance or objectivity but "the experience and attitudes of several thousand mentalities making up the several thousand poems and fragments of poems which Mr. Lowell's poem imparts and receives according to the reader." "Such is the destiny of a very good poem," he continues, "to become the creation of innumerably different minds." The idea that the reader writes the poem they read echoes with the creative and critical reading/listening practice we saw in *A Word by Wallace Stevens* and suggests something about Hill's larger purpose in these programs: to show how close reading practices are useful insofar as they enable one to apply the difficult questions raised by modern poetry toward the development of an individual, ethical, and socially engaged subjectivity.

But isn't the reader-listener in this drama still locked in a "private room" of the mind? Where is the vision of how these "innumerably different minds" might communicate with one another?[77] At one point, the voice of Moore's narrator even calls into question the mind's ability to communicate with itself, before meta-discursively drawing the listener's awareness once again to their participation in making the radio text:

You will have noticed that this role, read by Mr. Hill, is a complete abstraction. Now that is the principal novelty of our program, to which we call attention. The forebrain, of course, does not converse with itself like a radio actor; on the other hand, it is rather like these sounds as they pass between the transmitter and your loudspeaker.

> In that state, we call them waves, which, as you know, do not exist, but stand for something intangible that does.

The apparent point of this analogy is to compare the way the brain communicates with the rest of the body through electrical signals to radio transmission. But there is another analogy at work here, in which radio reception is made analogous to the way literary reception is supposed to operate in an idealized print culture sphere, in which individuals transform (rather than passively receive) the information they consume through the act of reading or listening, and in doing so become participants in an imagined public.

Hill's "experiments" in poetry broadcasting, like the Waldport Fine Arts experiment, focused on the inward transformation of the individual as the basis for bringing about a peace culture in ways that also corresponded with Hill's vision for Pacifica, and that claimed a special role for poetry in the future of broadcasting and the peace movement. But if the American public had lost their "ear for verse" and developed a skepticism about the opaque academicism of modern poetry, Lowell, whose early formalism might be heard to contain something of "the monotony of a code," hardly seems the poet to revolutionize poetic listening.[78] Earlier, I noted that Adorno critiqued radio's "illusion of closeness" that in his view "dispense[s] with the intermediary, objectivating stage of printing which helps to clarify the difference between fiction and reality."[79] Many postwar experimental poets would seek a poetry that would do just the opposite: bypass the intermediary stages of print to communicate instantaneously with the individual reader. The efforts by Pacifica Radio's founders to seize the mass medium of radio to communicate to "an audience of one" thus corresponded to a parallel dream in American poetry, in which, as Kenneth Rexroth put it, the poem would "presume to speak directly from person to person, each polarity, the person at each end of the communication fully realized."[80] Many of these poets would find their way to Pacifica Radio, some even during KPFA's very first years on the air, and it is their experiments in broadcasting that would help transform the network into the voice of the counterculture.

2

KPFA AND THE SAN FRANCISCO RENAISSANCE

The idea to establish a noncommercial, pacifist radio station in Berkeley may have originated with Lewis Hill, but to hear Kenneth Rexroth tell it, KPFA-FM owed its existence as much to him and his anarchist reading group as it did to the goals of its founder. Rexroth had started the reading group, known as the Libertarian Circle, after the war, with the ambitious goal "to refound the radical movement after its destruction by the Bolsheviks and to rethink all the ideologists from Marx to Malatesta."[1] At one of the group's weekly meetings, "a tall thin man with a long dead white face and a soft, propulsive manner of speaking" "showed up unannounced" to make his pitch for Pacifica Radio to the anarchists, labor unionists, intellectuals, and poets assembled there (*Autobiographical Novel* [rev. ed.], 519). In Rexroth's account,

> He presented what was really a very simple thesis. There had been a great structural change in society, and the days of street meetings and little pamphlets were over. New, far more effective means of communication were available. It was comparatively easy and inexpensive to set up a cooperatively run listener-supported FM radio station whose signal would cover at least the entire Bay Area, and which could be supported by subscriptions without any commercials.
> Unfortunately, this was presented not simply, but in the mystifying argot of a sociology professor. It was difficult enough for the younger college educated people to follow. For the elderly Jews,

Italians, and Spanish—who after all had been reading revolutionary theory all their lives—it was totally incomprehensible.... Perhaps it was rude of me, but I had to act as his interpreter.[2]

Mocking Hill's reputation for abstraction, and characteristically aggrandizing his own role, Rexroth downplays the intellectual might of the Libertarian Circle's regular attendees, who, in addition to "elderly" anarchists well-versed in radical theory, included among the "younger college educated people" poets like William Everson, Robert Duncan, Philip Lamantia, Richard Moore, Thomas Parkinson, and Jack Spicer.[3] Hill's pitch apparently did make some impression on those gathered, though. As Rexroth accurately notes, "In the early days, many of the people in [KPFA's] administration had been members of our Circle," and many more would appear on air as program producers and guests (*Autobiographical Novel* [rev. ed.], 519). Rexroth himself hosted a weekly book review program on KPFA for more than twenty years, which made him one of Pacifica Radio's defining early voices. In fact, Rexroth first delivered this account of Hill's visit to his reading group on KPFA in the late 1970s, when he returned to Pacifica's airwaves to dictate his autobiography.[4] It was for the ears of KPFA listeners in particular, then, that Rexroth offered up his mocking description of the network's venerated founder, while cheekily claiming that KPFA should be considered one of the "most significant products" of his own circle (519).

It would be more accurate to say that the Libertarian Circle and Pacifica Radio were both products of the WWII radical pacifist movement and its postwar legacy in San Francisco. Rexroth was right, however, to emphasize the significant role that he and other San Francisco poets with anarcho-pacifist leanings would play in the history of KPFA. These poets would markedly shift KPFA's sound and aesthetic, so that, by the late 1950s, "broadcasts of the austere and formal experiments of ... modernists much admired by Hill gave way to the polymorphous cultural eruption of the Beats, where jazz, poetry, and sound effects filled the airwaves."[5] This movement toward a recognizably Beat aesthetic was precipitated by poets like Rexroth, Moore, Everson, Spicer, Duncan, Allen Ginsberg, and Lawrence Ferlinghetti, all of whom appeared on KPFA in the 1950s. As these writers brought the oral and coterie poetics of the San Francisco Renaissance onto KPFA's airwaves, they contributed to a radical reimagination of radio and its audience that would prove influential on the aesthetics and cultural politics of the FM revolution of the 1960s.

The story of the San Francisco Renaissance, particularly as it overlaps with the Beat movement, is one of the most frequently told and mythologized literary histories of the twentieth century. It is a history easily evoked by reference to a few iconic names, events, and places: the Berkeley Renaissance of the late 1940s; the 1955 Six Gallery reading; the *Howl* censorship trial, the publication of *On the Road*, and the "San Francisco issue" of *Evergreen Review*, all in 1957; the sensationalizing features on "the Beat generation" in *Life* and *Playboy*; the 1965 Berkeley Poetry Conference. Its cartography maps the locations of Berkeley cottages and North Beach bars, coffeehouses, and jazz clubs and expands to outposts in Big Sur, Bolinas, and the Sierra Nevada. Yet for all its association with specific places (now tourist destinations) in the Bay Area, the myths of the San Francisco Renaissance are also about transience and virtuality, defined by dramatic literary entrances and exits, restless journeys across country by car and train, and transnational circuits of travel, exchange, and celebrity—not to mention the pilgrimages taken by scores of young people to San Francisco, City Lights paperbacks stuffed in their jean pockets, transistor radios tuned to KPFA. If we think of the San Francisco Renaissance as, in part, a radio phenomenon, then we might first take this figuratively as indicative of the ways that the renaissance was at once locally sited and virtually "in the air": diffuse, ephemeral, ubiquitous.

The San Francisco Renaissance can be thought of as a radio phenomenon in another, more literal sense, given that KPFA, though often given only brief mention in literary histories of the era, was instrumental in creating and disseminating the "enabling fictions" of the San Francisco Renaissance.[6] Through their engagement with KPFA as program hosts, guests, and listeners, a small community of Berkeley and San Francisco poets in the 1950s came to hear their emerging poetics and nascent sense of community echoed back as a coherent West Coast avant-garde. The fact that KPFA was a radio station mattered, in that it enabled these poets to imagine literary community as, importantly, a community of listeners. In a 1961 essay, Berkeley poet and literary scholar Thomas Parkinson attributed the emergence of the San Francisco Renaissance to both the public performance and the public *broadcasting* of poetry: "Through the poetry readings in Berkeley and San Francisco and—when it began operation in 1949—over KPFA, a fairly large audience was created that accepted and took interest in poetry readings."[7] Like independent record labels such as Fantasy and Evergreen Records, KPFA helped to widen the reach of the oral poetics of the movement, but the significance of KPFA to the San Francisco Renaissance was also due to its status as a local media institution deeply embedded in a network of Bay Area academic and cultural institutions. As Lawrence Ferlinghetti and Nancy J. Peters note in their anecdotal reference work *Literary San Francisco* (1980), KPFA in the 1950s and 1960s was "an intellectual center of perhaps more temporary influence than the university," attracting "[p]ractically every important writer in the Bay Area," and especially those seeking intellectual and artistic community outside academia.[8]

This chapter begins by returning to KPFA's early years, when the mythos of a West Coast literary renaissance was still inchoate, the survival of KPFA (not to mention FM radio in general) was uncertain, and the silences of the McCarthy era were deafening, in order to better understand how the relationship between KPFA and the San Francisco Renaissance was forged. I take two programs as case studies: Jack Spicer's live folk music show on American ballads, which aired from 1949 to 1950 during KPFA's first year on the air, and Kenneth Rexroth's *Books*, the review and commentary program that Rexroth started taping for KPFA in the early 1950s, and which continued into the 1970s, eventually broadcasting over the expanded Pacifica network. These programs differed significantly from each other, and neither was exclusively about poetry, yet each played a role in the developing poetics, social formations, and reception of the Berkeley and San Francisco Renaissance. Spicer and Rexroth also each contributed to—and subverted—KPFA's early programming, broadcast aesthetics, and modes of address. Disregarding aesthetic norms for what constituted "good sound" in radio, each of these poets, in his own way, repurposed radio's intimate address to hail not an "audience of one," as Lewis Hill had conceived of it, but a listenership more akin to a literary coterie.

"Most Educational Folk-Song Program West of the Pecos"

In Jack Spicer's "An Apocalypse for Three Voices," written soon after his arrival in Berkeley in 1945, the poetic speaker imagines himself as a disc jockey:

> Or say I turn the records in a great
> Electric station, our reception famed
> As far as May or Babylon and back again.
> My great turntable is inevitable; it whirls
> Around, around, a convoluting day
> A night of static sleeplessness; it plays
> Requested favorites, universal things,
> And millions listen[9]

From his invisible studio, the poet-DJ controls the airwaves and the masses with almost godlike power, spinning his "inevitable" turntable for what might be an eternity of "static" nights and "convoluting days." That is, until the ghosts in the machine, the spirits in the ether, requisition the frequency with "[t]heir flat electric voices":

> But listen to the chorus
>   When we dead—
> Those flat and tuneless voices
>   When we dead—
> The aching chorus is broken
>   When we dead awaken
>   We will do the singing.
>   We will do the singing.
>
>   (*MV*, 12)

In this early poem, the image of a poet unwittingly broadcasting signals from a ghostly underworld anticipates the radio metaphors that Spicer would later use to describe his theory of poetic dictation, in which the poet receives rather than creates the poem, like a radio set tuned to the subversive chorus of these "flat and tuneless voices."[10] But if Spicer dreamed of broadcasting out from "a great electric station" to the receptive ears of "millions," his actual experience as host of a live folk music program on KPFA participated in a vastly different model of broadcasting, one that aimed at using the new medium of FM to communicate to a small, intentional, even singular audience.

In what follows, I try to resurrect the ghostly voices of Spicer's radio program, of which there are no known recordings, by recontextualizing Spicer's radio work in relation to the early history of KPFA, FM radio, and postwar folk music. I argue that Spicer's engagement with radio in his life and his poetry had a reciprocal effect on the medium, giving new valences to his later poetic assertion that "[t]he poet is a counterpunching radio" (*MV*, 374). My attention is therefore focused here on Spicer's radio days rather than his radio poetics, which I take up in the next chapter. Both were informed, however, by contradictory notions of publicity and reception that structured Spicer's writing life: from his desire to write an Orphic poetry that would move large audiences, to his refusal to let most of his work circulate beyond a small coterie of readers in San Francisco. These contradictions are linked to Spicer's experiences as both a radio producer and listener during a period of profound instability and innovation in American broadcasting, poetry, and politics that unfolded over the two decades in which Spicer wrote most of his poetry, from 1945 to 1965.

Spicer likely knew about the Pacifica Radio project before the establishment of KPFA. A member of Rexroth's Libertarian Circle, he may even have been at the meeting where Lewis Hill pitched his idea for an alternative radio station. It was at another meeting of the anarchist reading group in 1946 that Spicer had first met Robert Duncan—an event so auspicious for both men's lives that Spicer would sometimes identify 1946 as his birth year.[11] Spicer introduced Duncan to Robin Blaser, and soon a vital, erotic, and competitive friendship developed between the three poets who formed a coterie they mythologized as the "Berkeley Renaissance." Spicer, Duncan, and Blaser's use of the term *renaissance*, unlike its more general use in the San Francisco Renaissance a decade later, expressed their shared interests in medieval and early modern history. These interests were influenced by the German historian Ernst Kantorowicz, whose celebrated University of California lectures on medieval theology and politics they attended, and whose former connection to the mystical, homosexual circle of poet Stefan George appealed to their own coterie sensibilities. Kantorowicz's lectures were also attended by the young poet and dancer Richard Moore, who had recently returned to Berkeley in 1948 with his wife, Eleanor McKinney.[12] After hearing Hill's pitch at Rexroth's circle, McKinney left her job as a radio producer at a local NBC affiliate to devote her energies to Pacifica Radio—an effort that Moore soon joined, too.[13]

Spicer's entry into radio would result from his participation in this network of poetic, anarchist, academic, and sexual connections that created the electric ether of the Berkeley Renaissance and helped spark the launch of KPFA. Around the same time, he became increasingly interested in the question of how poets could reach new audiences by restoring to poetry its connection to orality and song and by engaging new media. In 1949, Spicer contributed a short essay to the University of California's *Occident Magazine* for a feature titled "The Poet and Poetry—A Symposium," which he opened with "an embarrassing question": "'Why is nobody here? Who is listening to us?'"[14] The question, it seems, is not only rhetorical, as Spicer goes on to claim that the lack of widespread public interest in modern poetry is due not to its difficulty but to the tyranny of print. "If a lack of intelligibility makes a work unpopular with the public, why is it that there is always at least one song with nonsense lyrics near the top of the Hit Parade?," he asks, observing that "phonograph records" of Edith Sitwell and Gertrude Stein "have made the two writers (who are hardly paragons of intelligibility) perfectly acceptable to a large audience" (*House*, 229) because they offer "entertainment" (230). In this vein, Spicer enjoins his fellow poets to reject the decontextualized, page-bound, *boring* view of poetry espoused by the New Critics—who "have taken poetry (already removed from its main source of interest—the human voice) and have completed the job of denuding it of any remaining connection with person, place and time." Instead, he suggests, they should emulate popular radio entertainers: "There is more of Orpheus in Sophie Tucker than in R. P. Blackmur; we have more to learn from George M. Cohan than from John Crowe Ransom" (230).[15]

But Spicer came to KPFA less out of a desire to entertain audiences with spoken poetry than out of his acquaintance with Moore. When KPFA went live on April 15, 1949, the first program to air after Hill's statement of introduction was a selection of folk music recordings that Moore curated.[16] Moore's *Folk Music Series* started as a daily fifteen-minute program of recorded folk music with a special half-hour live program on Saturdays with local musicians, musicologists, and record collectors as guests. That same spring, Moore invited the twenty-four-year-old Spicer to the station to interview him about the annual poetry festival at the San Francisco Museum of Art.[17] In the interview, according to a feature on Spicer that was later published in the *Folio*, Spicer "mentioned his interest in [folk] ballads," and was thereafter "trapped into giving a ballad program on KPFA."[18] Spicer initially appeared on the *Folk Music Series* as a guest, but by the summer of 1949, he was hosting his own live installment of the program every week, usually accompanied by friends and fellow folk music enthusiasts James Herndon and Dave Fredrickson.[19] Loosely

(63)

focused on Anglo-American folk ballads, the show featured folk-singing by Herndon and Fredrickson (and the tone-deaf Spicer), scholarly and mock-scholarly commentary by Spicer, visits by other local musicians and record collectors, and occasional poetry.

"'Most Educational Folk-Song Program West of the Pecos' Jack called it over the air," Herndon would later recall, in an informal account of his early friendship with Spicer written at the request of Blaser and published in the appendix to *The Collected Books of Jack Spicer*. Since this document offers the most substantial description of Spicer's radio show from Herndon's perspective as a participant, I quote from it at length. According to Herndon, despite his and Fredrickson's protestations, Spicer would loosen them up before each of their live shows with wine:

> Drunk, we would then do what Jack wanted us to do, which was to join his view of "folk-songs" a view which wasn't ours at all. Jack wanted "American" 20th century versions of songs—we had learned our songs from records, from books like Randolphs North Carolina collections (which Berg gave Dave, which was a fine book, which Jack hated—"of course its a good book," he'd tell Dave, all the time persuading drunken Dave to make terrible changes in some revered "authentic" version, so it would go along with a statement Jack planned to make to the effect that Dave had learned it on the Santa Monica pier from an old bus-driver fishing for shiners) or from Child Ballads, or from the radio. (Only after reading *Lorca* could I understand why Jack wanted to do this.)
>
> (Naturally, Randolph *is* American, but not American enough. Jack wanted association, *not* authenticity, at least not in the sense of the folk-song purists.) If he had to make up the history on the spot, that was OK with him. As always . . .[20]

Iconoclastic and drunkenly spontaneous, Spicer's folk music show took aim directly at KPFA's educational mission ("Most Educational Folk-Song Program") and the ethnomusicologists and "folk-song purists" who sought an American folk music tradition isolated from the corrupting influence of popular, commercial culture. Vance Randolph, referenced in Herndon's account, represents one such "folk-song purist": Randolph's field recordings of Ozark folk music in the early 1940s were commissioned by Alan Lomax for the Library of Congress and became the foundation for the well-known anthology *Ozark Folksongs*. Herndon's claim that even

Randolph's anthology was "not American enough" for Spicer indicates it was precisely the *in*authentic, the commercial, the hybrid, the associative, and the profane that defined Spicer's "American" folk aesthetic. Indeed, Spicer's "view of 'folk-songs'" aligned with his view of poetry, in that he saw artifacts of the past as material for creative composition in the present. As Herndon belatedly realized ("Only after reading *Lorca* could I understand"), Spicer's insistence on "association, *not* authenticity" on his radio show could be linked to his developing interest in the serial poem, first realized in his 1957 book *After Lorca*, with its assemblage of "good" and "bad" translations, original poems passed off as translations, and epistolary correspondence with the dead Federico García Lorca.

As Herndon tells it, KPFA listeners unwittingly swallowed Spicer's "terrible changes" to traditional folk songs at first, but eventually the profanity could not be ignored, leading to a showdown between Spicer and the station in early 1950:

> So we went on awhile making up phony takes of "oral tradition" and singing fake verses composed by Jack (singing them the while, horribly) but it wasn't good enough. Letters came in by the hundreds to the station about how great the program was. So we had to go into profanity. Dave was very stubborn and moral about this, but Jack kept at him and his great triumph was the night Dave, in a burst of wild anger on the program sang or yelled Skip, Skip you son of a bitch! instead of the usual refrain for Skip to My Lou. That tore it. Up til then, our profanity had delighted the Berkeley hills audience and students—being profane they thought it more "authentic" and "real" I guess; after the Skip incident, we got all unfavorable complaining letters on account of the fact that Skip was a childs song and we were desecrating it. Jack was delighted. The station & Richard Moore in particular issued an ultimatum about profanity, and Jack got to confer with them and talk about narrow-minded Stalinists and fake liberals and so on and quit after issuing several ultimatums of his own—all impossible. We quit too—Jack was certainly tired of the whole thing anyway.[21]

Herndon's representation of Spicer's rebellious provocations reinforces the poet's reputation as *l'enfant terrible* of Berkeley. But like his "view of 'folk-songs,'" Spicer's insistence on profanity and antagonism in his folk music show can also be read as an extension of his developing theories about poetry and literary and queer coteries. From the Berkeley Renaissance to his North Beach bar circle, Spicer's practices of literary community emphasized competition, dissension, exclusion, secrecy, and invective alongside forms of play and magical ritual.

Given KPFA's provisional license, and the FCC's mandate to regulate "obscene, indecent, or profane language" in broadcasting, a live program that regularly tested those limits would be reasonable grounds for cancellation, though the conflict around what Herndon calls "the Skip incident" did not immediately lead to Spicer's resignation; he stayed on the air a few months longer until the spring or early summer of 1950.[22] In a memo to Spicer dated February 28, 1950, Lewis Hill alluded to "the Skip incident" and sought to defend himself from Spicer's accusations that he was a hypocrite and a censor. Hill explained that he supported Spicer's use of profanity on the air in instances in which it was "native" to the folk music but did not see the purpose of using it "irrelevantly," pointedly asking, "What has 'sonofabitch' got to do with Skip to My Lou?"[23] Clearly, Hill missed the iconoclastic point. But in the same letter he also articulated his vision for KPFA as a station that would be aggressive in pushing the normative and FCC boundaries for acceptable speech in broadcasting: "[W]e are the people who Let Things Be Said on the Radio. We have kicked out the sacred code. No one else has done it. Only we." Hill's words presaged Pacifica Radio's future as a recognized leader in the fight for free speech radio in the 1960s, in part through its commitment to broadcasting the profane speech of San Francisco poets. In this instance, though, Hill drew a line, admonishing Spicer that "the danger of profanity for its own sake is simply that of a loss of faith."[24] Spicer's program was fated to end anyway. In August, KPFA went off the air to raise funds for a new transmitter and did not return to broadcasting until May 1951. Spicer, too, was on his way out; after refusing to sign the University of California loyalty oath, he left the city late that summer to take a teaching assistantship in linguistics at the University of Minnesota. When he returned to the Bay Area in 1952, he did not resume his role at KPFA, though he did tune in as a listener, and the station would later broadcast recordings of his poetry readings, workshops, and lectures.

Other documents from Pacifica's early history, however, suggest that the reception of Spicer's folk music show by KPFA insiders and listeners was more nuanced than Herndon and Spicer's subsequent critics have implied. Early descriptions of the program by KPFA make no claims about the authenticity of the folk songs heard on it, celebrating instead Spicer's "folk music free-for-all" as exhibiting an improvisational, playful approach to folk-singing that captured a youthful folk spirit.[25] The *Folio* feature on Spicer that recounted the origins of his program, for example, characterizes his credentials as follows: "In spite of Spicer's inability to carry a tune, he has been interested in folk songs since early adolescence and he has a large and inaccurate memory of their lyrics" (fig. 2).[26] Far from overlooking the "inaccuracies" of Spicer's lyrics, or naively assuming that his altered lyrics were, as Herndon speculated, "more 'authentic' and 'real,'" the *Folio* profile addresses an audience assumed to be in on the joke and far from fastidious about the purity of origins (or purity of voice) of the songs they heard. Other documents also distinguished Spicer's program from others in the *Folk Music Series* that took a more folklorist approach, such as broadcast commentaries by the Berkeley musicologist Vincent Duckles, recordings from the Library of Congress's collection, and original field recordings "made by KPFA's wandering folk music consultant, Sam Eskin."[27] An internal report produced for the Pacifica Foundation board highlighted the diversity of the series, noting especially Spicer's and Eskin's contributions, and praised it as "perhaps as extensive a review of authentic (and occasionally questionable) folk music as was ever broadcast."[28] Far, then, from pursuing a rigid, narrow definition of folk music or culture for the *Folk Music Series*, KPFA's early leaders were characteristically interested in a plurality of perspectives and in the use of live radio to promote community engagement.

The station expounded on its own "view of 'folk-songs'" in a cover essay titled "Folk Music, Quid Est? . . ." in a 1950 issue of the program guide. "No clear explanation has ever been given of why KPFA is especially interested in folk music," the essay begins, conceding that folk music might not have been an apparent programming choice for a station whose musical offerings otherwise emphasized, like many early FM radio stations, recorded classical music.[29] In answer to the question posed by the title, the writer first attempts to define folk music according to positive criteria of amateurism, spontaneity, simplicity, and nativism. But exceptions abound, and the essay settles, unsurprisingly, on a negative definition of folk music as any music that is not produced for commercial ends (even if, as they acknowledge, some folk songs have been sold commercially):

2. GREAT BOOKS
   Tuesdays, 8:00 pm
   Directed by Lawrence
   Berger

Tuesday, Jan. 17
   To be announced

Tuesday, Jan. 24
   To be Announced

3. PSYCHOLOGY OF MODERN MAN
   Tuesdays, 4:30 pm

Tuesday, Jan 17
   "Psychiatry and Alcoholism. Dr. Ralph Weilerstein, Donald Thomson, Elmer Olson, Richard Kahan

4. CALENDAR OF EVENTS
   Fridays, 4:30 pm, rebroadcast Saturdays, 7:45. Constance MacKay Describes current Musical events, art shows, and Little Theatre performances.

KPFA PROGRAM PRODUCERS

JACK SPICER'S program on the Folk Music Series is heard each Tuesday night at 7:30. It combines the singing and guitar playing of local folk music enthusiasts with Jack Spicer's comments.

Spicer was born in Hollywood, California, in 1925. His father is a former I.W.W. organizer who ultimately went into the hotel business.

In spite of Spicer's inability to carry a tune, he has been interested in folk songs since early adolescence and he has a large and inaccurate memory of their lyrics.

Before coming to Berkeley in 1946, he worked as a private detective and attended the University of Redlands. For the past two years he has divided his time between his job as Teaching Assistant in English in the University of California and the writing of poetry, which has been published in various little magazines.

He was trapped into giving a ballad program on KPFA when he came to the studios to be interviewed about a Poetry Festival in which he was appearing. He mentioned his interest in ballads, and has been producing his weekly broadcast ever since. Jim Herndon and Dave Fred-

Figure 2. Profile of Jack Spicer. "KPFA Program Producers," *KPFA Interim Program Folio* 1, no. 17 (January 15–28, 1950). Courtesy of the Pacifica Radio Archives.

"in an age of violent extremes the commercial music industry is a categorical extreme, and of folk music one can say—it is not that. The phony, the commercially banal, the commercially standard, have no place in folk music."[30] This is what drives KPFA's emphasis on folk music, the essay concludes, as "staff members discussing this problem found that they share a peculiarly emotional wish to get at the indigenous in their own culture and the archetypal in human life."

Pacifica historian Matthew Lasar further explicates KPFA's interest in folk music as reflective of what he describes as the station's early "hybrid highbrow" aesthetic, which he argues developed in alignment with the class values, generational sensibilities, and political commitments of its early Berkeley staff and listeners.[31] In the 1950s, KPFA's small but devoted group of subscribers were, according to station surveys, predominantly white upper-middle-class professionals, highly educated, and left-liberal in their politics.[32] These listeners, according to Lasar, "had inherited a deep appreciation not only for Mozart string quartets but for what they saw as the 'authentic' cultural expressions of the economically disinherited" that they absorbed from the Popular Front culture of the 1930s and 1940s.[33] As progressive folk music and folk musicians came under siege in the rising anticommunism of the post-WWII and early Cold War years, KPFA opposed the politicized silencing of the American folk-song movement by making recorded and live folk music part of its daily programming. In doing so, the station helped keep the sounds of the cultural front in the air, where they circulated, ready to be picked up by a younger generation of Berkeley listeners, musicians, poets, and New Left activists.

As one of KPFA's earliest producers of folk music programming, Spicer (alongside Moore) helped to lay the groundwork for this cultural transmission between the Old and New Left, but he also jammed the signal by disrupting KPFA's "hybrid highbrow" aesthetic, subverting the liberal romanticizing of "people's songs," and mocking Berkeleyites' "peculiarly emotional wish to get at the indigenous ... and the archetypal in human life." Instead, Spicer pursued on both his radio show and in his poetry a more radically performative and postmodern view of folk music traditions as driven by creative lyrical forgeries and recombined cultural detritus that could include mass-produced commercial songs.

As Herndon suggested, we can see this alternative, subversive theory of folk music that Spicer advanced on his radio show developed in his later poetry, which frequently incorporates creative rewritings of folk and pop song lyrics. In the poem "Transformations II" from *Language*, for example, Spicer traces the adaptation of the traditional folk ballad "Barbara Allen" as it moves from seventeenth-century Britain to the contemporary American West, picking up "terrible changes" along the way:

> It is not that the name of the town changes
> (Scarlet becomes Charlotte or even in Gold City I once heard
>   a good Western singer make it Tonapah. We don't have
>   towns here)
> (That sort of thing would please the Jungian astronauts)
> But that the syntax changes. This is older than towns.
>
> (*MV*, 390)

As folk songs and tropes migrate across centuries and continents through the bodies of various performers, regional specificity and historical references necessarily change. But for Spicer, the "transformation" is more structural, operating on the very "syntax" of the singer's language, as the imported lyric form forces singers into utterances that disrupt normative linguistic structures. "We make up a different language for poetry," he writes, "[a]nd for the heart—ungrammatical" (*MV*, 390). The folk song creates correspondences across time and place not through a Jungian archetypal continuity but through its repeated disruptions to the structure of language that realizes an "ungrammatical" mode of speech that is unique to poetry, song, and love.[34]

"Transformations II" gives a descriptive account of how the folk song changes the structure of language, but another poem from "The Book of Galahad" section of *The Holy Grail* (1962) shows how Spicer performed these disruptions in his own poetry through a compositional practice of assemblage. Juxtaposing allusions to Arthurian legend and T. S. Eliot's *The Waste Land* with lyrics from Woody Guthrie's "Ranger's Command," the untitled poem translates Sir Galahad into the cattle ranger of Guthrie's song:

> To drink that hard liquor from the cold bitter cup.
> I'll tell you the story. Galahad, bastard son of Elaine
> Was the only one allowed to find it. Found it in such a way that
>   the dead stayed dead, the waste land stayed a waste land.
>   There were no shoots from the briers or elm trees.

I'll teach you to love the Ranger Command
To hold a six-shooter and never to run
The brier and elm, not being human endure
The long walk down somebody's half-dream. Terrible.

(*MV*, 351)

Rejecting the restorative quest of both the grail legend and Eliot's own modernist assemblage, in Spicer's version, Galahad's discovery of the grail means "the dead stayed dead, the waste land stayed a waste land," his "six-shooter" substituting for the life-renewing "shoots from the briers or elm trees." It is through such a logic of playful substitution and transformation, though, that the poem lets something else in (like in the substitutions of Tonapah for Scarlet Town or "Skip you son of a bitch!"). Subtly modifying the lyrics to Guthrie's song—which was already a forgery of sorts, an original composition by Guthrie made to sound like an old cowboy ballad—Spicer rewrites or mishears Guthrie's line, "I'll teach you *the law* of the Ranger's Command" as "I'll teach you *to love* the Ranger Command."[35] Across Spicer's poetry, *love* is a word that frequently appears to jam or reroute a message—or, in other words, to queer it. Here, the substitution of *love* for *law* foregrounds the homosocial love that binds these fraternal orders of knights and cowboys and may remind us that Arthurian legend has often inspired homoerotic interpretations. Certainly, the grail quest, already completed by the poem's third line, appears less important than this love, though the final lines undercut even this affective register by drawing reflexive attention to the poet's coercion of "the brier and elm" into unwilling set pieces for his maudlin, "terrible," "half-dream" of a poem.

Spicer's playful rewriting of Guthrie in this poem resonates with the approach to folk music that by accounts he performed on his radio show more than a decade earlier. It also resonates, as Stephen Fredman has argued, with Harry Smith's collagist approach to assembling the massively influential Folkways *Anthology of American Folk Music* (1952).[36] If Spicer's view of folk songs differed, then, from that of KPFA and its liberal elite audience, for whom folk songs expressed an authentic culture uncorrupted by commercialism and modernity, it corresponded more closely to the folk imaginary of the 1960s folk revival, which had its origins in a new understanding of folk music that began to emerge in the late 1940s

(71)

CHAPTER 2

in connection to collectors like Smith and singers like Guthrie and Pete Seeger. In the late 1940s, Spicer and Smith would hunt for rare records together in the Bay Area; Smith, by some accounts, also appeared as a guest on Spicer's radio show.[37] The recordings Smith collected, many of which had originally circulated in the "race" and hillbilly record trades of the 1920s and 1930s, became the basis for the *Anthology of American Folk Music*, which Smith thought of as "an art object" and "a collage," and which sonically conjured, through its collage aesthetic, the imaginary of what Greil Marcus (riffing on a phrase from Kenneth Rexroth) calls the "old, weird America."[38] In Fredman's reading, Smith's compositional method of decontextualizing and reassembling musical artifacts shared with Spicer's poetics of dictation the "primary goal of effacing the poet's ego," or the desire "to reveal correspondences among objects while performing a Zen disappearing act."[39] One could say something similar of Bob Dylan's interest in folk songs, or of the function of folk music among the predominantly white young folk revivalists of the 1960s, for whom the singing of folk songs became, in historian Robert Cantwell's words, primarily a way to achieve, through impersonation and performance, "the effacement of received social identity, on the one hand, and the construction of a new cultural ecology, on the other."[40]

Spicer, though, never quite pulls off the vanishing act. After all, as Herndon's account of his radio show and recordings of his poetry readings attest, Spicer was a terrible singer. A recording from 1957, for example, of Spicer reading "An Apocalypse for Three Voices" at the Poetry Center at San Francisco State College, captures his comically bad, high-pitched rendition of the ghost choir whose "flat and tuneless voices . . . [f]ill the sky" (*MV*, 12).[41] A tape of Spicer reading *The Holy Grail* at the Berkeley Poetry Conference on July 15, 1965 (given just days before his sudden collapse from liver failure), records in contrast a more muted, hesitant performance reflective of his deteriorating health and increasing anxiety about public readings.[42] Even here, though, the monotone delivery is interrupted when Spicer sings lines lifted from song lyrics, bringing into relief the book's humor and its disjunctive, collage form. This includes the lines adapted from Guthrie's "Ranger's Command," which Spicer sings in a wavering imitation of a country-western twang, sliding tunelessly and comically around the notes.[43]

Spicer's poor Guthrie imitation reveals the double bind of Spicer's poetics, in which no matter how hard the poet works to become a medium for the transmission of something beyond the self, "[y]our tongue is exactly the kind of tongue that you're born with" (*House*, 8). But that also means that the failure or refusal to carry a tune can be an oppositional strategy, a way to resist the ghosts, to jam the signal. In a late lecture delivered in Vancouver not long before his reading at the Berkeley Poetry Conference, Spicer explained that in poetry, "you have to learn how to sing off key in some way or another. . . . You can make the vocabulary the off-key thing, . . . or you can make the metrics the off-key thing, or you can make the whole structure, or anything else, and then the ghosts come and decide differently" (141). I will return to this lecture and Spicer's "counterpunching" poetics of dictation in more detail in the next chapter, but let it suffice to say here that this in part why the public performance of poetry was important to Spicer, even as he shied away from it later in his career: the poetry reading allows the "human voice" to distort what he described in his 1949 *Occident* essay as "the dull horror of naked, pure poetry" (*House*, 230). Just as Harry Smith inscribed into the microgrooves of the new technology of the LP the scratchy sounds of old 78s, Spicer, on his early KPFA radio show, took advantage of the live broadcast to transmit over FM radio—a medium prized for its pure and clear sound—the "off key" and profane.

Spicer's subversive approach to radio, moreover, paved the way for future experimental live and folk music programming on Pacifica Radio. The folk music program *Midnight Special*, for example, produced by Gertrude Chiarito for KPFA in the late 1950s and early 1960s, featured live performances by musicians like Pete Seeger, John Fogerty, and the young Jerry Garcia, while Henry Jacobs's eclectic *Music and Folklore* program extended Spicer's spirit of forgery and avant-garde assemblage by broadcasting original tape collages, *musique concrète*, parodies of folk songs, interviews with fictional musicians and real ethnomusicologists, and "want ads" written and performed by Lawrence Ferlinghetti.[44] These programs influenced the birth of freeform radio, and by the mid-1960s, a listener tuning in to Bob Fass's late-night freeform show on Pacifica station WBAI–New York might catch Bob Dylan singing off-key, under-the-influence, censor-taunting performances of rewritten folk songs from the *Anthology of American Folk Music*. In this context, Spicer's folk music show seems less like an outlier or biographical curiosity than an early example of FM innovation.

One could be forgiven, though, for asking the "embarrassing question" about Spicer's radio show that he had posed to poets in that early essay: "Who is listening?" (*House*, 229). Eight months after KPFA went on the air, the station had managed to garner only 115 subscribers, some of whom paid more for the idea of Pacifica Radio than for its actual programming, which they couldn't access.[45] Even for those who did own FM radio receivers, the station's weak signal barely reached beyond Berkeley to the rest of the East Bay, much less to San Francisco; Edward Meece, KPFA's chief construction engineer at the time, later recalled that he "could just barely pick it up on Broadway in Oakland with an old pilot tuner."[46] The extreme narrowness of KPFA's reach in its provisional first year, which primarily targeted the university and affluent Berkeley Hills communities, meant that Lewis Hill's conception of KPFA's ideal listenership as an "audience of one" could be taken almost literally. It also meant that Spicer's provocations of his audience's folk pretensions were rather specifically directed—not only to the Berkeley community in which he lived and worked, but to the staff and volunteers at KPFA itself, who ironically could be considered among the station's primary listeners. Moreover, to the extent that there was a listenership for Spicer's radio show, it would likely have drawn significantly from his social circle. One could speculate, then, that Spicer may also have used his broadcasts to transmit even direct or coded messages for particular listeners. Such uses would align with his poetic interest in how poetry might construct a "private language," address and admonish specific individuals, and queer the lyric address (*MV*, 313).

The revival of local and independent radio in the postwar years supported a short-lived resurgence of regionalism in the U.S., and to an extent we can see how, a decade later, KPFA would help to shape the broader reception of the San Francisco Renaissance as a regional avant-garde. But during the station's early years, we might understand its signal as mapping less a geographic region than the social contours of a community or even a coterie. As KPFA and Pacifica Radio grew, the shadow of a more intimate, socially exclusive, even secret form of radio would continue to shade its broadcasting and reception. For some San Francisco poets, the passage from the Berkeley to the San Francisco Renaissance signaled a movement away from coterie poetics and toward a literary regionalism that quickly dispersed into the air as the broadly countercultural, mass media spectacle of the Beat movement. Spicer (like Duncan) would resist this momentum, in part out of his commitment to the social and literary forms of queer coterie. Rexroth, on the other hand, would become one of the most prominent voices to claim the San Francisco Renaissance as a regional avant-garde. He also, over the same period, became one of the most prominent and polarizing voices on KPFA.

Kenneth Rexroth's *Books*

In Jack Spicer's only novel, begun in 1958 and published posthumously as *The Tower of Babel*, the protagonist John James Ralston, an East Coast poet and academic, travels to Berkeley in hopes of overcoming his writer's block by immersing himself in the Beat scene; once there, he gets caught up in the intrigue of a noir detective plot. About halfway through the novel, Ralston writes a letter to his wife in which he compares his poetic quest to a kind of radio listening. If he could only tune out "[t]he announcer of common sense" in his own mind, he explains, he might begin to hear the voices of inspiration:

> [T]here is a station underneath trying to get through (like those Mexican stations that make a ghostlike interference to the programs I listen to on my portable radio here)—a mysterious bit of almost unheard music or five words uttered in a strange tongue—and I will not believe that, good or bad, the sounds are merely static.[47]

Radio figures here, as elsewhere in Spicer's work, as metaphor for poetic dictation, though in the context of the novel it also signifies as a metaphor for Ralston's repressed homosexuality, as becomes evident when the character asks himself, "And where in the last few days had he heard even a hint of the ghostly voice of the Mexican radio station? With the fish perhaps—and he turned the whole radio off" (*Tower*, 104). Earlier in the novel, a young bohemian poet, Rue Talcott, had given Ralston a dead fish with a poem stuffed in its mouth; Ralston's misinterpretation and refusal of the gift indicates his inability to recognize both real poetry and his sexual attraction to Rue, to the extent that, as he says, "he turned the whole radio off."

Immediately after posting this letter, Ralston visits the home of another poet, Arthur Slingbot, where he encounters a much different radio voice. As Ralston climbs the stairs to Slingbot's study, he "hear[s] the echoing tones of Slingbot's public voice humming like the sound of a thousand bees" (104), and, upon entering the room, finds him recording onto "an enormously expensive piece of tape-recording equipment" his "books broadcast for KARE . . . a highbrow FM station over in San Mateo" (105).

Ralston "vaguely" recalls the station from his college days at UC Berkeley: "It had no commercials (being financed by a Ford Foundation grant or something) and ran . . . to string quartets, sopranos singing English sea-chanteys, and panel discussions about local and liberal subjects" (105).

KARE is, of course, a fictionalized KPFA, and Arthur Slingbot is recognizable throughout the novel as a thinly veiled caricature of Kenneth Rexroth. As the scene in Slingbot's study unfolds, Spicer creates a satiric portrait of Rexroth's book review program, which Rexroth did in fact tape on a home machine in his study, and which, at the time of the novel's composition, aired on KPFA every Thursday evening and Sunday morning. In the novel, Slingbot registers Ralston's arrival by switching off the recorder, and throughout the scene Spicer's narration tracks how Slingbot shifts between a private voice addressed to Ralston and a public voice addressed to the hyperbolically "vast, invisible, and future audience of KARE" (106). As Ralston enters the room, Slingbot greets him in a "voice, private this time" (104), boasting that he enjoys baiting the station engineers who edit his tapes with "off-the-cuff remarks," which he demonstrates by recording, "in a public voice," a rumor about the Archbishop of San Francisco being "arrested in the men's room of the San Diego Zoo for indecent exposure" (105). Reassuring Ralston that his remark will be cut by the station—while unwittingly reminding Ralston of the risks he would take if he were to act on his homosexual attraction to Rue—Slingbot then proceeds to recommence his review of a new edition of *Beowulf*. His commentary moves wildly between impressive displays of erudition (Ralston is surprised to discover that the book is not a translation but a new edition of the poem in Anglo-Saxon) and outlandish conspiracy theories, which culminate in Slingbot's assertion that "*Beowulf* is a hoax, an enormous fake," evident to "anyone who bothers to examine the poetic contents of it—who is not a professor or an idiot" (106). When Ralston asks if he really believes this, Slingbot's answer is that he dislikes the poem and that "[p]eople have to be shaken up"—an irreverent ethos that might remind us of Spicer's own KPFA show (107). Ralston's challenges to Slingbot's authority, though, cause the latter's control over his public and private modes of address to break down, as he speaks to Ralston first in a "half-public" register (105) and then in a "fully public" tone (106).

Spicer also depicts his Rexroth-inspired character as using his radio platform to publicize his own causes and address specific listeners directly. Concluding the recording, Slingbot teases his next episode:

"Next week I will also tell you . . . about the persecution of a fine Negro artist in a manner more appropriate to Jackson, Mississippi, than to San Francisco" (106). Slingbot refers here to the plight of Washington Jones: an African American Beat artist that Spicer loosely based on Bob Kaufman and Stephen Jonas. Washington Jones, the central figure in the novel's detective plot, has been wrongly accused by the character Sonia, a white woman and the lover of Rue, of physically attacking her after a party of which Jones, suspecting he was drugged, has no memory. When Ralston questions the wisdom of publicizing the allegations on the radio, Slingbot responds that he intended the remark specifically for the ears of Sonia, who he believes is lying to blackmail Jones and whom he hopes to intimidate, and begs Ralston not to tell his lawyer about the broadcast, since he "doesn't like publicity" (107). Publicity, of course, is the point; as Slingbot had stated earlier, "they [the station] don't pay me anything but it's good publicity" (105).[48] At any rate, Ralston could hardly keep a public radio broadcast a secret.

The seeming indistinction between mass publicity and secret communiqué adds to Spicer's dramatization throughout the scene of the interference produced when public and private speech, public and private identities, and public and private domains coincide. This is a common theme in Spicer's work, and it also evokes radio discourses about the way that the onset of mass broadcasting disrupted—and redrew—the boundary between the public and the private.[49] But Spicer is accurate in his representation of Rexroth's radio show as having transformed the intimate address of radio to reconceptualize the FM radio audience and reinvent the persona of the public poet-critic. In KPFA's early years, as we've seen, Hill and the other early staff variously and contradictorily appealed to an "audience of one," a "minority audience," and, to borrow Spicer's words, "a vast, invisible, and future audience." Matthew Lasar reflects on this early confusion about KPFA's intended audience by asking, "Did the first Pacificans create KPFA to reach out to the masses or as an avenue of internal communication, a voice for the San Francisco Renaissance?"[50] Though I doubt that the anarcho-pacifist and anticapitalist Hill would have described his ideal audience as "the masses," Lasar's phrasing captures the contradictions and confusion of terms around reception that circulated around both KPFA and the San Francisco Renaissance. Indeed, if KPFA began to sound in the 1950s like "an avenue of internal communication, a voice for the San Francisco Renaissance," it would not be too much of an exaggeration to attach that voice specifically to Rexroth. With the exception perhaps of Moore, who left KPFA in 1953, no single Bay Area poet had as great or as contentious an impact on KPFA as Rexroth, who arguably did more to realize Hill's dream of transforming radio into an experimental medium for poetry than Hill himself.[51]

Rexroth was not, however, initially eager to lend his voice to the machinery of radio. In a retrospective account, Moore recalled his initial attempt to recruit Rexroth to review books for KPFA:

> Forget it! Not only did Kenneth not own a car, he could not, he told me his voice rising in rage, be turned on and off like some switch. Finally I got him to agree, but on the following conditions: I was to bring him a tape recorder, teach him how to use it, and leave it behind! I brought him a then current tape recorder. It was in a wooden cabinet and looked more like a victrola. It was 1950. When I listened to Kenneth's first recording which he mailed in, I was dismayed. It sounded like someone rummaging in an attic and mumbling furiously to himself.[52]

Despite his initial dismay, Moore aired the tape, and week after week, year after year, Rexroth would stubbornly continue to tape his radio show at home, much to the chagrin of the station's sound engineers and many listeners.[53] Rexroth's unconventional approach to recording his radio show, and the unscripted and digressive nature of his reviews, could nevertheless be seen from a certain angle as fulfilling Pacifica's early promises to deliver authenticity, individualism, and "conversation" over the radio. Rexroth's reported refusal to be "turned on and off like some switch" even echoes Hill's critical portrait of the commercial radio announcer, who "in daily entering a studio, open[s] his mouth before a microphone, and simulate[s] the use of his own faculties in a communication of values he does not believe or possess."[54] Certainly no one could accuse Rexroth of speaking on behalf of anyone or anything but himself, even if he lacked the "restraints, candor, respect" that Hill also promoted as "common to all productive human relations."[55]

The notoriously bad sound quality of Rexroth's program, moreover, contributed to KPFA's efforts to redefine the sound of noncommercial FM radio against AM standardization. These efforts developed through two contrary aesthetics: on the one hand, a "hi-fi" aesthetic for classical music programming and (initially) drama and literature that utilized FM's superior sound quality to cultivate sophisticated audile techniques among its listeners; and, on the other, a defiantly "low-fi" aesthetic for many of its live programs that subverted broadcasting conventions to foster listener participation and affirm its anti-commercialism. Spicer's radio show would obviously be considered part of the latter, and KPFA actively promoted these low-fi productions; as one program guide put it, "The programs in which listeners participate are liable to be among the most successful which we produce, not because they are 'professional,' but because, for all the occasional bumbling around, they include thought that is as raw and—hopefully—as honest as you would expect to hear in your own living room."[56] Rexroth was not, strictly speaking, a KPFA listener—he even claimed in a 1955 letter to Hill that "I dont [sic] own an FM and never listen to the radio FM AM or any M"—but his radio show definitely had a "raw" home-recorded sound, given that it was literally recorded at home by Rexroth himself.[57] And while many listeners wrote to complain about the "intolerable acoustics" of Rexroth's program that derived from the nonstudio conditions, the technological limitations of early tape recording technology, and Rexroth's own flagrant disregard for recording or elocutionary conventions ("his alternating whispering and bellowing into the microphone, or occasionally sounding as if his voice came from a closet, are intolerable," wrote one listener),[58] others praised the program as representative of the unique sound of KPFA itself: "Please! Keep Rexroth just as he is. He can cough, belch, expel air in any way he chooses and we shall applaud. We love those motorcars that zoom through the room too. We ... feel that Rexroth *is* Pacifica."[59] As Brook Houglum has argued of Rexroth's radio program, these "non-lexical and ... non-vocal sounds and pauses ... contributed to the production of precisely the colloquial, immediate speech [Rexroth] aimed for," creating the poet's unique "vocal signature" that also, I would argue, became inseparable for a time from KPFA's own sonic signature as a noncommercial FM radio station.[60]

Beyond its sound quality, the content of Rexroth's book review program could also be seen as supporting Hill's belief that radio could revitalize the public sphere and transmit a pacifist world view by acting as an auditory supplement to print culture. Rexroth followed an Emersonian view of the uses of literacy—but with a self-consciously West Coast distancing from the centers of elite culture—that rejected passive conformism to an institutional canon in favor of the active, spontaneous, creative integration of written forms of knowledge with individual experience. The point of any given episode of *Books*, then, was always less about the critical evaluation of specific books than about Rexroth's dynamic performance of a unified life of the mind. Lasar nicknames Rexroth "the omnivore," describing him as "the perfect literary sage for KPFA's audience, an accredited radical with a gentle voice who could talk about the Bloomsbury group, imperialism, Lenin, and Trotsky in one breath and tell his listeners what to get their Scout nephew or niece for Christmas in the next."[61] Leaving aside for the moment the questionable modifier "gentle" for Rexroth's radio voice, it is clear that *Books* demonstrated the eclectic, erudite, and voracious reading habits of a poet whose formal education ended with his expulsion from high school but who earned an international reputation as a public intellectual.

A photograph of Rexroth published in a 1958 issue of the *KPFA Program Folio* conveys, almost archly, the Western style with which Rexroth imbued his autodidactic intellectualism: dressed casually with his hands in his pockets and eyes directed just to the side of the camera, the poet-critic leans against a full bookshelf next to which a cattle skull is prominently displayed (see fig. 3).[62] On air, Rexroth's performance of this persona also took on a tone of political dissent, as week to week Rexroth held forth on subjects generally considered taboo in 1950s American society and almost completely absent from discussion in mainstream broadcast media, such as Soviet communism, labor unionism, and anarchism; racism, segregation, and sexism; and banned books and censorship.[63]

As is already evident, Rexroth's radio reviews ranged far beyond the genre of poetry, but when he did review new books of poetry, he especially promoted West Coast poets as well as other "outsiders" from the East Coast literary establishment (much as he did in his print reviews and criticism, his public lectures, and his advisory role to James Laughlin of New Directions). These included poets like Amiri Baraka, Robert Creeley, Diane di Prima, Robert Duncan, William Everson, Lawrence Ferlinghetti, Carolyn Forché, Allen Ginsberg, Jessica Hagedorn, Philip Lamantia, Denise Levertov, Gloria Oden, Kenneth Patchen, Jerome Rothenberg, Gary Snyder, and Philip Whalen—all of whom had their work reviewed by Rexroth on the air. The wide-ranging and idiosyncratic scope of Rexroth's program also created a multigenre, transhistorical, and international context for these poets. In 1955, for example, Rexroth reviewed on his radio show the excerpt from Kerouac's *On the Road* that had been published in *New World Writing* as "Jazz of the Beat Generation." Praising Kerouac's

KPFA FOLIO

PROGRAM

May 25-June 7, 1958

KPFA (FM) 94.1 MC Vol. 9, No. 5 KPFB (FM) 89.3 MC

KPFA PROGRAM PARTICIPANTS: Kenneth Rexroth

Kenneth Rexroth's program "Books," broadcast on KPFA since 1951, has excited considerable controversy among the station's listeners. Ranging in subject from reviews of literature, contemporary and historical, to pungent criticisms of our social and civil ills, the broadcasts have aroused intense reactions over the years. Mr. Rexroth is a poet, writer, critic, painter—and broadcaster. He studied at the New School, the Art Student's League, and the Chicago Art Institute — but he claims that no school taught him anything —except the Art Institute.

A skier and climber, much of his creative writing has been done in the high Sierras. His published works include: IN WHAT HOUR?, THE PHOENIX AND THE TORTOISE, THE SIGNATURE OF ALL THINGS, THE ART OF WORLDLY WISDOM, BEYOND THE MOUNTAINS (Plays), THE DRAGON AND THE UNICORN, 100 POEMS FROM THE JAPANESE, 100 POEMS FROM THE CHINESE, and IN DEFENSE OF THE EARTH.

Rexroth's poetry and some of his prose works have been translated into a wide variety of languages, including Japanese, Lithuanian, Greek, Bengali, and Chinese. Recent articles, primarily literary criticism, have appeared in New World Writing, Perspectives USA, Arts Digest, Art News, The New Republic, Evergreen Review, the New York Times, and the Nation.

As a lecturer and reader of his poetry, Rexroth has appeared before audiences in many colleges in the United States, including Harvard, Bard, Universities of Kansas, Buffalo, Chicago, Washington and British Columbia.

In recent years nationwide publicity has been given to Rexroth's Jazz-poetry recitals in night clubs, the Jazz Concert Hall in Los Angeles, at Reed College in Portland, and many other places. He has just returned from a successful series of East Coast appearances. He has been awarded two Commonwealth Club medals, two Guggenheim Fellowships, The Tietjens Award from Poetry Magazine, and recently the Shelley Memorial Award from the Poetry Society of America.

In addition to this long list of activities, Rexroth's influences and encouragement of contemporary poets has had a marked effect on the flourishing activity in

(Continued on Page 10)

GEORGE FOSTER PEABODY AWARD

FOR PUBLIC SERVICE RADIO

Figure 3. "KPFA Program Participants: Kenneth Rexroth," *KPFA Program Folio* 9, no. 5 (May 25–June 7, 1958), 1. Courtesy of the Pacifica Radio Archives.

prose as ranking alongside that of Jean Genet and Louis-Ferdinand Céline, Rexroth brought his listeners' attention to an as-yet-unknown writer.[64] The generosity of Rexroth's praise at one moment, however, did not guarantee its continuance to the next, especially when it came to the Beats and their many imitators. As Kerouac knew perhaps better than anyone, Rexroth could turn harshly critical and even vindictive in his print and broadcast reviews.[65] Nevertheless, Rexroth's savvy use of local, national, and international media was instrumental in scripting the mythos of the San Francisco Renaissance as an autochthonous West Coast literary movement that expressed a larger generational revolt against war, quietism, and commercialism in an "international idiom."[66]

My own experience listening to archival recordings of Rexroth's radio show generally supports the characterizations that have been made in various accounts of it, though relatively few tapes have survived considering the show's decades-long run.[67] Tapes of two early programs from 1952 preserved with Rexroth's papers at UCLA, for example, capture the remarkable breadth of genres represented in Rexroth's reviews, which in these two episodes include recently published books in archaeology, paleontology, history of science, drama, art criticism, literary criticism, science fiction, psychology, religious studies, and young adult nonfiction.[68] They also capture Rexroth's flippant, bombastic style: on one of the programs, Rexroth's generally positive review of Herbert Read's *The Philosophy of Modern Art* turns into a rambling critique of the "barbarous taste" of most modern art criticism, while his review of Ray Bradbury's *The Golden Apples of the Sun* begins with the declaration that he prefers older science fiction, and ends with Rexroth stating that he has already forgotten what Bradbury's book was about.[69] The shifting volume, pitch, and pace of his vocal delivery, the unplaceable accent, the arch asides, the coughs and throat-clearing, the mumbled and swallowed words, the ever-shifting proximity to the microphone: these oft-mocked sonic qualities of Rexroth's "vocal signature" are audible, too.

Indeed, I cannot describe these tapes without recalling their noisy materiality, not all of which can be blamed on Rexroth. As Lytle Shaw observes, the tape recording as artifact has "a tendency . . . to embed within itself a series of abyssal gaps, noises, and registrations of contingent sound that challenge the medium's storage and retrieval protocols" and stymie a listener's attempt to treat the recording as a transparent medium.[70] This was certainly true of my experience listening to archival recordings of Rexroth's radio show, few of which have been digitized, and some of which have become essentially inaudible due to the deterioration of the tape. I often found my auditory attention distracted away from the content of Rexroth's speech by an electric hiss, a broken splice, or warped tape; by a child's cry or cat's meow in the recorded background; or by the many technical and bodily distortions of Rexroth's rollicking voice. Even when listening to tapes of Rexroth's radio show that have been carefully preserved and digitized, the effects of time, multiple layers of mediation, and Rexroth's recording practices still meant that my listening experience never felt transparent or conducive to close listening—if close listening implies that one treats the technological medium as a transparent window onto a performance or event. Yet my experience and frustrations with listening to Rexroth in the archive made me feel more affinity for Rexroth's contemporaneous radio listeners, who sometimes struggled to distinguish the words of the poet-critic from the ambient sounds of the environment and technology in which his voice was embedded. As one listener complained, "[p]erhaps with him, as with me and this damned typewriter, his tape recorder stands between him and his audience."[71]

I dwell on these material aspects of the tape recordings because listeners and Pacifica staff so frequently commented upon them, and because it is noteworthy that the same electronic technologies that poets saw as conducive to more direct, participatory forms of communication (tape, typewriters, FM radio) also frequently operated as barriers to it. This is not a new claim; Rexroth's contemporary Marshall McLuhan made the phrase "the medium is the message" into a slogan. I'm interested, though, in how the particularized reception by local poets in the Bay Area—by which I mean their reception not only of the content of Rexroth's program but of its unique sound, produced through a material assemblage of audiotape and FM radio—helped to foster their investment in the mythos of a San Francisco avant-garde. Like the Libertarian Circle and poetry salons that he curated, Rexroth's radio show fostered a social space for poets to connect with one another, only this space was simultaneously virtual and site-specific.

Indeed, listening to Rexroth's radio program became something of a ritual pastime for San Francisco poets, who tuned in not so much for his reviews but to hear his take on last week's visiting reader at the Poetry Center or to find out who he would defame or scandalously expose this week. And they listened not only privately, as an "audience of one," but socially, scheduling listening parties to tune in with friends or even joining Rexroth as he taped (as Spicer depicted in his novel).[72] Michael McClure, for example, recalls watching Rexroth tape his program from his home study: "He would pick up a book and hem and haw in grand style while flipping the pages and eyeing the front and back material, and then deliver a learned, unrehearsed review to the machine."[73] David Meltzer writes that he and other younger poets used to listen to Rexroth's radio show just "for snotty laughs and eye-rolling groans" at "this windbag just going on and on," but we should note that they still tuned in.[74] The many colorful descriptions of Rexroth's radio voice by poets also testify to how much the bizarre sound was also part of the program's appeal to this community of listeners. Meltzer's is my favorite: "[I]t was like listening to W.C. Fields playing the Wizard of Oz on the boards of a medicine-show chautauqua. His voice a rolling drone where many voices would emerge, ranging from cracker-barrel rube to imperious high-cult Brahmin."[75] McClure recalls that "[m]any of us had our own imitations of Kenneth's voice," though "no two of the imitations sounded alike."[76] Rexroth even had his own take on the oddness of his radio voice; as he wrote in a 1952 letter to Babette Deutsch, "I play back tapes and shudder—sounds just like a B gangster pitcher."[77]

Rexroth's radio program thus played a role in cultivating a sense of community among Bay Area writers, but it did so just as often by amplifying disagreement, competition, and antagonism as by promoting consensus or collaboration. When Rexroth and Robert Duncan had a bitter falling out in 1957 over a dispute about a reading Rexroth was scheduled to give at the Poetry Center, Rexroth escalated the conflict by airing his grievances on his radio show, falsely claiming that Duncan had canceled the reading because Rexroth had criticized the Archbishop of San Francisco for his role in the *Howl* censorship case on his radio program.[78] The dispute essentially ended the relationship between Rexroth and Duncan, and even threatened the institutional partnership between KPFA and the Poetry Center.[79] But when Duncan wrote to Eleanor McKinney to express his anger at being slandered over the radio, he also acknowledged his own experience as a listener to Rexroth's *Books*: "I'm sure that Kenneth's remarks on his radio program are understood in context. I at least so understand his attacks on Pound or Sartre[,] Olson or Creeley or whomever happens to be handy—it is not the truth of a statement but the use of a statement that determines his impulse."[80] One way to understand the "use" of Rexroth's inflammatory statements is to see them through the modernist lens of avant-garde coteries, which need their insiders and outsiders, new initiates and excommunicated members, and alternative forms of publicity.

Lawrence Ferlinghetti, for one, consistently played the role of an insider: the ideal listener for Rexroth's missives. Ferlinghetti once claimed that his "real education began with Kenneth Rexroth on KPFA," and if we recall that Ferlinghetti arrived in San Francisco in 1951 with a doctoral degree from the Sorbonne, we might speculate that what he found in Rexroth's radio show was an alternative to the academic model of the public poet offered by Eliot and the New Critics.[81] Ferlinghetti also knew how to take Rexroth's vitriol. In a 1959 episode of *Books*, Rexroth's review of *The Sacred Mushroom: The Key to the Door of Eternity* by paranormal researcher Andrija Puharich devolved into one of his by that time increasingly common attacks on the Beats. "I'm all for the sacred mushroom," Rexroth sarcastically declared. "I hope that somebody sends Allen Ginsberg and Jack Kerouac and Robert Creeley—all them real gone cats—I hope somebody sends them each about 30 pieces chocolate coated."[82] Ginsberg and Kerouac were often baffled by Rexroth's about-face on their work, but Ferlinghetti (who never identified himself as a Beat writer) enjoyed the attacks as productively hyperbolic satire intended for an in-the-know audience. "The put-down of the mushroom beats was good," Ferlinghetti wrote in a letter to Rexroth in response to the program. "Keep up the bad work.... How about a real broadside attack on the Beat—to be published by City Lights?"[83]

Listening to Rexroth's radio show also inspired Ferlinghetti to get involved with KPFA as a frequent guest and promoter. Even before his first book as a poet and publisher, *Pictures of the Gone World*, appeared in 1955 from City Lights Books, Ferlinghetti was reading his poetry on KPFA's airwaves; a program guide from the summer of 1954, for example, lists a studio reading by Ferlinghetti of a long, unpublished poem, "Palimpsest," described as "a work in progress ... begun, the author notes, because of the existence of a KPFA, and the stimulus its audience provides."[84] City Lights Bookstore also sold FM receivers (which could be hard to find in the 1950s) with KPFA subscriptions for the express purpose of growing the station's audience. Later, Ferlinghetti had the questionable honor of being the subject of Pacifica Radio's first official FCC investigation into allegations of obscenity for KPFA's broadcasting of a recording of

Ferlinghetti reading in Chicago at a 1959 benefit for the censored little magazine *Big Table*. The investigation, which was eventually dropped, was prompted by language in Ferlinghetti's reading of the poems "The Great Chinese Dragon" and "Tentative Description of a Dinner Given to Promote the Impeachment of President Eisenhower." At the same event, Ferlinghetti had also read his poem "The Insoluble Problem," the title of which, he explained to his in-person Chicago audience, came "from a phrase of Kenneth Rexroth's—a sentence one night on his KPFA radio program: 'All history is an insoluble problem.'"[85]

While KPFA's relationship with San Francisco poets was a local phenomenon, its effects could therefore carry far beyond KPFA's signal range, including to the offices of the FCC. In 1959–1960, the potential listening audience for Rexroth's program exponentially expanded, as Pacifica Radio established stations KPFK in Los Angeles and WBAI in New York, both of which aired Rexroth's *Books* during their first years on the air (though not necessarily with the support of these stations' local staff and listeners).[86] Rexroth himself, however, continued to figuratively limit the range for his program to an exclusive group of listeners, directly addressing friends and acquaintances by name on the air and rhetorically appealing to his audience as an intimate community of associates. In archival correspondence written to Rexroth, his friends frequently respond to his radio broadcasts as if they were intended as personal letters, and indeed Rexroth did sometimes read and respond to letters on the air. Other listeners would write to Rexroth via the radio station to request more information about a book reviewed on the program or to seek feedback on their own poetry. These forms of audience engagement are relatively conventional in radio, with precedents in the popular poetry programs of the network era.[87] What is unusual, though, and in ways that speak to how local, noncommercial FM radio was redefining the relationship between the broadcaster and the listening audience, was how often Rexroth engaged in private reciprocal correspondence with his listeners that in some cases became real-life relationships. The most extreme example is Rexroth's relationship with Carol Tinker, his fourth wife: the couple first met in 1963 when Tinker responded to a plea that Rexroth made on his radio show for live-in secretarial and childcare services.[88]

Rexroth also used his KPFA program to stay connected with his local social circle even when he himself was absent from San Francisco. In 1959, while traveling in Europe on a fellowship, Rexroth continued to record and mail tapes of his program to KPFA. When he ran out of books to review, he started taping memories and reflections on his childhood and early life, which he intended to later transcribe for his autobiography. "Speech seems to me to give one a more natural approach to this subject matter than does a typewriter or pen," he explained on one of the tapes: "Doing a book this way initially for the audience of KPFA, a very large number of whom I look on as personal friends, reduces or elevates the whole procedure to the level of conversation."[89] In his emphasis on the immediacy of the spoken word, Rexroth conveys his investment in the oral poetics of the New American Poetry. But his characterization of KPFA listeners as "personal friends" was not just a radio fiction. Rexroth's radio missives from Europe were, in fact, received by his friends as intimate, insider forms of communication. In a letter to KPFA station manager Harold Winkler, Rexroth's ex-wife Marie Rexroth wrote that while "the 'average' listener" might find Rexroth's autobiographical ramblings "tedious and dull," they found their truest audience among "those friends of Kenneth's in the bay area who have been close to him and in some way feel real love for him."[90] Like the much smaller audience that Spicer addressed on his radio show, Rexroth's audience not only was mediated by KPFA but also included KPFA staff among his intimate listenership. As Winkler wrote in his reply to Marie Rexroth, "In many significant ways I think of Kenneth Rexroth as I think of KPFA."[91]

Winkler's comment registered, however, a sense of a nostalgia about a station—now a network—that was on the brink of change. A year later, in 1960, Winkler published an essay in the *National Association of Educational Broadcasters (NAEB) Journal* titled "Pacifica Radio—Room for Dissent," in which he characterized KPFA's early years as "one of... lively intellectual curiosity," where "[t]he listener... found himself confronted by persons who talked without fanfare, and with obvious sincerity, as if they were friends present in the room."[92] However, he asserted, the network had now reached a crossroads where it would have to more boldly assert the right to dissent over calls for bland "balance" in the face of the escalating Cold War crisis and civil rights movement ("Pacifica Radio," 99). Still, he expressed the hope that its stations would continue to commit to airing "the intellectual 'shocks' that have been characteristic of KPFA from its inception," including "the Ferlinghettis of the literary world" (98).

By 1960, KPFA's close connection to the San Francisco Renaissance and Beat movement would have been apparent to all who listened. As Winkler noted, a recent "seven-month period" of broadcasting had included "forty-nine major programs of poetry readings," including "a poet's workshop program, with Kenneth Rexroth of the San Francisco Renaissance as moderator" ("Pacifica Radio," 101). But that had not always been the case. In 1955, a listener had written to the station in admonishment, "What have you in mind that you don't record at least some of the Poetry Readings in San Francisco and in Berkeley. The last one in S.F. had over 200 people there! Where was KPFA?"[93] KPFA did broadcast some of the large poetry readings of the mid-1950s, but it is true that the sensibility of San Francisco Renaissance poets like Spicer, Rexroth, Duncan, Ginsberg, and Ferlinghetti was initially somewhat at odds with KPFA's early "hybrid highbrow" aesthetic, sense of educational purpose, and modernist literary tastes. Yet by addressing (and mocking) their listeners "as if they were friends present in the room," these poets, and Spicer and Rexroth especially, did concretize KPFA's ideology, aesthetic, and reception. It was the *Howl* obscenity trial in 1957, however, that made KPFA fully embrace its association with the poets who had been broadcasting on its signal for some time. The first station to broadcast Ginsberg's "Howl," KPFA would play an important role in the long, unfinished struggle against the censorship of the poem in print and broadcast media. But for San Francisco poets like Spicer and Rexroth, as well as for Ginsberg, the *Howl* trial also brought to the fore the contradictions and complications of bringing a coterie poetics into the organs of mass media.

3

"THE POET IS A COUNTERPUNCHING RADIO"

> The poet is a radio. The poet is a liar.
> The poet is a counterpunching radio.
> —Jack Spicer (*MV*, 374)

On a late December evening in 1956, KPFA broadcast a poetry reading by a young, relatively unknown writer whose first book had just appeared that fall from City Lights Books. Allen Ginsberg had recorded the tape in KPFA's studios a few months earlier, reading three poems from *Howl and Other Poems*, including the long title poem. It was his first appearance on radio and the first sound recording of "Howl" to reach a public audience.[1] While that audience would undoubtedly have been small by the standards of commercial radio, Bay Area listeners who did tune in would have heard an early recording of one of the most influential poems of the twentieth century, one that would have a profound local impact on the San Francisco literary community and Pacifica Radio itself in the coming months and years. Listeners also would have heard a groundbreaking moment in the history of LGBTQ+ media. As David Lamble, a Bay Area reporter, cultural critic, and queer media innovator, would later assert, "the first truly gay broadcast occurred whenever Allen Ginsberg first 'Howled' on Pacifica Radio's KPFA."[2]

A few months later, *Howl and Other Poems* was embroiled in the infamous censorship case that began with the attempted seizure of the book's second printing by U.S. Customs officials on the docks of San Francisco in March 1957 and culminated in the trial and acquittal of Lawrence Ferlinghetti for the sale of obscene material. KPFA covered the case as it unfolded, with Ferlinghetti, Kenneth Rexroth, and Lewis Hill defending the book on the station's airwaves. At the trial, the defense attorney cited KPFA's broadcasting of "Howl" in his closing remarks as evidence that the work had been publicly received as having literary and social value.[3] Of course, the mass media spectacle that attended the *Howl* trial and its aftermath went far beyond Berkeley's local noncommercial FM radio station, launching Ginsberg into new heights of literary celebrity and plugging him into an increasingly globalized communications network. Over the next decade and beyond, Ginsberg's poetry, public appearances, and peripatetic travels would be inflected with a deep ambivalence about the forms of mass publicity that he both embraced and resisted. San Francisco, in the meantime, crystallized in the national imaginary as the center of the counterculture. Though Ginsberg had lived for only two consecutive years in the city, he would continue to haunt its literary scene in his absence, as local poets found themselves swept up by the all-consuming Beat media machine.

Jack Spicer was one of the poets who sparred with Ginsberg's ghost and avatars in the bohemian and gay bars of North Beach, where Spicer nightly held court with an exclusive coterie of young poets, disdaining the tourists and would-be beatniks that flocked to the city in the late 1950s and early 1960s. Spicer may have once called on poets to "become entertainers" (*House*, 230) in the style of golden-age radio celebrities, but after Ginsberg's rapid rise to fame, Spicer became increasingly critical of what he disparaged as "[t]he fix" of selling out to a rigged game (*MV*, 361). "I have seen the best poets and baseball players of our generation caught in the complete and contemptible whoredom of capitalist society," he wrote in a 1962 poem, hanging it on the wall of Gino & Carlo's bar (*MV*, 361).[4] In his lifetime, he published almost exclusively in local small-press books and little magazines (several of which he founded or edited), even going so far to insist that his publications not leave the Bay Area. But, like his poetic forebearer Emily Dickinson's limited publication during her lifetime, Spicer's restrictions on his poetry's circulation did not mean he lacked ambition or desire for an audience; his poems and letters often self-consciously address a future public and even scholarly readership. And, as had often been the case for him, opposition and antagonism proved

"THE POET IS A COUNTERPUNCHING RADIO"

generative for his poetry, his (largely one-sided) quarrel with Ginsberg helping to drive his most prolific period of poetic production. These years were also, however, ones of loneliness, poverty, and addiction. When Spicer died from complications related to alcoholism in 1965 at the age of forty—his final poem written as a direct address to Ginsberg—he was largely unknown beyond San Francisco and the small poetry communities in New York, Boston, and Vancouver where he and his work had circulated.[5] The few early poems of his published in *The New American Poetry* remained the only widely available works by Spicer until nearly a decade after his death, when Robin Blaser edited *The Collected Books of Jack Spicer* (1975).

In the late 1950s and 1960s, then, it might have appeared that Spicer and Ginsberg were broadcasting on different frequencies. But the supposed obscurity of Spicer and the publicity of Ginsberg are both part of the story of Pacifica Radio—of KPFA's role in the Berkeley and San Francisco Renaissance and the Beat movement, and of the network's own transformation from an obscure radio station with pacifist origins in Berkeley to a bicoastal public radio network and leader in the free speech radio movement. Pacifica's story in the 1950s and 1960s is also indicative of that of FM radio in general, which experienced a precipitous decline in the number of stations and listeners in the 1950s only to crawl back to viability in the 1960s as the underground medium for the counterculture. We might even characterize the difference between these poets by way of their involvement with Pacifica. Spicer's early experience as host of his own folk music show on KPFA was followed by only scant appearances in subsequent years; after his death, Pacifica stations would occasionally broadcast recordings of his poetry and lectures, helping to keep his cultlike status alive when it was hard to find print copies of his work. In contrast, Ginsberg's recording of poems from *Howl* for KPFA in 1956 inaugurated what would become a lifelong relationship between the poet and the alternative radio network, with Ginsberg appearing so often on Pacifica's airwaves that I often think of him as Pacifica's poet laureate.

To read Ginsberg and Spicer as poets of the radio, however, is to consider not only their appearances on radio but radio's appearances in their poetry. And in the case of both poets' work, radio is a ubiquitous motif. Spicer, as we've already seen, employed radio imagery in his poetry as early as 1945. In the mid-to-late 1950s, inspired by Jean Cocteau's film

Orpheus (1950), he began to use radio as a metaphor for a mediumistic poetic practice, in which the poet receives the poem the way a radio set receives transmissions from the ether. The figure would become dominant in Spicer's books *The Heads of the Town Up to the Aether* (1962) and *Language* (1965), as well as in his late lectures. Ginsberg, too, used radio imagery in his early poetry. In the 1952 poem "345 W. 15th St.," for example, the poet depicts himself engaged in a kind of radio transcription:

> I turned on the Radio   voices strong and clear
> described the high fidelity   of a set without a peer.[6]

And in the 1953 poem "The Green Automobile," Ginsberg imagines, "in the wan light of this poem's radio," an ecstatic, erotic road journey with Neal Cassady, "blasting the dashboard with original bop."[7] In "Howl," radio is not a dominant image, but, as I will argue, it operates powerfully and ambivalently in relation to the series of figures Ginsberg uses to describe his own magical, immanent poetics in ways that anticipate Ginsberg's more overt, critical engagement with radio in *The Fall of America*.

Indeed, as many readers have observed, Ginsberg's poetry of the mid-1960s is deeply engaged with radio, capturing a transitional moment in American radio history when Top 40 music formats (punctuated by news bulletins, weather reports, and commercials) had become standardized on AM commercial radio, while the dissident sounds of an FM underground were beginning to emerge. In Ginsberg's famous poem "Wichita Vortex Sutra," for example, the car radio spews a "Black Magic language" (*Collected Poems*, 401) of consumerism and imperial war that the poet attempts to disrupt by capturing the toxic "language, language / proliferating in airwaves" on his portable tape machine (402), and by jamming its transmissions with a spontaneous, poetic spoken word: "I lift my voice aloud, / make Mantra of American language now, / I here declare the end of the War!" (407). The pervasive evil of radio for Ginsberg, however, is not only that it had been co-opted by consumer culture ("you're in the Pepsi Generation" [398]) and by Vietnam War propaganda (Senator George Aiken on CBS's *Face the Nation*: "McNamara made a 'bad guess'" [398]), but that radio technology had become structurally embedded in the U.S. military industrial complex ("Vortex / of telephone radio aircraft assembly frame ammunition" [395]), and in U.S. policing, which turns a surveilling ear on its queer, dissident, but also increasingly popular poets:

"THE POET IS A COUNTERPUNCHING RADIO"

>   PERSON appearing in Kansas!
> ....
> Police dumbfounded leaning on
>   their radiocar hoods
> While Poets chant to Allah in the roadhouse Showboat!
>
>   (394)

The predominance of radio imagery in both Ginsberg's and Spicer's poetry, then, is linked to but not overdetermined by their actual experiences appearing on the radio. This means that while I begin with the story of the sounding (and censorship) of "Howl" on KPFA, this chapter eventually turns away from Pacifica Radio to offer revisionary readings of the multivalent figure of radio in "Howl" and in Spicer's poetry and lectures of the early 1960s. My central argument is that the figure of radio is queered in these respective works, by which I mean that both Ginsberg and Spicer contest the ceaseless transmission of heteronormative and homophobic discourses by American Cold War media, while also transforming radio into a vehicle in their poetry for queer poetics and queer connectivity. This is not to suggest that either poet represents the desire for queer connection as fully realized or realizable; on the contrary, the function of radio in both of their poetics appears to lie in part in radio's structural *failure* as both metaphor and medium.[8]

To see Spicer and Ginsberg as mutually, though differently, engaged in the project of queering radio overcomes the simplistic critical opposition between these two poets, including the one erected by Spicer himself. The fact that Ginsberg is remembered both as a Beat coterie poet and the exemplar of the public, popular poet in the mass media age, and that Spicer's critics are divided on whether he should be read exclusively in relation to his coterie or as "a poet of publics and publicity," should tell us something about the incoherence of the terms *coterie poet* and *public poet* at this historical moment.[9] Moreover, the mapping of sixties poetry through a coterie/public binary by literary critics, implicitly rehearsed in my introductory framing of this chapter, has often obscured the extent to which these terms are inseparable from modern discourses on homosexuality. Lodged in a signifying chain with private/public, feminine/masculine, obscurity/clarity, occult/exoteric, apocryphal/canonical, and elite/democratic, the binary categories of coterie/public are, as Eve Kosofsky

Sedgwick would suggest, inescapably marked in modern discourse by the homo/heterosexual binary.[10] This is especially true during the post-WWII, pre-Stonewall decades when Spicer and Ginsberg came of age and started writing and publishing, a period of heightened surveillance and repression of homosexuality and gender nonconformity in the U.S. that both poets resisted as gay rights activists.[11] The making of San Francisco into a center for Beat and literary counterculture, moreover, was connected to the city's related emergence as a center for gay and lesbian subcultures and the homophile movement.[12] Figuratively speaking, it is during these postwar years that a queer, underground frequency could be said to have been sent out from San Francisco, calling to the city those empowered to tune in.

In the previous chapter, I asked what happens when radio begins to address literary coteries, reimagining radio's putative mass public and the ideal of the private individual listener by cultivating what I described as coterie listenerships. This chapter reverses the question to ask what happens to a coterie poetics when it is filtered through the mechanism and rhetoric of radio. More specifically, what happens when a poet takes up radio as a medium or a metaphor for imagining queer coteries, or for the impossible possibility of a queer public? If "the poet is a counterpunching radio," as Spicer put it, then which signals get blocked, which are lost in the ether, and which, against all odds, come through?

Broadcasting "Howl"

When Ginsberg arrived in San Francisco in the summer of 1954, he was eager to find his way into the local poetry scene and hoped to find an entrée through Rexroth, with whom he had initiated a brief correspondence two years earlier. Rexroth was vacationing away from the city when Ginsberg arrived, but he put him in touch with Ruth Witt-Diamant, who had just launched the Poetry Center at San Francisco State College. Through Witt-Diamant and the Poetry Center, Ginsberg met Robert Duncan and Kenneth Patchen and, sometime after that, Spicer. At the time, Spicer was in the process of launching an exhibit and performance space with five students from the California School of Fine Arts—the Six Gallery—which opened in 1954 on Halloween. Ginsberg, meanwhile, continued to plunge into the growing San Francisco and Berkeley poetry and arts scene. In December, a chance meeting brought him into contact with a young painter's model and student, Peter Orlovsky, with whom he fell instantly in love.

During these same months, Ginsberg was also drafting the fragments of dreams, hallucinatory visions, and ideas on prosody that would become "Howl." A journal entry dated October 17–18, 1954, recounts Ginsberg's vision while on peyote of the Sir Francis Drake Hotel as an "[i]mpassive robot (antennalike structures)" and "an evil monster—A tower in Hell[,]" images that would inspire the second section of "Howl."[13] Another precursor to "Howl," the draft poem "Dream Record: June 8, 1955," Ginsberg sent to Rexroth.[14] Rexroth's response was lukewarm, but Ginsberg continued to work out the syntax of ellipsis in a new poem. In mid-August 1955, he sent the first draft of part 1 of "Howl" to Jack Kerouac in Mexico City, along with a letter inviting him to San Francisco. Noting that "[a]n art gallery here asked me to arrange [a] poetry reading program this fall," Ginsberg added, enticingly, "also we can record and broadcast whatever we want on Berkeley radio station KPFA."[15]

Kerouac made it to San Francisco in time to attend the legendary Six Gallery reading on October 7, 1955, when Ginsberg first performed part 1 of "Howl" in a program alongside readings by Philip Whalen, Gary Snyder, Philip Lamantia, and Michael McClure, with Rexroth as MC. Kerouac would enshrine the evening as "the birth of the San Francisco Poetry Renaissance" in *The Dharma Bums* (1958), and those in attendance were drawn, drunk on Kerouac's wine, into the incantatory rhythms of Ginsberg's performance.[16] Spicer, though one of the gallery founders, was notably absent from the event, having left the previous summer to seek his fortunes in New York. He would not be able to escape, however, the buzz that Ginsberg's reading generated for the as-yet-unpublished poem—a buzz heightened after Ginsberg's subsequent performances of part 1 of "Howl" at the Poetry Center on November 20, 1955, and of the full three-part poem at the Berkeley Town Hall Theater on March 18, 1956, in an event billed as a "re-creation" of the original Six Gallery reading.[17]

KPFA, as Ginsberg had suggested in his earlier letter to Kerouac, would have appeared to be a promising outlet for "Howl." Indeed, back in the summer or early fall of 1955, when he was finishing part 1, Ginsberg had sent a tape recording to KPFA in hopes of getting his poetry on the air. But KPFA proved to be a bit more selective than Ginsberg might have assumed from his experience listening to Rexroth, Ferlinghetti, and other poets on its airwaves. Eleanor McKinney auditioned the tape as program director, writing in her letter of reply that while she "found the imagery and rhythm very compelling," she "wished the poem might have been condensed so that its power was not over-extended into a kind of tract, to which I felt the poet was not committed in sympathy or resolution."[18] Dated October 17, 1955, McKinney wrote her letter of rejection ten days after the Six Gallery reading, and incidentally one year to the day from Ginsberg's vision of the antennaed face of Moloch on the Drake Hotel. I do not know (though it is tempting to imagine) whether Ginsberg had sent KPFA a recording of the first part of "Howl."[19] If he did, it would have been the earliest known recording of the poem, possibly even preceding its first live performance.

Speculation and missed opportunities aside, almost exactly a year later, the station reversed its opinion, and in the fall of 1956, coinciding with the first City Lights Books printing of *Howl and Other Poems*, Ginsberg recorded in KPFA's studios a reading of "A Supermarket in California," "In Back of the Real," and the three-part "Howl" (not including "Footnote to Howl"). The tape appears not to have been broadcast until a few months later; a program of Ginsberg reading from *Howl and Other Poems* is listed on the *KPFA Program Folio* schedule for December 8, 1956, at 10:30 p.m.[20] The recording, copies of which have been preserved by the Pacifica Radio Archives and PennSound, opens with the click of a recording device and the sound of the poet's voice, close to the mic, introducing the book:

> OK, I'm going to read *Howl and Other Poems* by Allen Ginsberg, I guess, published by City Lights Pocket Book Shop in San Francisco in 1956. Library of Card Catalog [*sic*] Account Number et cetera 56-8587. The first poem I'll read is one I did here in dear old Berkeley, called "A Supermarket in California"—it being the supermarket down on or by Grove and University, on a rainy lonely night. Of course, I wrote this after I had written a lot of great poetry, so this is sort of like coming down off of the post-coitus tryst, so to speak. ("KPFA Pacifica Studio Recording")[21]

With a light, winking, conversational tone, Ginsberg addresses KPFA's invisible and future listening audience as intimates and fellow Berkeley residents, setting the scene for the poem's stroll through the local supermarket and back "home to our silent cottage."[22] Although Ginsberg undercuts the poem's importance in his introduction, while building the listener's anticipation for the "great poetry" of "Howl," "A Supermarket in California" boldly announces his poetic and erotic kinship with Walt Whitman, the muse of the poet's "tryst." The poem, as many readers have noted, recasts the supermarket—an icon of Eisenhower America and the heteronormative, middle-class nuclear family—into a site of gay flânerie, where men like the speaker cruise "[a]isles full of husbands" and sample and steal from the consumer excess (*Howl*, 29). Rendered "absurd" in this postwar landscape of "brilliant stacks of cans" (29), "blue automobiles," and suburban houses, the speaker and his "graybeard" muse "stroll dreaming of the lost America of love" (30)—a democratic America realized through homoerotic rather than consumer desire. But if that America is "lost," or never consummated, traces of its possibility live on in what Ginsberg depicts as the lonely comradeship of gay life—a life that takes place, Ginsberg implies to his KPFA listeners, right here in "dear old Berkeley." The familiar, intimate address of Ginsberg's introduction and reading style imagines and invites the in-the-know listener who will apprehend not only the local particularity of the Berkeley supermarket but the poem as a gay text. The performance thus figuratively jams the dominant transmissions of American radio in at least two ways: by subverting its usual commercial purpose in ways that KPFA's founders could only approve; and by subverting its heteronormativity, broadcasting an address to queer listeners in the margins of the FM band.

Ginsberg follows "A Supermarket in California" with the short poem "In Back of the Real," but soon expresses an impatient desire to "get rid of all these earlier poems and read 'Howl'" ("KPFA Pacifica Studio Recording"). In his introduction to "Howl," however, he begins to express uncertainty about the mediated context of his address:

> Actually, it should be read, the way it should be read, is with people or in front of people, the way I have been reading it recently, this way, except I've read it too much and so the heart has gone out of me for reading it. However, the way it should be read is kind of ecstatically if possible, but it would take ecstasy to read it. What I'm going to do is read it quietly and give it a silent chance, and if I can work up into any kind of real rhythm, I'll try and deliver that—which I would like to do, but it's very difficult to do because it requires a certain kind of openness on my part. And a sense of openness on the audience part, too, actually, for transmission, really.

CHAPTER 3

Speaking rapidly, Ginsberg indicates that the poem's ideal communicative power is realized in and through oral, public performance, in which an "ecstatic," erotic "openness" between poet and audience facilitates the mystical, communal "transmission" of the poem. But this enactment of receptivity and participation by poet and audience could prove a difficult balance even in live public readings. If, as Ginsberg lamented elsewhere, the motivating desire "to communicate a live poetry" in front of audiences could easily become "more a trap & duty than the spontaneous ball it was first," what to do, then, with the conditions of this studio recording for radio, which separated voice from body, the poet from an unknown and invisible future audience, and even the time of utterance from the time of reception?[23] While the published print text of the poem relies on similar conditions of distance and mediation, this only appears to reinforce Ginsberg's oft-repeated claims that the auratic power of poetry can be only fully realized through present, embodied performance.[24]

Considering the extent to which postwar oral poetics in general, and Ginsberg's early poetry in particular, was defined in opposition to a commodity-oriented, mass-mediated culture, it's not surprising that Ginsberg expresses skepticism here about his ability to overcome the double mediation of studio recording and radio broadcasting (even on a noncommercial radio station). Such skepticism about radio would become common in Ginsberg's sixties poetry and especially in *The Fall of America*. In "Bayonne Turnpike to Tuscarora," the poet's speech is characteristically pitched against the car radio, its "antennae'd car dashboard vibrating / False emotions broadcast thru the Land / Natural voices made synthetic, / phlegm obliterated."[25] Insisting that "[t]he Super-Hit sound of All American Radio," with its "commercial jabber Rock & Roll Announcers," is as "False False False" as the lies it spins, Ginsberg accuses commercial radio of having "[l]ulled into War" a passive public (*Collected Poems*, 469).[26] Drawing on these poems, scholars have often contrasted Ginsberg's critical view of radio with his simultaneous use of the tape recorder as a compositional tool for an "auto poesy," highlighting his ambivalence about sound technologies.[27] Michael Davidson, for example, argues that in Ginsberg's sixties poetry "the orality of the tapevoice stands in direct opposition to the reproduced heteroglossia of incorporated sound" associated with mainstream commercial radio.[28] Yet Ginsberg's close relationship to Pacifica Radio inaugurated in this first broadcast reflects the complexity of both his media practices and the postwar media landscape, and contradicts critical assertions that rely on an overly neat opposition between tape and radio in Ginsberg's work, or in media history generally. What fascinates me about KPFA's recording of "Howl" is how it reflects both the participatory possibilities of FM radio that Hill and other early Pacificans championed, and the ways such possibilities could be co-opted into new forms of power.

Despite Ginsberg's stated reservations about his ability to perform "Howl" for radio, he is able on this recording to build from a relatively quiet, hesitant reading to a more intense, incantatory rhythm. Gone is the conversational, intimate tone of "A Supermarket in California," and in its place is the nonstop, repetitive, energy-sapping "howl" of the prophet, and without an audience present to heed his warning. In Ginsberg's performance of part 3, he begins with a slow, casual delivery of the first lines ("Carl Solomon! I'm with you in Rockland / where you're madder than I am"), choosing not to vocally register the exclamation point in the text while putting a slightly ironic emphasis on "madder" (*Howl*, 24; "KPFA Pacifica Studio Recording"). But as the anaphoric repetition of subsequent lines progress, his monotone delivery becomes more insistent, gradually rising in volume, pace, and pitch.[29] The microphone even registers the strain in his voice at certain moments, as when it slightly gives way at the start of the line, "I'm with you in Rockland / where you accuse your doctors of insanity and plot the Hebrew socialist revolution against the fascist national Golgotha" (*Howl*, 25; "KPFA Pacifica Studio Recording"). The intensity peaks at the start of the poem's penultimate line—

> I'm with you in Rockland
>> where we wake up electrified out of the coma by our own souls' airplanes roaring over the roof they've come to drop angelic bombs the hospital illuminates itself   imaginary walls collapse   O skinny legions run outside   O starry-spangled shock of mercy the eternal war is here   O victory forget your underwear we're free
>>> (*Howl*, 26; "KPFA Pacifica Studio Recording")

—and then quickly resolves, as Ginsberg slows the pace of his relentlessly long breath-lines with distinct pauses, and a falling cadence brings the whole poem to a sense of sonic closure. In listening to this radio reading, I am especially struck by the audible isolation of the poet in the recording studio, which to my ear amplifies the sense of desperation in the poem

CHAPTER 3

while conjuring the walls of enclosure against which his voice reverberates. Ginsberg's "howl" from within the "private room" of KPFA's studio also recalls for me Lewis Hill's "private room" analogy for the postwar communication crisis and the isolation of the commercial broadcaster—a crisis that Pacifica's economic model and aesthetics of authenticity were supposed to circumvent.

I find, moreover, that listening to Ginsberg's paradoxically close yet distant voice conjures not *conversation*, the trope that was so prominent in the early rhetoric of KPFA, but *surveillance*. Am I listening to the poem as its intended addressee, or am I an invisible auditor, eavesdropping, overhearing, "listening to the Terror through the wall" (*Howl*, 10)? This anxiety and uncertainty about address is communicated in the poem, which registers a desire for the lyric's intimate address to the beloved but complicates that desire in at least three ways: in the first instance, by proliferating the poem's beloved addressees (Carl Solomon, Jack Kerouac, Neal Cassady, William S. Burroughs, and, implicitly, Naomi Ginsberg); in the second instance, by aspiring to a broadly public address in a Whitmanic auto-ecstatic dissemination, "scattering their semen freely to whomever come who may" (13); and, in the third instance, by evoking the specter of the unintended addressee who triangulates and co-opts the message for other, potentially nefarious ends. This last form of address is likewise part of a lyric tradition that, at least since John Stuart Mill, has understood poetry to be fundamentally a kind of speech that is "*over*heard" rather than heard.[30] In Ginsberg's poem, however, and within the context of Cold War surveillance society, the reader's sense of "overhearing" takes on more ominous connotations. Considering the poem's representation of homosexual and heterosexual promiscuity as well as incestuous desire, the threat of the spying eye and ear is pervasively active in the text.

In "Howl," radio figures as one mechanism through which a bureaucratic authority devours any effort at authentic human connection and speech. In an early draft of the poem, "moloch the radio" is part of a long catalog of such authorities that includes "moloch the soldier moloch the teacher moloch the congress," and so on.[31] In the poem's final version, radio is imagined to issue news updates on those minds driven to madness and ecstasy by a repressive society: "I'm with you in Rockland / where your condition has become serious and is reported on the radio" (*Howl*, 24). Reversing the trope of the paranoid schizophrenic who thinks the radio is sending secret messages meant only for them, Ginsberg describes a world where our most intimate experiences are made perversely public, broadcast for all to hear, and where the inhuman systems of power produce sinister concern about the specifics of our bodily and mental health under their biopolitical management.[32] As Ginsberg wrote in a 1959 letter to the *San Francisco Chronicle*, "[mass communication] media are exactly the place where the deepest and most personal sensitivities and confessions of reality are most prohibited, mocked, and suppressed."[33] There is a Foucauldian logic at work here, in which, by sending his "Howl" into the highly regulated commons of the airwaves, Ginsberg invites both the prohibitive "policing of statements" through the mechanism of censorship and "a veritable discursive explosion" about sex that, in the actual case of the publication and attempted censorship of *Howl and Other Poems*, was initiated by the state justice system.[34]

Ginsberg's reservations about reading "Howl" over the radio thus echo the broader concerns raised within the poem about the ability to communicate authentically in any form, including through poetry, in a mass-mediated society of authorities. The industrial architecture of radio and television broadcasting is also part of the hellish urban landscape of "Howl," which transforms Ginsberg's vision of the Drake Hotel to "Moloch whose smokestacks and antennae crown the cities!" (*Howl*, 21). Moloch's monstrous antennae conjure industrialized means of control (robots) and naturally occurring antennae (insects), giving Moloch the disturbing hybridity and uncanny sentience of a human-made monster. But in their association with broadcasting, antennae also become the visible signs of an invisible, wireless, electromagnetic atmosphere through which mute signals pass in the ethereal "machinery of night" (9), transmitting messages seemingly instantaneously across "gaps in Time & Space" (20).

In citing these phrases from the poem, I'm deliberately connecting radio to the series of figures that Ginsberg uses to explain the formal and transcendental project of "Howl": to "[make] incarnate gaps in Time & Space through images juxtaposed" (20). Like the cinematic jump cut and "the alchemy of the use of the ellipse the catalog the meter & the vibrating plane" (19), the structure of broadcasting reveals and relies on a gap between transmitter and receiver through which transmission occurs and on which its instantaneous communication depends. For Ginsberg, materializing the gaps prompts the listener-reader's mind to create the missing connection, and thereby to alchemically reconstitute loss into presence. In doing so, the poem becomes the medium for the transcendent enactment within time of the beyond-time, figured at the end of part 1 as the incarnation of Logos in the body of Christ, who "rose reincarnate in the ghostly clothes of jazz in the goldhorn shadow of the band and blew the suffering of America's naked mind for love into an eli eli lamma lamma sabacthani saxophone cry that shivered the cities down to the last radio" (20). In the blasts of jazz music transmitting over the radio, the poet hears the intimate publicity of Christ's cry, broadcast from the Cross to that invisible, absent ear of God.

The "gaps" in the 1956 KPFA recording of "Howl," however, become most audible in the literal ellipses created by censorship. Listeners who tuned in to KPFA on that late December night may have noted a few moments of self-censorship by the poet, where he verbally substituted a "blank" or "asterisk" for a word, but they would more likely have been astounded by the language that they did hear than by what they did not ("KPFA Pacifica Studio Recording"). Six months later, in June 1957, after the arrest of Ferlinghetti and Shigeyoshi Murao for the sale of obscene material at City Lights Books, KPFA aired a special live program titled *The "Howl" Controversy*.[35] Lewis Hill moderated the program, which featured a roundtable discussion on the obscenity charge with Ferlinghetti and four other guest panelists, each of whom had close ties to the case or to free speech advocacy.[36] Hill no doubt saw the program as an opportunity to use his noncommercial radio station to advocate for the freedom of expression. In the discussion, the panelists unanimously and vigorously defended *Howl and Other Poems* against the obscenity charge, citing legal precedent, prevailing definitions of obscenity, and the book's literary and social value (though they differed somewhat in their opinions on whether it was a "responsible" work of art).

As a prelude to the discussion, Hill rebroadcast an edited version of KPFA's recording of Ginsberg reading "Howl." Given the subject of the program, Hill acknowledged in his introduction that listeners would not be hearing the poem in its entirety. Noting that the original recording "was made at KPFA several months ago, before the censorship controversy about the poem had arisen," and "broadcast . . . very late one evening," he explained:

> it should be mentioned that Mr. Ginsberg's reading, if compared with the printed text of the poem . . . reveals that the poet himself deleted for radio broadcasting one or two passages. . . . Moreover,

for this particular broadcast, and specifically in consideration of the hour at which this broadcast occurs, KPFA has edited out two or three words or brief passages in the poem, simply as a matter of taste. I think you may feel assured, however, in what you are going to hear that the full essence of what has provoked the San Francisco Police Department into the arrest of Mr. Ferlinghetti is still present.[37]

Whether he intended it to or not, Hill's defense of the station's decision to edit out some of the profane and sexual content of the poem as "simply a matter of taste" had the effect of calling attention to these moments of institutional silencing by KPFA, leading several listeners who phoned in during the program to ask about them. The first listener question that Hill paraphrased for the panel, for example, asked whether "the words and phrases that . . . were deleted" in the recording contained "the essence of obscenity, which we might assume caused Mr. Ferlinghetti's arrest." The panelists responded by echoing Hill's appeal to taste, but callers continued to express skepticism. "We've been showered by questions from listeners," Hill reported at the end of the program, noting that these listeners appeared "as much concerned with the censorship they've heard this evening and indeed see in the book . . . as about the anxiety of the San Francisco Police Department or [Ferlinghetti's] legal plight." The failure to adequately address the station's own complicity in the censorship of the poem—or to make any substantive distinction between broadcast and print media in the eyes of either the law or station management—undermined the program's larger defense of free speech.

Certainly, listeners did not hear "the full essence" of "Howl," since the additional words and passages edited out by KPFA were predominantly descriptions of sex, and thus essential to Ginsberg's depiction of liberated sexuality. For example, whereas Ginsberg had vocalized his self-censorship of "fucked" by substituting "blanked" in his otherwise faithful reading of "who let themselves be fucked in the ass by saintly motorcyclists, and screamed with joy" (*Howl*, 13), KPFA staff excised the entire line, thereby removing the poem's most explicit and celebratory description of gay sex.[38] Moreover, several of the lines that KPFA cut from the recorded poem—including the line just quoted—were read aloud at Ferlinghetti's trial by the prosecution, affirming listeners' suspicions that the missing passages were those that had motivated the obscenity charge.[39] It is not my aim to deny KPFA its groundbreaking role as the first radio

CHAPTER 3

station to air "Howl," even in a censored version, in the repressive climate of the mid-1950s. But in choosing to edit out some of the sexual content of "Howl," KPFA exposed itself to criticism over the betrayal of its mission. As one could imagine Hill himself asking, how could open dialogue about this particular case—how could communication in general—occur in the context of censorship?

These questions would become pressing ones at Pacifica Radio in the years that followed, though Hill, who tragically died by suicide a few months after this broadcast, would not live to see either the conclusion to the *Howl* trial or Pacifica's future battles with the FCC. KPFA's early broadcasts of "Howl" did not attract the attention of the government agency, but within a few years Pacifica Radio became subject to several FCC investigations into obscenity allegations over its literary programming: first over Ferlinghetti's 1959 *Big Table* reading, and then over broadcasts of literary works by Robert Creeley and Edward Albee (as well as a groundbreaking program on homosexuality, *Live and Let Live*, featuring a conversation among gay men in New York) that in 1963 led the FCC to temporarily block Pacifica's license renewals until all obscenity charges had been cleared. The 1963 controversy, which dovetailed with a Senate subcommittee hearing on alleged communist infiltration at Pacifica, cemented the network's influential status as a staunch defender of the First Amendment just in time for the eruption of the Free Speech Movement at the University of California. Pacifica was cleared of these allegations, but the fight for free speech radio was far from over. In 1978, the Supreme Court ruled against Pacifica in the landmark *FCC v. Pacifica Foundation* by upholding the FCC's censure of Pacifica Radio for a daytime broadcast of George Carlin's "Filthy Words" comedy routine on WBAI, thereby affirming that the FCC had the power to regulate "indecent" speech in broadcasting. These powers expanded again a decade later when, after a successful lobbying effort by the religious right, the FCC revised its standards for determining and penalizing indecency in broadcasting. After they were adopted in 1987, all five Pacifica stations broadcast an interview with Ginsberg titled *Why We Can't Air "Howl"*; Ginsberg's refusal, in protest of these standards, to allow his poem to be broadcast with language edits led to a de facto banning of the poem from the terrestrial airwaves that continues to this day.[40]

Before I leave Ginsberg behind, however, I want to turn back to the line of questioning posed by KPFA's listeners in 1957 to inquire after the meaning of censorship within the poem "Howl"—in both its print and broadcast versions, including as imposed by Ginsberg himself. Let us return, then, to the "private room" of KPFA's recording studio in the fall of 1956, where Ginsberg reads from his copy of *Howl and Other Poems*, in which, we might imagine, there are annotations that indicate which passages to read with emphasis and which to omit or change. One is already printed in the book: "with mother finally ******" (*Howl*, 19). When he gets to this line he vocalizes the omission, despite the disruption it produces in the sound of the line: "with mother finally asterisk" ("KPFA Pacifica Studio Recording"). Elsewhere, as we've seen, he admits the awkward substitution of a "blank." Other "dirty words" censored in the first printing of the book he chooses to restore and read aloud for the radio audience.[41] And still elsewhere he silently passes over whole lines of text, at times without apparent reason, as in the omission of the line "who cowered in unshaven rooms in underwear, burning their money in wastebaskets and listening to the Terror through the wall" (*Howl*, 10).

In these moments, Ginsberg again makes audible the presence of the unintended addressee: the invisible, surveilling ear that overhears; the Moloch in the self and in the ether that consumes authentic speech. But I'm interested in the way that the vocalization of censorship also disrupts the listener's auditory experience of the poem, jars the listener out of absorption into its incantatory rhythms, jamming, so to speak, the poem's own message. This is a technique that we will see again when we turn to Spicer's "counterpunching" tactics. As for Ginsberg, he would later reflect that in writing "Howl" he had "thought to disseminate a poem so strong that a clean Saxon four-letter word might enter high school anthologies permanently and deflate tendencies toward authoritarian strongarming."[42] His decision to substitute asterisks for the four-letter word "fuck" in both printed and performed versions of the line "with mother finally ******" may appear to contradict such claims, but it's my contention here that in *inscribing* and *vocalizing* censorship in "Howl"—in this case, by putting into speech the unspeakable taboo of incest—Ginsberg materializes at once both the omnipresence of authoritarianism and the gaps or omissions that constitute its limit. As he writes in the notes to the facsimile edition, he "replaced letters with asterisks in final draft of poem to introduce appropriate element of uncertainty."[43] Like the juxtaposition of two contradictory images, this "uncertainty" produces a gap that the reader must reconstitute into meaning. The poet's "obscene odes," then, may finally be written not textually or phonographically but telepathically, "on the windows of the skull" (*Howl*, 9).[44]

It is important to emphasize here, however, that obscenity would have meant more to Ginsberg and his readers than the simple use of a few "clean Saxon four-letter word[s]." In a society that defines homosexuality itself as a form of obscenity, *any* expression by the gay writer risks censorship and silencing, just as the gender and sexually nonconforming body is exposed to violent attempts at erasure or expulsion by the heterosexist social order. Yet it is ironically the awareness of this exposure that created for Ginsberg the condition of possibility for writing "Howl." As he later explained, it was only after writing the line "who let themselves be fucked in the ass by saintly motorcyclists, and screamed with joy" that the "author was left free to write thenceforth what he actually thought, from his own experience," precisely because it "militated against author's [sic] thinking of the writing draft as 'poetry' or 'publishable.'"[45] By vocally putting back into speech this impossibility of poetry in his performance for radio, Ginsberg transforms the authoritarian mechanism of censorship, and the heteronormative cultural form of radio, into telepathic technologies for the transmission of queer desire.

Jack Spicer's Radio, or the Queer Sound of Static

In September 1957, Spicer attended the *Howl* trial, joining what the *San Francisco Chronicle* described as a "sellout crowd" for the literary event of the year.[46] In the packed court gallery, he met and flirted with Russell FitzGerald, a young painter and poet who had recently moved to the city, while the deputy district attorney read out lines from "Howl" in his cross-examination of the defense's expert witnesses.[47] So far, 1957 had been a good year for Spicer, and one that he would mark as a turning point in his life as a poet. He'd just completed his first full-length book, *After Lorca*; run a successful "Poetry as Magic" workshop under the auspices of the Poetry Center; given a few public readings; and had poems published in the "San Francisco scene" issue of the *Evergreen Review*. He would also soon begin a serious (and tumultuous) relationship with FitzGerald and was settling into a routine that he would more or less keep for the rest of his life. Days he could often be found in Aquatic Park with his portable transistor radio, nights at North Beach bars like The Place, and Sunday evenings at a poetry salon headed by Duncan and himself. Where he was, other poets gathered, especially younger gay men for whom Spicer served as a mentor and source of knowledge about a queer literary tradition. The Berkeley Renaissance triumvirate of Spicer, Duncan, and Blaser that had formed in the late 1940s had broadened and changed for Spicer into a wider circle that included poets like Helen Adam, Donald Allen, Ebbe Borregaard, Joe Dunn, Allen Joyce, Joanne Kyger, George Stanley, and John Wieners, among others. But coterie as both a social and a literary practice never meant for Spicer an intimate community constructed around consensus, shared affects of attachment and belonging, or even experiences of marginalization. Isolation, provocation, suspicion, and even outright resistance to the social as such were paradoxically part of Spicer's social practice of queer community. As in the Berkeley Renaissance, Spicer's North Beach circle thrived on competition and insularity, performing, in Michael Davidson's words, "certain rites of exclusion, acceptance, and initiation in relation to a potentially hostile outside world."[48] Only not just a *potentially* hostile world: evidence of the homophobic violence of the San Francisco Police Department, supported by the Bay Area justice system and political leadership, was ever-present in North Beach bar life in the 1950s (to say nothing of the homophobic hostility of most U.S. academic and literary institutions at the time).[49]

Spicer's poetry of this period is deeply connected to his coterie. The habit of dedicating poems to personal addressees—other poets, lovers, friends, rivals, acolytes—that had emerged in the writing of *After Lorca* became the basis for his next book, *Admonitions*, in which each poem is titled as a personal dedication (e.g., "For Ebbe," "For Russ," For Robert"). Like *After Lorca*, *Admonitions* also includes prose letters alongside poems, but whereas the letters in the former had been addressed to the dead Spanish poet, the letters in the latter are "real" letters sent to Spicer's friends Joe Dunn and Robin Blaser (though the distinction between fact and fiction is perhaps less important than one would assume). *Admonitions* thus announces itself as fully a coterie text, but, true to its title, one that is equally engaged in a long tradition of lyric invective and obscenity. In the letter to Dunn that opens the book, Spicer defends his use of obscenity—without defining what the term means to him—on cryptic grounds, writing that "[i]n these poems the obscene (in word and concept) is not used, as is common, for the sake of intensity, but rather as a kind of rhythm," an "unnecessary ... disturbance," analogous to the rhythmic "tip-tap of the branches throughout the dream of *Finnegans Wake*, ...

a cheering section at a particularly exciting football game," and "the beat in jazz" (*MV*, 157).

In time, I will return to this quote as part of my inquiry into how the keywords *obscenity* and *censorship*—so important, as we've seen, to the queer telepathy of Ginsberg's "Howl"—mediate a discourse on sexuality in Spicer's own poetics. But first we need to understand how the coterie poet became the poet of impersonality. Given my description so far of Spicer's complex commitments to his social circle and to coterie poetics after his return to San Francisco in 1956, it may be surprising to know that Spicer himself described this period as a turning point for his poetry toward a radically de-personalized writing practice, one that required, in his words, a rigorous "censoring"—if not of obscenity then of one's own intentions and desires for the poem (*House*, 7). Ritual, magic, games, play, the mediumship of the seance, the mystery of the tarot: these mystical practices had always been part of Spicer's poetics since the days of the Berkeley Renaissance. But Spicer seems to have experienced the writing of *After Lorca* as finally achieving a correspondence with something outside himself and his immediate social circle, the poems arriving as if dictated directly from Lorca—"a game," as he puts it in the last Lorca letter, "like Yeats' spooks or Blake's sexless seraphim" (*MV*, 153). It is the fundamental unknowability of the source for poetry that becomes central to Spicer's concept of the "Outside"; as he explains in the Vancouver lectures, it matters little "whether it's an id down in the cortex which you can't reach anyway, which is just as far outside as Mars, or whether it is as far away as those galaxies which seem to be sending radio messages to us" (*House*, 5).[50]

The image of the poet as a radio receiver picking up alien signals is the most well-known (though by no means only) figure for Spicer's poetics of dictation. Yet despite the enduring association of Spicer with his radio metaphor by readers and critics, there has been relatively little sustained analysis of it, with the notable exception of Peter Gizzi, whose indispensable afterword to Spicer's collected lectures, published in 1998, unpacks some of its sources and significations.[51] Prior to this, critics tended to either ignore the radio motif altogether or reiterate it as a self-explanatory metaphor for an impersonal or hauntological poetics.[52] Yet as early as 1989, Michael Davidson was already expressing a sense of exhaustion with Spicer's radio metaphor, arguing that it fails to capture the complexity of Spicer's poetics—a criticism that has been reiterated in more recent scholarship.[53] Spicer is to some extent responsible for this critical skepticism; his own use of the metaphor is frequently undermined by meta-poetic expressions of doubt and ambivalence. Davidson, for example, cites the well-known lines of *Language* from which the title for this chapter is drawn—"The poet is a radio. The poet is a liar. The poet is a counterpunching radio" (*MV*, 374)—as support for his claim that "Spicer himself seems to have become dissatisfied with his radio motif toward the end of his life."[54]

Spicer's "dissatisf[action] with his radio motif," however, is apparent from the very first instances of its appearance in his work. What I find remarkable, then, is not the unsuitability of radio as a metaphor for Spicer's poetics but its persistent appearance in his work despite or, as I want to suggest, *because* of its unsuitability. For most critics, Spicer's radio motif is understood to be aligned with an anti-expressive, anti-Beat poetics of impersonality. This dominant critical understanding is heavily indebted to Spicer's Vancouver lectures, which were delivered just two months before his death, and which "have become almost as important a part of Spicer's legacy as the poems."[55] In the lectures, Spicer describes dictation as a rigorous, even spiritual practice of self-abnegation in which the poet works to become a medium for the Outside by suppressing personal intentions and desires. As he states at one point in the lectures, "The point is that you're not the thing which is broadcasting. You're the receiver. If you're good enough, you can get so much out of yourself that you're almost as empty as a radio tube or a transistor or whatever you're using, and the message comes through" (*House*, 77). In Michael Snediker's reading, statements like these position radio as one of several "erotically neutered metaphors" used by Spicer to present a version of poetic impersonality in the lectures that centers on "the conversion of a poet from a desiring, wanting, person into a poetic conduit."[56] For Snediker and others, Spicer's account of his poetic practice in the lectures, and his use of the radio metaphor, seems to disavow the homoeroticism of his actual poetry.[57]

In what follows, I argue for a revisionary interpretation of Spicer's poetics that reads both his theory of dictation and the associated radio motif as continually troubled by disturbances that signify as queer. Contrary to the critical tendency to read the lectures back on Spicer's poetry (or the countertendency to downplay their significance), I read the radio motif forward as it develops in his work from the mid-1950s on in order to show how it opens dictation as well as the lectures to queer readings.

CHAPTER 3

Radio, I will argue, *is* the dominant figure of Spicer's late work, but one that ironically works only in its failure to function properly as a metaphor for a de-eroticized impersonal poetics. This rhetorical and mechanical breakdown of sorts, which Spicer suggests is subversively instigated by the poet in the space-time of composition, introduces an uncertainty of meaning like static noise into the poem. To put it bluntly (and somewhat reductively), if the demands put upon the poet by the poem sound at times like the self-abnegating demands of heteronormativity, then the structural impossibility of getting the channel clear materializes in a queer kind of static. Radio is therefore hardly an "erotically neutered metaphor." On the contrary, Spicer re-engineers the radio to imagine an alternative frequency or spectrum of frequencies—another kind of Outside—that could sound within the dictated poem the vibratory materiality of queer bodies and desires as something other than meaningless white noise.

To recover the eroticism built into Spicer's radio metaphor, we need to first return to its origins in Spicer's poetic engagement with Jean Cocteau's *Orpheus*, in which the image of a poet receiving poems through radio dictation was already queered. Spicer saw the film *Orpheus* sometime after its U.S. release in 1950, and in 1956 attended a stage production of the original one-act play at the Poets' Theater in Boston. Many of the themes and images of both versions clearly resonated with Spicer—from the rewriting of the Orpheus myth (a foundational myth for Spicer's own poetics), to the depiction of internecine conflict among a homosocial poetic coterie, to Cocteau's incorporation of autobiographical and queer subtexts through casting choices and character names.[58] In *Letters to James Alexander*, a series of poetic letters written in 1958 to 1959 and addressed to a young poet who had recently moved from San Francisco to Indiana, Spicer alludes directly to Cocteau's *Orpheus*:

> We do not write for each other. We are irritable radio sets (but the image of the talking head of a horse on the wall in Cocteau's first Orpheus was a truer image) but our poems write for each other, being full of their own purposes, no doubt no more mysterious in their universe than ours in ours. (*MV*, 209)

The image of the talking horse head is from the stage version of *Orphée*, which preceded the film by a quarter century. In the play, there is no car radio transmitting otherworldly poems as there is in the film; instead, Orpheus receives his poems from a horse head with human feet ensconced in a wall that taps out the poems, letter by letter. In stating a preference for dictation by horse over dictation by radio, Spicer immediately undermines the metaphor that he later makes central to his theory of dictation. But even his reference to Cocteau's filmic representation of dictation by radio revises the image by making the poet a radio *set* rather than, as in Cocteau's film, a radio *listener*. Daniel Katz argues that Spicer's more "radical" image of the poet-as-radio makes the poet's "privileged relationship to death" even more pronounced, as it implies that poetic composition involves "a process of becoming less human, less alive, less distinctive, less oneself."[59] In Spicer's poem-letter, he and his correspondent are both "irritable radio sets," coerced into relaying messages that are exchanged between poems who silently "call to each other above the poet's heads" (*MV*, 209). Yet Spicer also leaves space for subtle resistances; a true radio set would not be "irritable," after all, and there are ways to read this text as allowing for that irritation to reverberate in the poem's calls to "revolution," or as imagining a channel on which Jack and James (or, for that matter, Spicer and Cocteau) could communicate (*MV*, 209).

Cocteau's radio similarly leaves open the possibility for a homoerotic line of connection to be made between two poets co-opted by poetry and death. In the film, Orpheus is not aware that the poems he receives via the Princess's car radio come from the dead poet Cégeste, whose death Orpheus witnessed at the beginning of the film, and who is resurrected and coerced by the Princess into transmitting the poems to Orpheus via radio and telegraph (figs. 4 and 5).[60] A walking corpse (albeit a beautiful one), Cégeste is essentially an automaton: his awkward movements, empty stupidity, and monotonous recitation make him little more than a vehicle for the Princess's will. He appears, in fact, not so different from the radio technologies he uses. But he is also a distorted or inverted reflection of both Orpheus—that original poet of Greek myth whose lyre's vibrations telekinetically moved nonhuman beings and objects—and Eurydice. Like the "irritable radio sets" at the two poles of Spicer's epistolary exchange, Cégeste and Orpheus communicate neither with each other nor with an audience or public elsewhere: they are both enthralled by poetry, which is to say, death. And yet, something *is* communicated between them. An unspoken yet palpable current of eroticism travels between the older poet and his younger rival in the film, subverting the terms of the mediumship and the metaphor, so that the poems (and the Princess) become instead the conduits of queer desire. What does the potential of this connectivity

CHAPTER 3

Figure 4. The Princess (María Casares) and Cégeste (Edouard Dermit), broadcasting via shortwave radio. Film still from *Orpheus* (1950), director Jean Cocteau.

Figure 5. Orpheus (Jean Marais), listening to the car radio. Film still from *Orpheus* (1950), director Jean Cocteau.

sound like? Perhaps like the electrostatic noise and coded, nonlinguistic signals that surround the radio transmission of the first poem in Cocteau's screenplay and the film's soundtrack:

PRINCESS: The radio!
Heurtebise turns the radio knob. Sound of static, then a short-wave signal and Morse code.
THE RADIO: Silence moves faster when it's going backward. Three times. Silence moves faster when it's going backward. Three times. (*Morse code*)[61]

It is this alternate version of Cocteau's radio—noisy and full of static, rather than the clear voice transmissions heard elsewhere in the film—that I argue becomes increasingly central to Spicer's poetics. *The Heads*

(112)

of the Town Up to the Aether, the long, densely intertextual, hybrid-genre work in three books that Spicer began writing at the same time as his *Letters to James Alexander*, continues the poet's dialogue with Cocteau.[62] Each of the subsections of the first book, "Homage to Creeley," is dedicated (after the titular dedication to Robert Creeley) to a character from the film *Orpheus*. In the second section, dedicated to the Princess, a poem titled "Booth Tarkington" (after the American novelist and dramatist) alludes to the film's representation of Cégeste's voice transmitting poems over the car radio:

> Begin to recall
> Cegeste's voice
> (Distrusted as if there were any number of statues speaking)
> Strange how the sound of wings comes through to it
> As if the act of having sex had a meaning
> Beyond
> Recalling.
>
> (MV, 266)

The "recalling" of "Cegeste's voice" here is a pun: a prompt to remember Cocteau's film, it also serves as an appropriately Orphic (and Echoic) callback to the absent other. The re-call, however, brings back neither the grain of Cégeste's voice nor the words he recites but the "[s]trange ... sound of wings," which metonymically suggests the presence of birds or angels—imagery associated throughout Spicer's oeuvre with homosexuality—but metaphorically evokes the sound of static.[63] Is the "sound of wings," in other words, signal or noise? Meaning or nonsense? The subsequent turn in the poem links this ethereal sound to the proposition that sex does not *mean* anything more (or less) than an Orphic "recalling" of that which is, presumably, irrevocably lost. But the simile itself feels strained, the "as if" too weak to carry the signal across.

The transfer of poetic meaning through explication is likewise strained. The lyric poems of "Homage to Creeley" are all underwritten by prose notes that appear on the bottom of the page, in an underworld of exegesis that more often distorts and redirects than explains. The notes to "Booth Tarkington" again remind us of the two versions of Cocteau's *Orpheus*:

> The recalling of Cegeste's voice was done on a horse in one version and on a car radio in the other. Both made it seem natural. A crys-

tal set, in this version of the legend, would not be inappropriate. However there is no crystal set. Cegeste never speaks after he is spoken to. (*MV*, 266)

To Cocteau's two versions of dictation, Spicer adds his own (before discarding it): a crystal radio set. A simple, shortwave AM radio receiver, crystal sets were popular in the 1910s and 1920s among amateur radio hobbyists, Boy Scouts, and spiritualists channeling the voices of the dead. But while these DIY receivers were easy and inexpensive to build, "there was no guarantee you would hear anything except auditory chaos"; as Susan Douglas explains, "static was a constant nuisance, as was blasting, a loud, grating noise that blew into your ears every time you changed from one station to another."[64] Spicer's reference thus recalls an older, weaker, and far noisier radio technology to denaturalize Cocteau's depiction of poetic dictation.

Spicer returned to the radio motif, as well as to themes of reception, communication, and eros, in *Language*, a long serial poem in five parts, and the last of Spicer's books to be published in his lifetime, in 1965. The first section, "Thing Language," further breaks down the battered vehicle of the poet-as-radio metaphor, distorting its capacity to carry meaning across, while amplifying the sound of the "[w]hite and aimless signals" that carry over its waves (*MV*, 373). The book's most indelible radio image, however, is the one from the poem "Sporting Life," which jams the metaphor in multiple ways. First, by negating radio as a suitable image for dictation: "The trouble with comparing a poet with a radio is that radios don't develop scar tissue." Second, by overloading the image with too much specificity, limiting its transferability: "The tubes burn out, or with a transistor, which most souls are, the battery or diagram burns out replaceable or not replaceable." And third, by using a mixed metaphor that crosses the signals and, furthermore, negates them—"but not like that punchdrunk fighter in the bar" (373)—which introduces interference into the metaphor, culminating in the image, cited in the epigraph to this chapter, of the poet as "a counterpunching radio" (374).

A few pages later, Spicer links his "counterpunching radio" to the car radio in the *Orpheus* film, whose deathly broadcasts abide "NO SPEED LIMIT" and thus appear to crash or shatter the receiver. Again, Spicer emphasizes the "[u]selessness" of the radio motif, only to give it a curious kind of embodied life:

> Finally the messages penetrate
> There is a corpse of an image—they penetrate
> The corpse of a radio. Cocteau used a car radio on account of
> > NO SPEED LIMIT. In any case the messages penetrate the
> > radio and render it (and the radio) ultimately useless.
> Prayer
> Is exactly that
> The kneeling radio down to the tomb of some saint
> Uselessness sung and danced (the radio dead but alive it can
> > connect things
> Into sound. Their prayer
> Its only connection.
>
> (376)

The radio "alive ... can connect things / [i]nto sound," but what can "the radio dead" connect or sound? Yet it is not, it seems, totally inert. In this *danse macabre*, the dead radio appears to be still a vibrating body and still vulnerable to penetration, and if it can no longer (or not yet) "connect things," it nonetheless creates the condition of possibility for "connection," its Orphic signal sent out without assurance of reception—like a prayer sent into the ether, like the erotic image of a "kneeling radio down to the tomb of some saint," or like an open parenthesis that never closes.

It is at this point that we arrive back at Spicer's late lectures, in which we might now hear in Spicer's explication of the radio as a flawed metaphor for an impersonal poetics something of the queer, "counterpunching" echoes of the motif as it appears in his poetry. Spicer delivered these lectures and poetry readings over three evenings on June 13, 15, and 17, 1965, in Vancouver in the private home of Warren and Ellen Tallman, far from (though networked to) the San Francisco poetry community. Spicer evidently hoped that the Vancouver poetry community would offer him a new professional and social start, but it also would have presented unknown risks to him as an openly gay writer.[65] Given Spicer's sensitivity to the social contexts in which his work was embedded, and his interest in issues of circulation, reception, and rejection, it is important to read the lectures as shaped by the particularities of this context. In doing so, we might also attune especially to those moments when Spicer directs his audience to listen suspiciously for the contradictions between what he says in the lectures and what the poems say.

CHAPTER 3

Early in the first lecture, delivered on the hundredth anniversary of W. B. Yeats's birth, Spicer lays out his basic theory of dictation through "the analogy of the medium..., which Yeats started out, and which Cocteau in his *Orphée*... used a car radio for.... That essentially you are something which is being transmitted into" (*House*, 7). As he gets into the complexities of the method, other tropes (the haunted house, the Martian invasion, the parasite, the baseball game, the dance) seem better suited as analogies, though he keeps returning to the radio figure. At one point, one of the members of the audience asks whether there is room for "individual abilities" in this model, or whether there is any difference between "[g]ood hi-fi sets or bad hi-fi sets" (17). Spicer answers by lamenting the inadequacy of the metaphor and suggests replacing the modern "hi-fi" set in the analogy with the anachronistic crystal radio: "as far as radio sets are concerned, it's not a good analogy now because even the worst transistor is built pretty good.... And I would think that we probably always will be crystal sets, at best" (17). In this context, the crystal set's propensity for static represents the poet's embodied limitations as a vessel for the Outside. As Spicer explains, "you don't get the radio program if the radio set has static in it" (15), implying that the poet's task is analogous to that of the sound engineer, to work on "getting the static out" of the poem as much as possible (115). Spicer characterizes this process as an active, even strenuous form of self-censorship, in which the poem is more successful "the more that you clear your mind away from yourself, and the more also that you do some censoring—because there will be all sorts of things coming from your mind... from things that you want, which will foul up the poem" (7).

Spicer is clear that the poet cannot actually become empty, and moreover that the poem ultimately comes through the poet's physical body and is assembled out of the poet's language, knowledge, memories, and skills by the Outside. What, then, are the "things" that need "censoring" or that "will foul up the poem"? As Katz and Snediker observe, Spicer appears especially focused on the poets' desires and "wants," with the term *want* appearing repetitively throughout the first lecture, and often in connection with sexual desire. For example, Spicer states that the poet will be assured of being on the right track when the "poems say just exactly the opposite of what he wants" (6), or when "the poem, when you're trying to seduce somebody, will make the person run five miles away screaming" (16). Spicer's performative negotiation throughout the Vancouver lectures of the "open secret" of his sexuality also implies in moments like these that the gay poet's public expression of a personal address or private "want" in a repressive, homophobic society will be received by its intended recipients as repellent and obscene—as, in effect, anti-social.[66] The fact that desire cannot, however, be completely removed from the time and space of poetic composition is the intractable problem that Spicer wrestles with in the lectures. The poet "tr[ies] to be a blank," but always "[t]here's this utter animal spirit which is coming out and saying, well, gee, can I lay this person if I write this line" that makes pure dictation "impossible" (*House*, 116).

This impossibility is also the site of resistance, since the inherent resistance of the object to its erasure as a medium produces static and makes static structural to the poem. This is the more subversive, "counterpunching" form of dictation that we find in Spicer's poetry—as he writes in *Heads of the Town*, "The poet thinks continually of strategies, of how he can win out against the poem" (*MV*, 301)—and though it appears less prominently in the lectures, it comes through in subtle moments, particularly through and around the readings. In the second lecture, for example, Spicer suggests at one point that the poet might strategically include in the poem what dictation seemingly would not allow: the erotically charged, private address to a proper name. After he reads a series of poems from his book *The Holy Grail*, which includes inscrutable references to two different individuals named Tony, an audience member asks him about the meaning of the name. Spicer, rather than explicating it as a reference to members of his social circle, offers this answer instead:

> The proper names ... are simply a kind of disturbance which I often use. I guess it's "I" rather than the poems because it's sort of the insistence of the absolutely immediate which has nothing to do with anything, and you put that in and then you get all of the immediate out of the [goddamn] poem and you can go back to the poem. ... It's like the "tap tap tap" the branches make in *Finnegans Wake*. (*House*, 58)[67]

Here the static produced by the "disturbance" of the personal appears not to require censorship but to be instead a byproduct of it. In other words, the use of a private proper name, a signature of coterie writing, is presented here as a paradoxical strategy used by the poet to momentarily jam the signals from the Outside in order to better receive them, to put in "the absolutely immediate" in order "to get all of the immediate out." The poem becomes a technology for de-personalizing but not, I argue, for de-eroticizing the poet's direct address; sending the address out into a public that cannot (or will not) receive it empties the name of signification but not of the power to circulate. This allows the name—and its erotic charge—to become impersonal, to be carried along with the poem as a "disturbance" untethered to a time or place or addressee, promiscuously available to be received by anyone. For a listener among Spicer's Vancouver audience, who would presumably not know the coterie references, the proper name Tony (unlike the proper names of Lancelot or Merlin) appears emptied of signification and presence, and therefore would in some sense operate as noise in the audience's reception of the poem's meaning. Knowledge of the name's referent does not remove the static, however; even a reader from within Spicer's circle would still find the appearance of the name to be a "disruption" in the poem's meaning, since it would seem to come from another discursive register.

As other critics have noted, Spicer's language in this passage, including the allusion to *Finnegans Wake*, closely echoes his cryptic defense of obscenity in the first letter in *Admonitions*, which I quoted in passing earlier:

> In these poems the obscene (in word and concept) is not used, as is common, for the sake of intensity, but rather as a kind of rhythm as the tip-tap of the branches throughout the dream of *Finnegans Wake* or, to make the analogy even more mysterious to you, a cheering section at a particularly exciting football game. It is precisely because the obscenity is unnecessary that I use it, as I could have used any disturbance, as I could have used anything (remember the beat in jazz) which is regular and beside the point. (*MV*, 157)

In the context of *Admonitions*, it is not immediately clear what Spicer means when he refers to "the obscene (in word and concept)" in the poems, which include some mild profanity but no explicit descriptions of sex acts or violence—little, in other words, that would draw the attention of state censors. Reading these two passages in conversation, however, allows us to interpret Spicer's reference to "the obscene" as relating to his intensive use of proper names throughout the text—as referring, in other words, to a queer coterie writing that uses invective to reject both the demand that the poet translate personal experience into something universalizable and, more radically, the demand of sociality and "the big lie of the personal" as such (*MV*, 150). The proper name is a "disturbance" because, in Derridean terms, it is both singular and iterable, personal and radically impersonal, disruptive and structural to communication. Just as importantly for Spicer's poetics, however, is the way that the gendered proper name, when used in the context of an erotic address, can appear "obscene" and as a "disturbance" to a heterosexist social order. Although an impersonal poetics of dictation would appear to be in opposition to the kind of eroticized coterie writing that we see in *Admonitions*, the correspondences between these two passages suggest that they are in fact closely related. Spicer's "mysterious" analogies thus encourage readers to listen not only for the poem's meaning but for those moments where the name or the word seems "unnecessary" or "beside the point." These are the moments that register the body in the machine, or the interference produced when the desiring body meets the de-subjectifying force of the outside.

To hear the static that arrives with the proper name in Spicer's poetry, I'd like to conclude by listening to the third and final book of *The Heads of the Town Up to the Aether*, which Spicer read in its entirety during his first Vancouver lecture. It is easy to forget when reading the published transcripts that Spicer's lectures were also poetry readings; listening to the recordings, now available on PennSound, allows one to hear the dialogic tension between poetry and prose, poetry and exegesis, and poetry and personal address that structure many of Spicer's books.[68] Titled "A Textbook of Poetry," the series of twenty-nine aphoristic prose poems demands to be taken in this context as a countertext to the pedagogy of the lectures. Spicer prefaces his reading by asserting that the book "is as near to dictation, without interference from me, as I've written," and instructing his audience to "listen . . . for differences between what it says and what I say" (*House*, 19). One of the book's central motifs is the image of a city, which appears variously as a heavenly city, an earthly city, a future city, a past city, a polis, a church, a gay bar, a "boy's club," a ghost town, a crowd (*MV*, 309). Yet this is a city where, as Spicer famously put it in a poem from *Language*, "No one listens to poetry" (373). Some "bastards . . . are not patient enough to listen," and others "are too crowded" (300). Still others try to "listen to it, read it, make comments on it . . . as if they or you observed one continual moment of surf breaking against the rocks" (313). These last are, the poem indicates, misled: "The real poetry is beyond us, beyond them, breaking like glue" (313). The broken metaphor of "breaking like glue," however, introduces a different kind of white noise in the transmission of poetic meaning that resonates with one of the most important, though obscure and difficult, lessons of this textbook: "Metaphors are not for humans" (300). Nor are poems; they "were written for ghosts." And ghosts don't listen either, because "[t]hey cannot hear the noise they have been making." Dictation thus appears in this poetic rendering like a lonely, deathly kind of work, less a direct transmission from gods or Martians than the jamming of all signals in a total negation of communication and the social: "'The public be damned'" (299). The messages "won't come through. Nothing comes through. The death / Of every poem in every line" (301). Poetry, it seems, "is not a simple process like a mirror or a radio" (300).

There are many anonymous ghosts in this strange book—"low ghosts" and "Logos"—but one has a name, a proper name, a name of private, erotic significance. Does it come through? In the larger text of *Heads of the Town*, this name has followed the poet on a journey through hell to paradise, first appearing in the submerged notes of "Homage to Creeley" in the moment of its disappearance: "The figure of Jim begins to emerge in the poem. The Poet uses all his resistance to us to try to create the figure of a person at once lost and unlikely. The unlikelyness [*sic*] is also the first hint of metaphor" (262). Spicer's Orphic recalling of "Jim" (James Alexander) by the magic of a private name does not call into presence the beloved, "lost and unlikely," but does leave in the poem a trace of the poet's "resistance" to poetry, the poet's failed attempt to encrypt "[a] private image" in the dictated poem (298). What is most "unlikely" about the private name or image is the idea that it could keep its likeness and specificity while being borne across distance and time by the poem. By allowing the phonic materiality of the name to resonate as disturbance or noise in its collision with the Outside, however, the poem also creates a frequency for queer eroticism to circulate freely across time and place.

In the final poem of "A Textbook to Poetry," which begins with the statement "That they have lost the significance of a name is unimportant," the name Jim returns, carrying in its absolute singularity all the vibratory multiplicity and excess of static:

> Now the things that are for Jim are coming to an end, I see nothing beyond it. Like a false nose where a real nose is lacking. Faceless people.

> The real sound of the dead. A blowing of trumpets proclaiming that they had been there and been alive. The silver voices of them.
>
> To be alive. Like the noises alive people wear. Like the word Jim, es-specially—more than the words.
>
> (*MV*, 313)

The translation of "Jim" from name to word entails a loss of its signification in reference to the real, singular person, so that he or it becomes another ghost to join the ghosts of poems. But in the death of signification resonates the "real sound" of loss, which is also an excess, a "noise" that paradoxically recirculates the living wor(l)d. Recall here the "sound of wings" that Spicer heard in Cégeste's voice, humming through the radio-corpse, and opening an alternative channel, both material and virtual, to carry queer desire (*MV*, 266).

In short, Spicer's transformative uses of the radio motif deconstruct everything a contemporaneous reader might assume about radio and, by metaphoric extension, about the compositional practice of dictation—including dictation's connection to the logics of metaphor, in the sense of transporting or carrying meaning from one place to another. We've seen how Spicer's radio privileges static over signal and sound, cites anachronistic rather than modern radio forms, and amplifies linguistic registers of ambiguity and ambivalence over clear signification. We've also seen how Spicer imagines radio as an Orphic medium that, rather than instantaneously transmitting a voice over vast distances, is perpetually turning backward, losing the voice and the poem to further distances. Moreover, Spicer's emphasis on radio as a technology of reception, and a poor one at that, subverts the general understanding of radio as a technology for broadcasting, making the poet-as-radio analogy into a figure for the queer poet's receptive capacities rather than the queer poem's public dissemination. The car radio in Cocteau's *Orpheus*, in other words, sounds nothing like the car radio in Ginsberg's *Fall of America*.

This contrast between radio's receptive and broadcasting capacities points to an important difference in Spicer's and Ginsberg's queering of the motif. While Ginsberg's broadcasting of "Howl" seeks to seize the mechanism of censorship to magically, instantaneously, directly transmit a queer signal to the mind of the listener as if by telepathy, Spicer's radio is too full of static to get the signal clear. As Spicer writes in *Language*,

"Telekinesis / Would not have been possible even if we were sitting at the same table" (*MV*, 394). Yet, in Spicer's poetics, the absolute indeterminacy and otherness of poetic reception—the impossibility of transmitting a message that would be sure to meet a receiver intact—is also what generates alternative frequencies and an ether of queer possibility. Christopher Nealon has argued that Spicer's image of the "counterpunching radio" "suddenly makes poetry a minor kind of radio, hitting back at 'major' radio, the real radio that would drown it out."[69] My reading of static throughout this section suggests that a queer poetics might be that "minor kind of radio" imagining alternative frequencies to both "major" radio and "major" poetry.

It may appear at this point that we are far removed from the types of radio and radio imaginaries that saturated 1950s and 1960s American culture, including those associated with the rise of FM radio. My argument, though, is that poets' creative and "counterpunching" uses of radio helped to create alternative cultural and social imaginaries to hegemonic media discourses that did feed back into FM radio aesthetics and politics, even if not always in direct or lasting ways. By re-making radio into a technology of queer mediumship, and by excavating older radio imaginaries for residual queer possibilities, both Spicer and Ginsberg contested the heteronormativity of dominant radio and literary cultures of the postwar U.S. Their radio and poetic work of the 1950s and early 1960s also looked ahead to the radical emergence of gay and lesbian media activism in the 1970s, including at Pacifica Radio stations. Ginsberg, of course, would participate in this movement directly. His ongoing appearances on Pacifica stations also helped the network to dramatically expand the reach of its countercultural signal. By the time of Spicer's death in 1965, the tiny, low-wattage, noncommercial FM radio station that in 1949 had given a live radio show to a young poet and folk music enthusiast with a tuneless singing voice and a penchant for profanity had become a public network broadcasting in three major metropolitan centers. But censor-taunting poets could still find a place on its frequencies, and with the acquisition of New York radio station WBAI in 1960, Pacifica Radio would generate new intimate listenerships and static dissonances that drew connection to an avant-garde poetry community that was forming around the public performance of poetry on the Lower East Side.

4

WBAI AND THE LOWER EAST SIDE SCENE

On a late December afternoon in 1960, Allen Ginsberg made his way to the midtown Manhattan studios of Pacifica Radio's newest station, WBAI-FM, to record an interview. He had returned to New York in 1958, moving with Peter Orlovsky into an apartment on East Second Street, just blocks from where he had lived with William S. Burroughs five years earlier. Though he continued to travel extensively, most recently in South America, the Lower East Side would remain Ginsberg's home for the rest of his life. In 1960, *Howl and Other Poems* was still his only published book, but he had recently completed *Kaddish*, the title poem of which, a long elegy to his mother, begins by tracing the poet's steps from "the sunny pavement of Greenwich Village" to "the Lower East Side—where you walked 50 years ago, little girl—from Russia."[1] The opening lines of "Kaddish" thus map a symbolic journey back in time, from the bohemian but gentrifying Village where Ginsberg, resident Beat poet, performed in famous clubs like the Gaslight, to the multiethnic, working-class neighborhood where the young Naomi Levy and her family first settled as Russian Jewish immigrants, and which appeared to her son half a century later—despite the post-WWII shifts altering the demographics and urban geography of the Lower East Side—as essentially unchanged, "the place of poverty / you knew, and I know" (*Collected Poems*, 210).[2] But Ginsberg's depiction of his eastward trek across downtown Manhattan was also prophetic in a sense, in that it looked ahead to the larger movement of artists, musicians, and writers from Greenwich Village to what became known, in the mid-1960s, as the East Village. This artistic influx made the Lower East Side the center of a dynamic poetry community that first coalesced in the early 1960s around reading series at local coffeehouses, little magazine and small press publishing, and social gatherings at the cheap lofts and cold-water flats that seemed far from the hallowed institutions of the New York art and literary establishment. And like the San Francisco Renaissance and KPFA, the Lower East Side poetry community would find its broadcasting outlet in Pacifica Radio station WBAI.

Pacifica Radio acquired WBAI in 1960 over the course of a transformative year for the network and U.S. radio more generally. In the summer of 1959, Pacifica was in the process of launching its second station, KPFK in Los Angeles, when its offices received an unsolicited call from the millionaire Louis Schweitzer offering to donate an FM radio station in New York City. Though office staff originally thought it was a joke, Schweitzer eventually got through to Pacifica president Harold Winkler, who jumped at the opportunity, recruiting KPFA's Eleanor McKinney and Alan Rich to oversee the quick transition.[3] In January 1960, Pacifica officially began broadcasting on 99.5 FM in New York. It was the dawn of a new era for Pacifica, and it couldn't have come at a more auspicious moment. Sales of FM radio sets in the U.S. had just exceeded one million for the first time; the payola scandal was dealing a blow to commercial radio; and massive layoffs and program cancellations at CBS and NBC radio would soon sound the final death knell for radio's network era. And with a presidential election in full swing, the civil rights movement gaining momentum, and the student movement about to take off, the opportunity was ripe for a broadcaster with a mission "to serve as a voice of free radio, free culture and free expression" to seize the moment.[4] By the end of the decade, BAI—as the station is affectionately known to its listeners—would be widely recognized as a bastion of free speech radio and a leader in the FM revolution, attracting the largest listenership and subscriber base of any station in Pacifica Radio's growing network, and "play[ing] a central, unifying role in New York's vast counterculture."[5] Over the same period, the Lower East Side, and especially the northern subsection of the neighborhood between Houston and Fourteenth Streets, became a contested center for that counterculture: the home of hippies and Yippies, the Peace Eye Bookstore and Diggers' Free Store, the Five Spot and the Fillmore East, the Poetry Project at St. Mark's Church, and the underground press.

At first, though, WBAI sounded like a transplanted KPFA—unsurprising given that much of its early staff and programming came directly from the Berkeley station, with Kenneth Rexroth's *Books* airing weekly alongside other KPFA stalwarts, like Anthony Boucher's opera program *Golden Voices* and the usual slate of Bach and BBC Third productions. But as at KPFA, WBAI management gave its staff wide license to propose new programming, and it wasn't long before a young radio producer, David Ossman, started creating original poetry programming. His interview program, *The Sullen Art*, brought many experimental New York poets to the station from 1960 to 1961, including Ginsberg, Ossman's most high-profile guest. When Ginsberg arrived for their interview in December 1960, he was eager to share some of his new consciousness-expanding work, but he had been emboldened since the *Howl* trial and his previous experience with Pacifica station KPFA to take a more assertive position against censorship edits. "Will they cut this tape," Ginsberg pointedly asked Ossman at the start of the interview, who assured him that station engineers "won't cut anything out of a poem."[6] Ginsberg emphasized his preference for reading poems over "conversation," insisting on the radical communicative power of the poetic spoken word: "Because everybody is God, and it's time they seized power in the universe and took over the means of communication and started communicating!"[7] With this introduction, Ginsberg read the poem "Magic Psalm," which apostrophizes the divine through a litany of epithets that includes "Asshole of the Universe into which I disappear."[8] Predictably, though, Ginsberg's effort to channel a queer, visionary frequency into the "Ear of the buildings of NY" was blocked; this poem and others were cut from the program before it aired (though, true to Ossman's word, the poems were not selectively edited). Instead, listeners had to settle for Ginsberg's and Ossman's conversation about "such subjects as dope addiction, the New York police, the poetic experience, Fidel Castro and 'the Beat scene.'"[9]

This chapter is about the co-emergence of WBAI and the Lower East Side poetry community in the early 1960s as more broadly representative of the intersections between sixties poetry, politics, and radio. The problem of communication, and specifically of how to create alternative institutions and media outlets for dissenting politics and culture, was a central question of the sixties and for the poets and broadcasters that I consider in this chapter, much as it was for the pacifists who founded Pacifica Radio in the wake of WWII. But while KPFA entered the U.S. broadcasting industry in 1949 with grand ambitions of seizing the means of communication for the cause of peace only to find itself transmitting to a small audience of Berkeley elites, Pacifica took control of WBAI on the cusp of an eruption of alternative media, free speech activism, and countercultural production that in New York included the rise of underground radio and an underground press with roots in the Lower East Side. The experimental poetry community was deeply engaged in these political and media dynamics, and in what follows, I recover the story of how poets and radio producers—starting with Ossman—helped to bring WBAI downtown, figuratively speaking, and how WBAI, in turn, contributed to the aural poetics and community formation of the Lower East Side poetry scene in the early 1960s. As in previous chapters, I am interested here in exploring the formation of this relationship as it initially took shape, and that in this case preceded and paved the way for the establishment of the Poetry Project at St. Mark's Church, the marketing of the East Village by property developers, and the FM revolution of freeform underground radio in the mid-to-late 1960s.

I focus especially on the different effects that this radio connection had on Paul Blackburn and Amiri Baraka, two of the principal architects of the Lower East Side poetry community of the early 1960s. Blackburn, who fostered the community by organizing and documenting a poetry reading series at the cafés Le Deux Mégots and Le Metro, was a participatory listener to WBAI, and from 1964 to 1965 he also hosted his own WBAI program, *Contemporary Poetry*, which broadcast poetry readings and conversations with poets recorded in the studio and from his personal tape collection. I argue that Blackburn's practices of taping the radio and broadcasting tapes informed the oral, "freeform," and narrowcast poetics of the Lower East Side scene. Baraka, too, played a central role in making the Lower East Side a center for New York's avant-garde through his work as a poet, editor, publisher, music critic, and activist who moved between various art scenes and across the segregated racial divides of postwar American society—which is not to say that he did so with ease. In fact, the period from 1960 to 1966 that saw the rise, fragmentation, and reformation of the Lower East Side poetry community corresponded with the so-called transitional period in Baraka's biography that led him to reject his position as LeRoi Jones, "King of the East Village," to become Amiri Baraka, leader of the Black Arts movement.[10] Baraka's political radicalization in the mid-1960s was, moreover, a media event of which WBAI and the Pacifica network were important broadcasters. Thus, while scholars have often noted the prominence of radio as a motif in Baraka's early poetry that looks back with ambivalent nostalgia on the "golden age" radio of his childhood, I consider how Baraka's first appearances on FM radio influenced (and continue to influence) the reception of his turn toward a "blacker art" in these years,[11] and contributed to his development of a critical poetics and praxis of listening that transduces in order to destroy the "white noise" of American media.

The New American Poetry, Radio Edition

"In New York, these days, if you're looking for excitement the place to go is downtown. Where the customers are tripping over iambic pentameter in the local coffee houses and saloons in their rush to hear poetry in action." So reported WCBS-TV announcer and sportscaster Jim McKay for the television program *Eye on New York* in a May 1959 segment about poetry readings in Greenwich Village, which featured interviews with Paul Blackburn, Amiri Baraka, Galway Kinnell, Denise Levertov, and Edward Marshall about the spectacle of the downtown poet-performer. With reference to the Village's history as the site of 1920s literary bohemia, and Jack Kerouac's *On the Road* as "start[ing] a new movement called the Beat Generation," McKay had one simple question: "Is it art?" Viewers were encouraged to decide for themselves from clips of Blackburn and Kinnell reading poetry on a set designed to simulate a downtown coffeehouse. "A renaissance.... Perhaps," McKay mused, "But certainly new and certainly vital ... living sounds ... person to person. HERE IN NEW YORK." With that, McKay ended the report, but before the cut to commercial he teased his next interview with another group of wild performers: animal actors representing "some of television's biggest talent on all fours."[12]

To many commercial media outlets and tourist spectators at the turn of the decade, Greenwich Village was an exotic zoo of bohemian specimens, the home of poetry-reciting beatniks, jazz hipsters, and guitar-strumming folkies. And while one could hardly expect to hear much iambic pentameter, it is true that by the late 1950s, San Francisco's poetry reading culture had come to downtown Manhattan, and with it the Beat sensationalism of both popular media and the literary critical establishment. As a result, New York poets who gravitated downtown in search of literary community couldn't avoid being painted with the Beat brush even when (as in the case of all the poets featured on the WCBS-TV spot) it didn't quite apply. The eastward drift of downtown poets and artists away from Greenwich

Village may have been motivated primarily by the search for cheaper rents, but as Daniel Kane observes, it "also had roots in artists' resistance to being co-opted by the kinds of mainstream activity commodifying the late 1950s West Village arts scene," including "sugar-coated media representations of bohemian theater and poetry."[13]

The 1960 publication of Donald Allen's anthology *The New American Poetry, 1945–1960*, by New York independent publisher Grove Press also promised to change the conversation by contextualizing and circumscribing the Beats within a more capacious poetic avant-garde. In his preface to the anthology, Allen announced the arrival of a "third generation" of American modernists whose work so far had only a limited circulation in print; "a larger amount of it," he wrote, "has reached its growing audience through poetry readings."[14] By centering the importance of the poetry reading and the little magazine, and by putting Charles Olson at the front of the volume, Allen gestured to the importance of oral poetics as a unifying thread for the "new" but made clear that it neither originated nor ended with the Beats. Allen's groupings of the poets into four quasi-regional movements (Black Mountain, Beat, San Francisco Renaissance, and New York School) and a fifth, more loosely defined group of mostly younger writers—as well as his selection of almost exclusively white male writers—proved especially influential on the critical conception of postwar American experimental poetry.[15]

For David Ossman, a twenty-three-year-old radio producer, actor, poet, and recent Columbia University graduate, *The New American Poetry* was a kind of "bible," and WBAI, now broadcasting as a listener-sponsored Pacifica Radio station, the perfect outlet to sound the word.[16] Ossman was one of the few staff members to carry over from WBAI's previous iteration as a commercial classical music station, and from 1960 to 1961 he produced some of the station's first original poetry programming, including the interview program *The Sullen Art*; a series of half-hour readings, *The Poet in New York*; and a radio documentary edited from these, *American Poetry, 1961*. In 1963, Ossman published an edited print selection of his radio interviews under the same title, *The Sullen Art*, with downtown publisher Corinth Books, which gave them a wider and more lasting circulation. Though the radio program went on the air a few months before Allen's anthology was published, *The Sullen Art* functioned in a sense as a kind of radio supplement to *The New American Poetry*. Like Allen, Ossman sought to cut through the Beat noise, albeit on the smaller and more local scale of FM radio, by highlighting the variety of poetry that was being published in little magazines and performed at public readings. Several of the poets featured on *The Sullen Art* (and *The Poet in New York*) also appeared in Allen's anthology, while others represented a wider network of experimental and often younger poets.[17] Most were not widely known beyond the small press circuits and literary communities in which their work circulated, with a few notable exceptions (like Ginsberg). And while a few more white women writers were featured on Ossman's radio programs than in Allen's anthology, Baraka was once again the sole poet of color represented, implying, as Aldon Lynn Nielsen observes of anthologies of the period, that "the public face of poetic innovation in New York was white, masking once more the significant contributions of black writers to the gathering forces of the new."[18]

Unsurprisingly, many of the poets who appeared on Ossman's WBAI radio programs lived in New York. More noteworthy, though, is how many had connections to the coffeehouse reading scene that was just beginning to emerge on the Lower East Side. Poets had been coming to the neighborhood since at least the mid-1950s to frequent the Five Spot jazz club and the abstract expressionist galleries on Tenth Street, but the origins of the Lower East Side poetry community have generally been traced to two poetry reading series that began in 1960–1961.[19] The first reading series, organized by Howard Ant and Ree Dragonette, started in 1960 at the Tenth Street Coffeehouse between Third and Fourth Avenues, a café owned by Mickey Ruskin. In 1961, Ruskin opened a new café on East Seventh Street, Les Deux Mégots, and the poets followed, establishing a regular weekly schedule of open community readings on Wednesday evenings and solo readings by an invited poet on Sundays. Paul Blackburn, Carol Bergé, and Allen Katzman joined Ant as organizers of the readings at Les Deux Mégots. Baraka, too, was a presence in the emerging Lower East Side poetry community, though he would more actively foster it through his work as editor of *Yugen*, Totem Press, and (with Diane di Prima) *The Floating Bear*, and through the parties that he and Hettie Jones hosted in their downtown apartments that attracted a diverse group of poets, artists, and jazz musicians. Over the next few years—during which time the reading series moved to café Le Metro—the East Side scene would foster "a gathering of the avant-garde tribes" that cut across and beyond the groupings of Allen's anthology.[20] The community was also relatively more integrated in terms of race and gender than other postwar avant-gardes, though the inclusiveness implied by the title of Daniel Kane's study, *All Poets Welcome*, was belied (as Kane acknowledges) by the fact that in the early 1960s it was still dominated by white men and an overarching ethos of racial tokenism and heterosexual masculinism.[21]

Ossman, who learned about the Tenth Street Coffeehouse readings from Blackburn and performed his own poetry at the open readings, was an early participant in this emerging community. Its influence on Ossman's radio programs was subtle, though, observable primarily in the poets he invited for readings and interviews—and those he did not. The absence of any of the New York School poets on Ossman's programs may have been largely for circumstantial reasons (John Ashbery, for one, was living in Paris at the time), but Ossman later recalled that his own sense was that the "New York School of poets . . . were somehow too 'uptown' for *The Sullen Art*. . . . The two communities of writers seemed further apart than the distance from Canal Street to the Museum of Modern Art."[22] As this community was still just forming, however, the more evident discursive background for a radio interview program on contemporary poetry circa 1960 was the so-called anthology wars set off by the publication of *The New American Poetry*, and one therefore finds across Ossman's interviews a recurring interest in topics that were major points of contention between the "raw" upstarts and the "cooked" formalists, including questions of craft as it concerned free verse poetry, and questions of audience, since the grouping of Allen's anthology had raised the criticism that the "new" poetry was too exclusive in its address, too much a coterie art.

In Ossman's interview with Blackburn, for example, which aired on WBAI on October 13, 1960, Ossman quoted praise from Paul Carroll that "Blackburn knows his craft" to ask about his approach to poetic form. Blackburn responded by explicating his poetics as jazz inspired, speech and breath based, and performance oriented, asserting that "a poem . . . is basically a *musical* structure" that "must tie together as a musical unit—however irregular it looks on the page, and even if it sounds almost free-form."[23] A poem read near the end of the program, "The Franklin Avenue Line," conveys this musical sensibility, as Blackburn's ode to the dilapidated Brooklyn spur line mimics the train's halting rhythm through its varied line lengths, heavy enjambment (marked by pauses in his reading), internal rhymes and alliteration, and metrical play that come to a punning conclusion when

vaguely in-
decisively   train and rain
come at the same
time
    to a measured
                    stop[.][24]

While "The Franklin Avenue Line" is refreshingly (at least for this reader-listener) free of the poet's objectifying male gaze—whose incessant cataloging in other subway poems of jiggling thighs, breasts, and backsides becomes a wearying sexist cliché—it might be noted that Blackburn likely chose this poem to read on the radio because it did not include language that could be subject to censorship.[25] Indeed, another subway poem, "The Once-Over," was cut from the program before broadcast because of its content. In the interview, Ossman and Blackburn had agreed that "the use of 'common speech' [is] the most common link between the new poets," but their discussion of "common speech" turned on the phrase's connotations as signifying vulgar or profane speech, with Ossman observing in the audio recording that many of Blackburn's poems contained words that, though now "eminently printable," were still verboten in broadcasting.[26] In response, Blackburn stated, "if you want to start from the point of view that ... common speech ... is a very fair and valid medium for poetry, you're going to find some people whose common speech is commoner than most. That would include a lot of the male members—ladies usually watch their language fairly carefully, and that's only right, too."[27] Blackburn's comment makes explicit the ways that a discourse on the poetics of "common speech" was often gendered to enforce "the compulsory homosociality" of the New American Poetry.[28]

Baraka's appearance on *The Sullen Art* a few months earlier had also touched on the poetics of "common speech," though here the conversation perhaps predictably segued into questions about the (in)audibility of race in Baraka's own speech-based poetics. To Baraka's explanation of his intention "to write the way I *speak* rather than the way I *think* a poem ought to be written," Ossman asked, "Does your being a Negro influence the speech patterns—or anything else ... in your writing?"[29] Baraka responded, "It could hardly help it," but went on to assert that, beyond his awareness of the "sociological" influence of race on his work,

(131)

"it doesn't have anything to do with what I'm writing at the time"—a view that he would soon radically revise (Baraka [Jones], "LeRoi Jones," 81). But it was the issue of coterie poetics as it concerned Baraka's role as an editor that came more vociferously to the fore. At the start of the interview, Ossman had pointedly questioned the twenty-five-year-old poet, whose first book wouldn't appear until the next year, about whether his little magazine *Yugen* was just another "'clique' magazine" publishing "a fairly restricted group" or "'stable' of writers" (77). Baraka did not reject the label, stating "[i]f it seems like a coterie—well, it turns out to be that way," but defended his editorial vision as no more exclusionary than the *Partisan Review*, more "various" in its selection of contributors than it might seem, and more influential as a tastemaker than Ossman implied (77). Noting that many of the poets who appeared in little magazines like *Big Table*, *Evergreen Review*, and *Black Mountain Review* "wouldn't have [been] printed if it hadn't been for . . . *Yugen*," Baraka rightly asserted his role in defining what Allen—and Ossman—were now championing as the vanguard of American poetry (78).[30] Ossman continued, however, by aggressively questioning the "validity" of a poem published in the last issue of *Yugen*: O'Hara's "Personal Poem," which famously recounts the poet's lunch date with "LeRoi," and which Ossman dismissed as too anecdotal and intimate in its references to be of interest to anyone except future scholars. Baraka countered, "I thought that anything . . . was fit material to write a poem on," arguing that "[a]nybody who is concerned with the *poem* will get it on an emotional level," whether or not they know "who the LeRoi . . . was" (78; italics in original). The fact that Baraka, especially, would be made to answer for the charge of (queer) coterie anticipates how central the question of "who the LeRoi was" would become—both to Baraka himself, and to white poets like O'Hara and Blackburn for whom the proper name "'LeRoi Jones' would soon mark a site of radical rupture and absence, . . . a sign of black life in white America and a mark of American blackness within their own lives and texts."[31]

That the position of being architect, token, and text in the downtown poetry community would become increasingly untenable for Baraka in the early 1960s—and that radio literally and figuratively became a site for this impossibility for Baraka—are key points in the narrative of this chapter, and I will return to them (and this early radio appearance) later. Here, however, I only want to note that the coterie poetics of Baraka,

Blackburn, and other downtown poets that Ossman invited onto *The Sullen Art* did not (as yet) influence Ossman's own crafting of his persona and approach on these radio programs. Nor does it seem likely that Ossman would have adopted a more intimate radio address at this time, given the skepticism he voiced about both coterie poetics and Beat publicity. By his own account, he saw *The Sullen Art* as an inquiry into "what was going on in contemporary writing" taken "on behalf of . . . a pretty un-hip listening audience," whom he might reasonably have assumed to be mostly hi-fi classical music listeners and older elites.[32] Even the title of his interview program, borrowed from Dylan Thomas's poem "In My Craft or Sullen Art," was chosen, as he explained, not for its "pejorative connotations" but because "'sullen' comes from the Latin *solus*—alone. These poets, and all poets, despite their contacts with the world, are ultimately alone. One creates, after all, by one's self."[33] It's a striking claim to make about poets whose aesthetic and social forms have often been understood to be inextricable. But that's presumably the point: contra O'Hara's bid in "Personism: A Manifesto" for a poetic narrowcasting that would be as direct as a telephone call or, better yet, a threesome, so that "[t]he poem is at last between two persons instead of two pages," the title of Ossman's program reflected a dominant midcentury belief (even among many of the New American poets) of the necessary solitude of the poet who, like the radio announcer, broadcasts out to an invisible, unknown public.[34]

The poets of the Lower East Side, however, were experimenting with a different model, one that, as Daniel Kane puts it, saw "the poetry reading as a staging ground for an alternative community" that was locally sited, intentionally formed, and uninterested in appealing to an abstract, universalized public.[35] From 1962 to 1965, the coffeehouse reading scene at Les Deux Mégots and Le Metro—and a corresponding eruption in mimeograph and small press publishing—took off alongside the burgeoning experimental theater, jazz, and art scenes on the Lower East Side. But Ossman would have to learn about its happenings from a distance; in 1961, he left New York for Los Angeles, though he would continue his radio career at Pacifica Radio station KPFK, creating literary, drama, and comedy programming with an increasingly experimental, countercultural, improvisatory bent.[36]

CHAPTER 4

Freeform, Narrowcast

In March 1963, the organizers of the weekly poetry readings at Les Deux Mégots moved the series to Le Metro on 149 Second Avenue, a café with a larger space and more foot traffic. Blackburn became the principal curator of the solo readings by invited poets, which he often recorded on his portable tape recorder, and both the solo and open readings attracted large, raucous audiences that filled the venue and sent lines out the door. The core group of poet-performers also expanded significantly over the next two years. Recent arrivals Ted Berrigan and Ron Padgett became active participants, with Berrigan eventually joining the organizing committee. Kathleen Fraser and Diane Wakoski attended and performed at the readings. Ed Sanders started publishing *Fuck You/A Magazine for the Arts* and opened the Peace Eye Bookstore. And the Umbra poets were now on the scene: Calvin Hernton and David Henderson, who first met at a reading at Les Deux Mégots where they were the only two African Americans present, formed the Umbra workshop with Tom Dent in 1962 to foster a community of Black writers and, through their literary magazine, a radical, internationalist Black aesthetic.[37] Copies of *Umbra*, *Fuck You*, Berrigan's *C*, and other mimeos circulated at Le Metro readings, as did Dan Saxon's *Poets at Le Metro*, the contents of which were solicited, handwritten, printed with a rexograph, and distributed between the start and end of a reading. And in the audience, you might find William S. Burroughs or Andy Warhol. Increased visibility, however, also meant increased surveillance (and vice versa); a 1964 effort by the New York Police Department to shut down Le Metro readings under the coffeehouse license law met organized and successful resistance by the poetry community.[38]

After Ossman's departure from WBAI in 1961, there was no regular radio program connected to the Lower East Side poetry community on the station until 1964, when Blackburn became the host of his own show. But that didn't mean that the connection was lost in the interval. WBAI's growing attunement to the civil rights movement in its public affairs and cultural programming brought more African American writers and jazz artists onto its airwaves, including those with connections to the Lower East Side. A listing in the *WBAI Program Folio* for August 30, 1963, for example, announces a program on *The Umbra Poets* that would feature readings by nine writers: Ishmael Reed, Joseph Johnson, Askia M. Touré

(Rolland Snellings), Lorenzo Thomas, Art Berger, Charles Patterson, Calvin Hernton, Tom Dent, and David Henderson.[39] As at Le Metro readings, where the Umbra poets often performed as a collective, the "powerful group presentation of these younger black writers" would have asserted a "prominence [that] allowed them to forcefully claim a space" on the airwaves of a radio station still dominated by white voices.[40] More significantly, A. B. Spellman, who was also part of the Umbra group, started hosting the WBAI program *Jazz with A. B. Spellman* in 1962, where he broadcast free jazz music and in-depth interviews with musicians like Ornette Coleman, laying the groundwork for his landmark work of jazz criticism, *Four Lives in the Bebop Business* (1966).[41] As one of the first African American program hosts at WBAI, Spellman helped to pave the way for other Black producers and jazz programming at WBAI and inaugurated the tradition of the poet-cum-jazz radio DJ that writers like Baraka, Nathaniel Mackey, and Erica Hunt would later continue.

WBAI was thus becoming part of the soundscape of the Lower East Side scene, which Blackburn, in addition to being one of the main organizers of the readings at Le Metro, cultivated as its audio documenter. The romantic portrait of Blackburn as a modern troubadour with a "tape-recorder ear" is cemented in the lore of the Lower East Side poetry community.[42] In a memorial program for Blackburn that aired on WBAI in 1972, after his early death from cancer, Joel Oppenheimer reminisced that his lasting "picture" of his friend would be of Blackburn "constantly hunched against the wind somewhere, going off into the night, schlepping an enormous tape recorder, off to another reading."[43] Decades later, Bob Holman recalled how Blackburn "would go from reading to reading, hauling his jumbo public-high-school issue Wollensak reel-to-reel, recording open and featured readings all over town. At night, he'd record jazz or rock off the radio, or read (rewrite?) his own poems on tape. He was a walking exponent of the oral tradition."[44] Blackburn's sense of the "the oral tradition," though, clearly also embraced the "secondary orality" of electronic and broadcast media.[45] His tape collection at the Archive for New Poetry at the University of California, San Diego, testifies to the breadth of material he recorded: public poetry readings, intimate readings in his apartment, drafts of his poems, audio letters, conversations with friends and family, miscellaneous sounds of everyday life, and—of particular interest to us here—radio broadcasts. An avid radio listener, Blackburn used his tape machine to record off his radio everything from popular and classical music to literature and drama to interviews, news reports, and live coverage of political events. And since much of the radio programming that appears in his tape collection originated from WBAI and other local FM stations, Blackburn's archive also offers a fascinating, personal document of 1960s New York FM radio from the perspective of one poet. And not only as a listener: the collection also includes recordings from Blackburn's own WBAI program, *Contemporary Poetry*.

In *Narrowcast: Poetry and Audio Research*, Lytle Shaw argues that postwar experimental poets used the new medium of tape not only to capture an oral poetry but to explore their environmental surrounds, conducting what he characterizes as a kind of sonic fieldwork into modes of poetic address embedded in embodied and social localities and durational time. The significance of the portable tape recorder to what Michael Davidson terms the "tapevoice" of post-1945 American poetry has been observed by many critics, but as Shaw observes, "[t]ape . . . registers environments and not merely voices; spatial situations and not merely oracular utterances."[46] For Shaw, poets' interest in the noise of tape is in part what makes the New American Poetry "[a] poetry of narrowcasting," though the term, he explains, would have to mean something "rather different from the word's common association with niche marketing," something more than "the empirical size of an audience" (*Narrowcast*, 24). Narrowcasting, in Shaw's usage, is therefore less a metaphor for coterie poetics—though it may describe works that "display a coterie logic, a provocative narrowness"—than a term to conceptualize how post-WWII experimental poets used tape to "specify, concretize, ground, or in some basic sense reject the generalized address" of mainstream radio and television (24).

In other words, for Shaw, it is tape not radio that narrowcasts; indeed, one of his central claims is that poets used tape recording to contest "dominant American media—radio above all" and to critique the whole "media apparatus of radio itself: its time, its space, its hail, its logic, its common sense" (*Narrowcast*, 2, 7).[47] Certainly it is true that many poets, including many whom I discuss in this book, were deeply critical of mainstream commercial radio for precisely the reasons that Shaw elucidates. But so, too, were Lewis Hill and the other founders of Pacifica Radio; we might recall, for example, KPFA's early refusal to run programming by the clock, or the various bodily, environmental, and technical noise on Rexroth's homemade tapes that frustrated and delighted his radio listeners, or even Ginsberg's ambivalence about who might be listening to the broadcast of "Howl." In a certain sense, Pacifica Radio was narrowcasting during KPFA's first years on the air, though it is only in the 1960s and 1970s, ironically with the expansion of the network, that Pacifica stations began to explicitly narrow their rhetorical address to audiences on the progressive left. Debates about the New American Poetry's challenge to literary universality had, moreover, an interesting parallel in radio in the 1960s, as the industry debated the viability of mass broadcasting in the post-network era. The short-lived revolution in freeform underground FM radio in the mid-to-late 1960s, which was also driven by a critique of the commercial standardization and political quietism of commercial AM radio, contributed to the belief among leftist artists and activists that audio media (tape, independent record labels, and FM radio) could be used to narrowcast an alternative culture.[48] To see poets' engagements with tape and FM radio in the 1960s not as opposed but as overlapping practices is therefore to account more fully for the multimedia assemblage that produced the "tapevoice" of post-1945 American poetry.

Blackburn is an exemplary case for this thesis because of how profoundly his oral and coterie poetics intersected with practices of tape recording, radio listening, and radio production. One of the original tape reels in his archive, for example, includes over three hours of recorded miscellany, much of it from WBAI programs that Blackburn taped off his radio over a period of several months in 1961, vividly documenting the feedback loop that flowed between WBAI and the Lower East Side scene. This includes David Ossman's *Sullen Art* interview with Ginsberg that I discussed at the start of the chapter, which aired on February 22, and a WBAI program of Blackburn himself reading from his translations, which aired on April 2. In addition, Blackburn recorded on this reel two WBAI broadcasts of BBC programs (a radio production of *King Lear* and a program of John Keats's poetry read by the late English actor Robert Donat) as well as broadcast music from various radio stations. At one point on the recording, the sounds of a typewriter in close proximity to the tape recorder accompany several minutes of classical piano music. That the piano music originates from a radio set is evident from the announcer's voice heard at its conclusion, who identifies the composition as Mozart's *Andante and Variations in G Major* and the program as WBAI's *Chamber Music*.[49] The first time I heard this recording, the sounds of the typewriter had a transformative effect on my listening experience, projecting me suddenly into a three-dimensional acoustic space, where it was easy to imagine Blackburn as the typist, working on a poem while his radio played in the background.

Taping the radio—a now mostly obsolete practice, but one that I nostalgically associate with my childhood and a bedside radio-cassette player that I used to record pop hits off my favorite FM stations—first became possible with the conjunction of the portable tape recorder and the transistor radio. Though it would take cassette technology to make this a widespread consumer practice, it's nonetheless true that by syncing up these two postwar technologies, a listener could, for the first time and without much technical know-how, capture and "own" an ephemeral broadcast. The ad hoc media assemblage could also enable listeners to redistribute broadcast content through informal tape exchanges—as Blackburn did, sending tapes with poetry, conversation, and jazz and pop music recorded from the radio to writers like Robert Creeley in New Mexico and Julio Cortázar in Paris. Tape exchanges extended the narrowcasting of not only the oral poetics but the whole aural culture of the Lower East Side poetry community beyond New York, fostering national and even transnational micro-networks of exchange.[50]

Blackburn's practice of taping the radio also fed into his poetry and compositional practices. One of the tapes in his archive, for example, records several news broadcasts about the December 1965 launch and space flight of NASA's Gemini 7 that Blackburn drew on in the composition of his poem "Newsclips 2. (Dec/ 6-7)."[51] The poem begins by reflecting on the drip of broadcast news that had becoming increasingly constant on radio in the 1960s—"The news keeps squirting in from all over, / it's like a leak in my head"—and then cites reports of the crew removing their space suits in flight to imagine a crassly comic scene of "a pair / of astronauts / orbiting earth for two full weeks / in their underwear" as sexual antics ensue.[52] In the poem's final stanzas, the speaker ventriloquizes (or is perhaps more accurately ventriloquized by) the broadcast voice of the newscaster:

Well, I'm about to the end of the broadcast.

High tides for today, Dec/ 7, at Sandy Hook

6:20   A.M. and 6:46 P.M.;   6:33 A.M. and 7:07 P.M. on

the North side of Montauk Point;

at the Battery   6:49 and 7:12   .

(138)

Temperatures yesterday were various:

88° and clear in Kingston, Jamaica
84 and cloudy in Acapulco
85 and partly cloudy in San Juan

(*Collected Poems*, 386)[53]

After the weather and tide report, and an announcement of a "'Cruise to Nowhere'" due to set sail from the New York harbor, the poem ends with a sign-off: "Don't miss it, boys and girls, and that's / all for tonight." The poet Robert Kelly later claimed that Blackburn was "the first person to put the tape recorder to a genuine compositional function," recalling how he would obsessively record and play back drafts of his poems, "collaborat[ing] with the tape recorder . . . to restore the poem on the paper to its proper indexical function."[54] But in "Newsclips 2," the poet's attunement of page to tape means indexing other voices and sounds in the poet's environment—including the highly mediated voices that transmit over his radio.

The transcript of "Newsclips 2" is rare in Blackburn's poetry, but other poems register radio as integral to the particularized New York soundscapes that the poet moves through with his "tape-recorder ear." In "Pre-Lenten Gestures," for example, a radio playing in a bakery on Third Avenue and Twenty-Fourth Street sets the tone for the poet's meditation on the sacred and the profane as he observes the everyday goings-on of the café:

Thank God one tone or
one set of decibels is
not all there is.   The
Dies Irae, the radio behind me, is,
due to the mad programmer we never know, followed
by a selection of military band music.
          How kind.

(*Collected Poems*, 238–239)

Here, Blackburn aligns radio form and poetic form: the "mad programmer's" juxtaposition of the dramatic orchestral and choral power of Mozart's requiem mass followed by the boisterous brass of a military march comes to figure the poet's own invisible artistry in arranging disparate observations and ideas into contiguous relation so that the poem "tie[s] together as a musical unit . . . even if it sounds almost free-form."[55]

CHAPTER 4

The musical juxtaposition also sounds like what one might find serendipitously arranged on one of Blackburn's tapes. It reminds me, too, of the kinds of irreverent musical segues, more jarring than this one, that one might have heard on an early freeform radio show helmed by a "mad" announcer with hours of uninterrupted airtime to go. In 1963, when Blackburn wrote "Pre-Lenten Gestures," the late-night hours at WBAI had been taken over by Bob Fass, a young actor from Brooklyn who, like Blackburn, used to lug his own portable tape recorder to the cafés of downtown Manhattan. Fass, one of the inventors of freeform radio and host of the legendary and long-running WBAI program *Radio Unnameable*, had performed in downtown theaters before starting as an announcer at the station in 1962. He soon got permission to take over the station's airwaves after its official sign-off at midnight, and in the early days he would often play tapes he had recorded in Village coffeehouses. "I wanted to put my culture on the air—the Greenwich Village *cul-chah*—politics and exotic people," Fass later explained of the origins of *Radio Unnameable*.[56] Over the years, he would invite many of the resident performers and activists of the West and East Village—including Ginsberg, Gregory Corso, David Henderson, Ed Sanders, Abbie Hoffman, and Bob Dylan—to the studio to play music, read poems, spin records, take listener calls, smoke weed, and hang out. By the late 1960s, *Radio Unnameable* would become a voice or more accurately the switchboard for a devoted audience of hippies, night owls, and night-shift workers, who called in to talk as much to each other as to Fass and his guests, and whom Fass addressed each night as his coterie, his secret "cabal."[57]

To be clear, I am not suggesting that Blackburn's "Pre-Lenten Gestures" alludes to Fass's program. The loose connection I want to draw between the invention of freeform radio and the "free-form" poetry of the early 1960s is more about listening for the rhyme created by their contiguity —particularly as they were heard over WBAI's airwaves—than about claiming any kind of direct influence or analogy. If we wanted to find one, though, we might look again to A. B. Spellman, who by 1965 had transformed his jazz program into the daily freeform morning show *Where It's At*. As fellow freeform DJ Steve Post later recalled, "at 99.5 you could wake up to the voice of poet A. B. Spellman ... reading early angry black poetry, giving news headlines off the A.P. wire, playing jazz or blues, or talking to a guest."[58] In contrast to the overwhelming whiteness of later underground freeform radio, Spellman's live morning show made connections between experimental jazz, poetry, and radio as part of a radical Black Arts aesthetic.

Blackburn also hosted a radio program on WBAI from 1964 to 1965, and though it was not, in any sense, a freeform program, it did amplify the oral and aural poetics of the downtown poetry scene. On some episodes of his *Contemporary Poetry* program, Blackburn invited local and visiting poets—most of whom had also performed at Les Deux Mégots or Le Metro—to the WBAI studios to record a reading and conversation in a format similar to, but more casually executed than, Ossman's *Sullen Art*.[59] On other episodes, Blackburn simply broadcast poetry recordings from his personal tape collection with minimal editing. An early program from December 1964, for example, featured two previously recorded readings by John Keys: the first, from a reading Keys gave at Les Deux Mégots on January 16, 1963, and the second from that same night, recorded, as Blackburn explained for listeners, "at my apartment on 9th Street over a quart of ale."[60] In his characteristically brief introduction, Blackburn noted that while Keys is "too rarely published" and "even news of [him] is highly elusive," Keys "has been on the Lower East Side coffeehouse poetry reading scene for years" and his "work is highly respected by his fellow poets when they can find it or have an opportunity to hear it read." Implicit in these remarks is the suggestion that Keys's work is best experienced through oral performance, and that his "elusiveness" is connected to his reputation as a poet's poet in an avant-garde scene where marginality reads as authenticity. The low-fi recording of Keys's reading captures the lively, informal, and noisy interaction between the poet and the audience at Les Deux Mégots, some of whom Keys addresses by first name, and who frequently interrupt the reading with laughter, jokes, and even conversations. The sociality of the scene is also part of Keys's poems, which reference poets and places known to his audience, often for laughs. That not all these exchanges (or all the poetry) are fully audible on the recording seems beside the point; the noise asserts that this is a communal poetry. On programs like this one, Blackburn showcased not only the poets and poetry of the Lower East Side but the whole social scene that took place in the coffeehouses and even private apartments where poets engaged receptive, participatory audiences indifferent to the expectations of a general or commercial public. Davidson writes that Blackburn's radio show "brought the new writing out of the clubs and bars of the lower East Side and made it available to a wider audience," and in many ways it did, but it would be just as accurate to say that Blackburn narrowcast to an audience who might come downtown, metaphorically but also literally, to join this poetry community.[61]

Blackburn's radio show captured the energy of a live scene, yet in some ways, it was also a retrospective. In his introduction to the program on Keys, Blackburn noted that the reading series at Les Deux Mégots was "defunct"; the readings at Le Metro ended a year later, after a physical altercation between café owner Moe Margules and poet Tom Dent at a reading in the fall of 1965 capped off a series of racial and political confrontations between Margules and African American poets and musicians at the café.[62] By that time, a more general fracturing of the Lower East Side community was underway, resulting in part from the growing sense of political urgency and disillusionment felt by many of the African American writers in the scene. Blackburn's WBAI show had also been canceled in March 1965, allegedly "because of the (even more than usually) rough language used by one of Blackburn's participating friends, LeRoi Jones."[63] The cancellation served as a reminder yet again of the federal limits on broadcast speech that ultimately separated even a free speech defender like WBAI from the other cultural outlets and exchanges that narrowcast the avant-garde. It also, as Aldon Lynn Nielsen suggests, figured "the ruptured broadcast and friendship of Blackburn and Baraka."[64] In the spring of 1965, around the time he was scheduled to appear on Blackburn's program, Baraka left the downtown poetry community that he had helped to build (and his wife and young daughters) and moved to Harlem, where he and a group of Black writers and artists from both the downtown and uptown communities founded the short-lived but influential Black Arts Repertory Theatre/School (BARTS). In a draft of a poem written late in 1965, Blackburn lamented in quasi-mocking terms the departure of several of his closest friends, including Baraka: "Roi's gone into the hills of Harlem / and we hear nothing from him / all winter long." Blackburn noted, a few lines later, another significant departure from the Lower East Side poetry community and WBAI: "A. B. Spellman's off the air."[65]

Blackburn, too, would find himself somewhat on the outs of the community that reformed around the establishment of the Poetry Project at St. Mark's Church in 1966, after he was passed over for the Poetry Project directorship in favor of Joel Oppenheimer, a decision that many of his friends saw as a slight. None of these changes, though, ended the connection between WBAI and the Lower East Side poetry performance scene, which would only become stronger in the years and decades that followed, as WBAI became an important outlet for the Poetry Project and the Nuyorican Poets Cafe.[66] And Baraka, far from being silenced on WBAI, became an increasingly prominent and controversial voice on its airwaves in the mid-1960s. In fact, his own relationship to WBAI, as it initially formed over the same period of the early 1960s, would have a profound impact on the reception of his work and his voice that continues to the present day.

Amiri Baraka on the Radio

Late on an evening circa 1962, Amiri Baraka joined Joel Oppenheimer at Paul Blackburn's apartment on Cooper Square for one of Blackburn's "Saturday night tapings"—just friends hanging out, drinking beers, and reading poems for the tape.[67] Blackburn selected a reel that he had previously used to record the WBAI broadcasts of his own *Sullen Art* interview with David Ossman and of Ossman's documentary *American Poetry, 1961*, and, advancing to their end, set the machine to record.

> BLACKBURN: Well, you want me to interview you, gentlemen?
> OPPENHEIMER: Sure, interview us.
> BLACKBURN: Is this *The Sullen Art*?
> BARAKA: Interview Joel, that'd be interesting.
> BLACKBURN: What's sullen about this art, Joel? What is sullen about the new American poetry?[68]

For the next few hours, and over two reels, the three men put on their own mock episode of Ossman's former show, taking turns interviewing one another and reading poems. On the recording, Baraka can be heard getting things started by formally introducing Oppenheimer ("Hey, you think I could get a job on the radio now?") and asking him whom he considers to be the most important contemporary poets (Oppenheimer's response: Olson, Creeley, Duncan, Dorn, Sorrentino, Ginsberg, Zukofsky, definitely Zukofsky, because of his "sense of what sound is").[69] On Blackburn's prodding ("Since you're here in our studios this evening, why don't you read us some of your poetry"), Oppenheimer reads from *The Dutiful Son* (1956), which had been recently reprinted by Baraka's Totem Press.[70] It's a long reading; Baraka falls asleep.

CHAPTER 4

OPPENHEIMER: Hey, LeRoi.
BLACKBURN: He doesn't have to wake up.
OPPENHEIMER: Yeah, well, I'd like to hear him read that poem.
BARAKA: *indistinct mumbling*
BLACKBURN: Could we interview you for a while, Mr. Jones?
BARAKA: *indistinct mumbling*
BLACKBURN: Mr. Oppenheimer's been interviewed extensively, and he's read his book, and now . . .
OPPENHEIMER: My voice is starting to give. LeRoi, why don't you read that poem?

With a bit more nudging and another beer, Baraka agrees to read "that poem," a new poem that he's brought with him for the occasion. Blackburn adjusts the microphone. Baraka begins: "This poem's called 'Black Dada Nihilismus.'"

To hear Baraka read "Black Dada Nihilismus" on this home recording from Blackburn's archive is, in a word, surreal. First published in the *Evergreen Review* in 1963, and then in *The Dead Lecturer* in 1964, it is one of Baraka's most well-known and controversial poems, an iconoclastic work of his so-called transitional period from Village bohemianism to Black nationalism that dramatizes the poet's cutting away at the anti-Black roots of Western culture and, particularly and intimately, from his predominantly white social circle. In the poem's most (in)famous passage, the poet calls on the eponymous spirit to enact a brutal vengeance—"Rape the white girls. Rape / their fathers. Cut the mothers' throats"—including against his "friends," who Baraka associates with homosexual decadence and a sadomasochistic fetishization of Blackness: "Black dada nihilismus, choke my friends // in their bedrooms with their drinks spilling / and restless for tilting hips or dark liver / lips sucking splinters from the master's thigh."[71] On this recording (which, if accurately dated, preceded the poem's first appearance in print), Baraka reads these lines as he does the rest of the poem, with a slow, casual, somewhat halting delivery.[72] Are they listening, these white friends? When Baraka finishes—praying to "a lost god damballah, rest or save us / against the murders we intend / against his lost white children"—there is no immediate response, only a pause, the sound of paper shuffling.[73] Oppenheimer breaks the silence to identify an allusion in the poem's ambivalent litany of Black ancestors to Asbestos, a blackface minstrel character from the horse-racing comic

Joe and Asbestos. He and Baraka share memories of reading the newspaper strip in the *New York Mirror* and decoding its secret racing tips, as if to reaffirm a friendship based on shared generational experiences of pop cultural consumption that Baraka's poem has just thrown into a critical light. Otherwise, there is no further discussion of the poem; the conversation moves on, though for a while it will circle, as if symptomatically, around issues of race and sexuality.

Years later, in an interview with William J. Harris, Baraka explained that references to "my friends" in *The Dead Lecturer* directly addressed the poets "who lived in the Village and the Lower East Side, who I saw all the time, who I had some commonality with but at the same time felt estranged from since most of them were running around saying that poetry and politics had nothing to do with each other, and I was getting much more political."[74] But "talking to those people and to that particular sensibility" soon seemed fruitless to Baraka, who, like the autobiographical narrator of his story "Heroes Are Gang Leaders," hoped but doubted "[t]hat I am not merely writing poems for Joel Oppenheimer and Paul Blackburn."[75] In 1964, the success of *Dutchman* made Baraka a literary celebrity, but the bigger platform only strengthened his sense, especially in the wake of the Harlem riots that same year, that he could no longer play the role of "LeRoi Jones Talking" about Black rage to the predominantly white East/West Village scenes and New York liberal media.[76] The political radicalization of Baraka and other Black nationalists in the 1960s has often been framed as unfolding in relation to profound shifts in audience and address, in which Black artists and activists stopped speaking to white audiences through white-dominated media and started addressing and fostering instead a Black counterpublic.[77] In Baraka's case, his move to Harlem in 1965 signified a performative rejection of liberal integrationist politics in favor of a cultural nationalism committed to building alternative institutions for Black artists, audiences, and communities. After BARTS collapsed a few months later, Baraka moved back to his hometown of Newark, where in the 1960s and 1970s he built a whole infrastructure of Black nationalist cultural institutions, political organizations, and media outlets, from Spirit House to the Congress of Afrikan People to Jihad Publications to the Black NewArk media group, this last of which produced radio programs for WNJR-AM, the original flagship station of the Mutual Black Network.[78]

My aim here is not simply to rehearse the narrative of Baraka's break

CHAPTER 4

with his white friends and family in his highly publicized turn to Black nationalism, but to ask how radio figures in this story—how Pacifica Radio, specifically, became an important broadcaster of Baraka's voice at a pivotal moment for the network and FM radio's emergence as a countercultural media form, and how Baraka's ambivalent attachments to radio shaped the aurality of his work over this transitional period. Because Baraka was *heard* even if not always listened to or understood. As James Smethurst rightly observes, "there is probably no other U.S. poet whose speaking voice was so clearly 'heard' and tracked by readers as well as auditors" attuned to changes in the actual sound of Baraka's performance style as an index of his political and aesthetic transformations.[79] Radio was instrumental in the dissemination of Baraka's voice beyond the printed page, extending the reach of his live performances and talks and LP records, and contributing to the multimedia archive of his work that still circulates today and informs his critical reception. Attending to the radio dimensions of Baraka's work therefore reorients the critical focus on Baraka's sound to include questions of auditory reception. In other words, if "How You Sound??," published in *The New American Poetry*, is the defining statement of Baraka's early projective poetics and a touchstone for critics like William J. Harris who track a "radical shift in Baraka's sound" in the 1960s, I want to suggest that a related question and assertion, which we might phrase after Baraka as *how you listen??*, is equally central to Baraka's political and hermeneutical quest for "the blacker art" that "Black Dada Nihilismus," more than any other poem of this period, has been heard to inaugurate.[80]

Before turning to two broadcasts of "Black Dada Nihilismus" that aired on Pacifica Radio in 1964, though, I'd like to first return to an earlier moment in Baraka's radio archive. When Baraka first appeared on WBAI on Ossman's *Sullen Art* in 1960, he concluded the program by reading a few poems from his forthcoming *Preface to a Twenty Volume Suicide Note* . . . . (1961), including "In Memory of Radio."[81] Though this is not documented in the published print versions of the interview, Baraka's reading does appear on the archival recording of the program housed with Ossman's audio collection at the University of Toledo. The archival recording, while not widely accessible, thus preserves an important early performance of Baraka and a radio reading of his best-known radio poem.

Baraka often traced his lifelong love of radio to a childhood spent enthralled by radio serials like *The Lone Ranger* and *The Shadow*, and in his early work, radio is a prominent trope that often registers the poet's ambivalent participation in the nostalgia for "golden-age" radio that first arose as a public sentiment in the 1950s with the waning of the network era.[82] In the opening lines of "In Memory of Radio," Baraka represents this nostalgia as a generational feeling, but in the Beat sense, as an affect that binds together a homosocial coterie of visionary outsiders who know how to listen for the subversive undertones of American mass culture:

> Who has ever stopped to think of the divinity of Lamont Cranston?
> (Only Jack Kerouac, that I know of: & me.
> The rest of you probably had on WCBS and Kate Smith,
> Or something equally unattractive.)[83]

Over the patriotic soprano highs of Kate Smith, First Lady of Radio, Baraka declares his allegiance to Lamont Cranston, alter-ego of The Shadow, distancing himself from radio's association with a feminized bourgeois culture to align himself with the masculinized (but ambiguously racialized) heroism of The Shadow—and, more intimately, with Beat hero Jack Kerouac.[84] In its pop culture references and naming of intimates, "In Memory of Radio" therefore exhibits the kind of coterie sensibility that Ossman had objected to in O'Hara's "Personal Poem," even as it also mocks the notion that a mass commercial production as popularly beloved as *The Shadow* could become a secret shared among an elect few.[85]

Yet as the poem (and Baraka's reading of it) continues, the death of radio implied by the title becomes less something that the poet mourns with his friends and more something that he alone might desire:

> & Love is an evil word.
> Turn it backwards/see, see what I mean?
> An evol word. & besides
> who understands it?
>
> (*Preface*, 12)

For the African American listener, a nostalgic love for Jim Crow–era "golden-age" American radio can only be ambivalent, haunted by its inverse, and the "evol" pun, which signifies in the relay between sound and writing, aurality and literacy, resonates in the poem as a kind of interference, disrupting the generational, economic, and racial logics of cultural transmission. Because it cannot be fully sounded in oral performance, however, its auditory transmission in this radio reading relies on the listener following Baraka's verbal instruction to "turn it backwards" in a kind of mental writing, a telepathic transduction.[86] In so doing, the listener joins the poet in a counterlistening practice that hears in the canon of American radio "a dark and abiding presence,"[87] a submerged and potentially subversive Blackness:

> What was it he used to say (after the transformation,
>   when he was safe
> & invisible & the unbelievers couldn't throw stones?)
>   "Heh, heh, heh,
> Who knows what evil lurks in the hearts of men?
>   The Shadow knows."
>
> (*Preface* 12-13)

Quoting the iconic opening to *The Shadow*, Baraka makes no attempt at imitation: he does not lower his pitch, and his "laugh" is a slow, deadpan *ha, ha, ha* that registers as textual, not spontaneous or theatrical, and more sarcastic to my ear than the print text's "heh, heh, heh."[88]

What one hears, in other words, is not the dynamic, improvisatory, vernacular, polyvocal voicings that define Baraka's celebrated Black Arts performance style, but neither is it a voice that hides (like The Shadow) behind the invisibility of the medium to assume an unmarked whiteness. Instead, in my view, by resisting certain voicings Baraka paradoxically vocalizes his inscription of a certain mode of *aurality* that transduces the "white noise" of American radio into a different kind of signal, and that he would elsewhere trace back to his childhood experiences of radio listening.[89] In his autobiography, Baraka recalls how he would secretly listen to late programs like *The Shadow*, converting the pervasive message of American media—"that evil needed to be destroyed"[90]—through a counterlistening practice:

> I transformed the radio in my transmutating mind so it told brown tales somehow. (Yet you understand the term brainwash and must acknowledge certain brain damage. Yet I claim the transduction of certain impulses, so that the output was not just white noise, but a heroic grimace when I smile that contains absolute desire for the destruction of evil.)[91]

On the page, "In Memory of Radio" enacts a similar transduction, converting the invisible, acousmatic power of the radio voice into the hermetic textual silence of "evol" to decode the evil at the heart of white American capitalist and carceral fantasies of omnipresence. By performing the poem for radio, Baraka extended this process of transduction, converting text back into sound in a (counterpunching) radio transmission, sent out "on the lower frequencies."[92]

But "who understands it"?[93] The sense of alienation that pervades *Preface to a Twenty Volume Suicide Note....* would reach its crisis point in 1964–1965 in works like *The Dead Lecturer, The Toilet, Dutchman*, and *The System of Dante's Hell*. In these years, and in large part due to the success of the Obie Award–winning *Dutchman*, Baraka became a more public voice, amplified by WBAI and other New York liberal media outlets as "not merely... a well-placed analyst of the rising tide of black anger, but ... its personification."[94] He also became increasingly estranged from the downtown community he had helped to build—a social consequence, in some ways, of his new media celebrity and persona. In a comic illustration of this, Lorenzo Thomas relays an anecdote from Ted Berrigan about an afternoon at Frank O'Hara's apartment when

> Suddenly another friend of O'Hara's bounded up the stairs and burst into the room, heart-attack-if-you-don't-slow-down written across his face.
> "Amiri Baraka's on the radio," the man gasped, red with alarm, "and he's talking about killing white people!"
> "Well," said Frank consolingly, "I don't think he will begin with you or me. Now sit down and have some wine."[95]

O'Hara's attributed rejoinder is characteristically witty, but as Thomas notes, "[t]he efforts made by Baraka and others to distance themselves from the Beats and downtown avant-garde created resentments and hurt feelings in many relationships."[96] The same violent rhetoric that might be accepted as performatively shocking in the context of a Le Metro reading, in the pages of a mimeo magazine, or on one of Blackburn's tapes was received by some in the downtown community as offensive when it was routed through broadcast and traditional print media.

I like to imagine that what O'Hara's friend heard, what sent him careening up the stairs in panic, was a broadcast of Baraka reading "Black Dada Nihilismus" on New York radio station 99.5 FM. WBAI and other Pacifica Radio stations did broadcast recordings of Baraka performing the poem, including from his reading at the University of California Extension

CHAPTER 4

conference "The Negro Writer in the United States," which took place at Asilomar in Monterey on August 5–9, 1964. At the conference keynote, which Baraka headlined with Gwendolyn Brooks, Baraka read poems from the recently published *The Dead Lecturer*, including "Black Dada Nihilismus," as well as unpublished work that would later appear in the "Sabotage" section of *Black Magic* (1969). Though Brooks was the more established poet and the clear favorite among the majority of the (racially mixed but predominantly white) audience of writers, teachers, social workers, and journalists who received each of her poems with enthusiastic applause, Baraka was the focal point of attention: the divisive figure of a new, defiantly Black masculine expression whose connection to the Beats only enhanced the aura of controversy that surrounded him.[97] Pacifica Radio recorded the reading and broadcast it, along with other conference talks and roundtables (including two contentious talks by Baraka), on all three of its stations.[98] The recordings were also later added to Pacifica's Tape Library (the origin of the Pacifica Radio Archives), which facilitated program sharing with other radio stations, educational entities, and individuals. As a result, Pacifica's recording of Baraka and Brooks's reading circulated beyond the original event and broadcasts—and continues to do so, as easily discoverable online copies have made this one of the more well-known and critically discussed of Baraka's recorded performances.[99]

In addition, a WBAI program titled "Black Dada Nihilismus" with the description "Leroi Jones reads his poems to special music performed by a group under the leadership of John Tchicai" appears in the station program guide for November 19, 1964.[100] As many readers will know, Baraka recorded a jazz poetry rendition of "Black Dada Nihilismus" with the Afro-Danish saxophonist John Tchicai and the other members of the New York Art Quartet (NYAQ; trombonist Roswell Rudd, bassist Lewis Worrell, and percussionist Milford Graves) for the ensemble's self-titled 1965 debut album with ESP-Disk.[101] The WBAI program, of which there are no known recordings, may have featured takes from the ESP-Disk sessions that were recorded earlier that month at Bell Sound Studios in New York, or it may have constituted a separate, unique performance at the WBAI studios.[102] Baraka and the NYAQ also returned to WBAI on January 17, 1965, to participate in a live day of broadcasting in celebration of the station's five-year anniversary; an aircheck recording of their live performance, on which Baraka recites his poems "Western Front," "Bad Mouth," and "In One Battle" as the ensemble (with Eddie Gomez on bass) performs original compositions by Tchicai and Rudd, was issued on record for the first time in 2013 on the limited-edition vinyl box set *Call It Art: New York Art Quartet, 1964–1965*.[103] Blackburn managed to tune in for this one; a recording of the live broadcast also appears on one of the tapes in his audio collection.[104]

Though Baraka's Asilomar reading and collaborations with the NYAQ are well known, the role that Pacifica Radio played in the making and reception of these recordings has not been considered of much relevance to critics otherwise interested in Baraka's multimedia and performance poetics. Nielsen, for example, writes that Baraka's reading of "Black Dada Nihilismus" at Asilomar "did not, after all, receive significant air play," which is true if the comparison is with popular music but less so if one considers the significance of Pacifica having broadcast the difficult, controversial poem multiple times on three radio stations in major metropolitan centers in the mid-1960s.[105] Even if we consider the public reach of these broadcasts to be narrow, the fact that the recording has been known and written about for decades testifies to the ways that radio, despite its supposed ephemerality, has contributed to the archive of recorded poetry. We know, moreover, that the radio broadcasts caught the attention of at least some listeners at the time; in 1965, the FCC once again investigated allegations of obscenity on Pacifica stations that cited "a poetry reading by LeRoi Jones, [that] was played at all three stations, featured by two of them, and is part of an archived important series of tapes made at the Asilomar Conference on Negro Writers, fall of 1964."[106] After having just survived high-profile investigations by Congress and the FCC that threatened the network's licenses, the Pacifica Radio Board responded to these newest allegations by not only defending Baraka's poetry from the charge of obscenity but identifying it as exactly the kind of content they wanted to be aggressive about defending in the future.[107] As for Baraka's performances with the NYAQ, while there is no doubt that the LP reached more listeners than the radio broadcasts (especially over time), it might be noted that as a small, independent New York record label that specialized in Esperanto music, experimental jazz, avant-garde rock, and poetry (including by Lower East Siders like Sun Ra and The Fugs), ESP-Disk was very much part of the same New York alternative media ecosystem as WBAI.

Baraka's performances at the Asilomar conference and with the NYAQ, and especially of "Black Dada Nihilismus," have nevertheless inspired numerous critical and creative responses that tend to center around the question of how these two recordings do and do not sound Baraka's turn toward a more radical Black aesthetic during the tumultuous year of 1964. The critical discourse has yielded strikingly divergent interpretations of Baraka's voice, with scholars debating, for example, even basic questions about his performance: for example, whether Baraka's reading style on the *New York Art Quartet* album differs significantly or not from his performance at Asilomar, or whether on either or both recordings he conforms to "white middle-class literary and verbal conventions," mobilizes restraint to radical effect, or vocalizes a Black vernacular or jazz aesthetic.[108] What becomes apparent from these debates, beyond the fact that poetry recordings are as productively open to interpretation as print texts, is how much the reception of Baraka's sound is shaped by expectations for what his style should sound like at a given moment in his career and by particular contexts, media technologies, and practices of listening.

Both the Asilomar and NYAQ performances are, in their own ways, also *about* listening—something that considering them in a radio context helps to make clear. When Pacifica stations broadcast the recording of Baraka and Brooks's reading at Asilomar in January 1965, they put the complete reading, including the audience Q&A, on the air. The controversy surrounding Baraka, and the divergent responses and racializing and gendered meanings that different conference attendees brought to their reception of his poetry, are therefore part of what this recording documents and what Pacifica broadcast. Moreover, the professional recording of Baraka's reading in the large conference hall represents, acoustically as well as in terms of its content, the poet as isolated and embattled, not without his defenders in the audience, but separated and even alienated from them.[109] This audible sense of alienation resonates with the poems that Baraka read at the event, including "Black Dada Nihilismus," in which a pervasive tone of alienation and ambivalence simultaneously drives and deadens the poem's call for the purifying catharsis of revolutionary violence. This ambivalence, as many readers have noted, mutes the "Black scream" in the poem, which even on the page is a "dull, un / earthly / hollering," the stark enjambment creating a visual and sonic stress on "un" as if to encode in the scream its own silencing.[110] The poem thus resists in certain ways the dictates of projective verse; as Fred Moten asks in his reading of the poem, "the spatial representation, the visual-ritual embodiment of the poem on the page, is supposed to indicate how it sounds, *how you sound*. But does it? Can it?"[111] Given the contradictory hearings that Baraka's reading at Asilomar provoked among present and subsequent auditors, it appears that not even Baraka's vocalization of the poem resolves this ambiguity, suggesting that what is at stake is not only *how you sound* but *how you listen*.

Baraka's recorded and broadcast performances with the NYAQ, in contrast, did not capture live audience reactions, but they dramatized a different kind of listening that creates a counterpoint with the alienation expressed in Baraka's work of this period. Both Nielsen and Anthony Reed respectively draw attention to the ways that, in the LP recording of "Black Dada Nihilismus," Baraka and the ensemble perform their listening: to one another, and in and out beyond the open field of the poem. Nielsen argues that the musicians "sound as if they have not only listened to Baraka's poem but have taken positions inside its stanzas from which to elaborate their contribution to the new ensemble structure built upon the poem."[112] Reed concurs, and expands on the point to argue that Baraka and the ensemble weave "a tapestry of concentrated, anticipatory listening" that withholds the cathartic yet easily co-opted sounding of revolutionary violence, in order to further "a tentative claim to modes of sociality not yet subsumed by capitalist spectacle."[113] The ensemble might appear, then, as a shadow version of the poem's hermetic coterie, its "secret men" and would-be practitioners of "the // blacker art" whose improvisatory creation of a fragmented, unsettled, percussive soundscape around the recitation of the poem leaves open the space of incomplete ritual as a site of listening.[114] The performance of listening in the recording thus enfolds within and beyond the ensemble, interior and exterior to the transduction of poem into sound into electronic media form so that a further transduction of feeling and power might be enacted, in which, as Baraka puts it in a later poem, "To turn their evil backwards / is to / live."[115]

By bringing onto radio Baraka's performances with the NYAQ, along with other readings, speeches, interviews, and press conferences from before and after his public break with the Lower East Side scene, WBAI resisted the media tendency to reduce his voice, and the complexities and contradictions of his literary and public personae, to an inflammatory soundbite. The radio station and network thus offered Baraka an important and importantly noncommercial media outlet open to the wide range of his creative, critical, and political work. But what it could not offer was a reliable channel to reach Black listeners. In the mid-1960s,

CHAPTER 4

WBAI was still a white liberal institution that had so far made only very limited efforts to engage Black audiences or other audiences of color or to diversify its programming and staff. FM radio in general was shedding its elitist associations, but the eruption of FM underground and progressive rock radio in the mid-to-late 1960s was driven by and appealed to a white male subculture that reinscribed the whiteness of FM radio, especially in contrast to the rise of soul and R&B radio stations that expanded African American representation on radio and spurred efforts to establish Black-owned stations and networks. Pacifica, though, remained somewhat apart from the FM underground radio trends (even as its expanded freeform programming tapped into them), as it continued to see its mission as dedicated to broadcasting noncommercial culture and free expression, especially by voices otherwise marginalized in mainstream media. As a result, WBAI and other Pacifica stations became sites of struggle in the late 1960s and 1970s, as activists and community members demanded that their local, free speech stations become more responsive to and representative of the diverse cities in which they broadcast.

Baraka, for his part, would increasingly see radio as a populist medium of the Black lower classes and a terrain of anticapitalist and decolonial struggle. In his Black Arts poetry, radio loses some of its association with golden-age nostalgia, appearing instead as the shortwave, transnational distress signal of "SOS" "calling all black people, come in, black people, come / on in,"[116] or the "beautiful radios" that Baraka imagines being seized and repurposed in the riotous uprising of "Black People!": "Dance up and down the streets, turn all / the music up, run through the streets with music, beautiful radios on / Market Street, they are brought here especially for you."[117] The multimedia and performance aesthetic of his Black Arts and Third World Marxist periods also ensured his continued involvement with (and ambivalence about) radio as a producer and guest. This includes WBAI, to which Baraka maintained his connection well beyond the mid-1960s. In fact, Baraka's many appearances on Pacifica across his decades-long career, which included a several-year stint as the host of a live freeform jazz show in the early 1980s, made him, like Ginsberg, one of the defining poetic voices of the network. But what he helped define for WBAI was its own contentious reinvention in the 1970s into a community radio station that devoted a substantial portion of its programming to the music, politics, and poetry of liberation.

5

THE POETICS OF FEMINIST RADIO

The classical music station
playing hour upon hour in the apartment

the picking up and picking up
and again picking up the telephone

The syllables uttering
the old script over and over

The loneliness of the liar
living in the formal network of the lie

twisting the dials to drown the terror
beneath the unsaid word[1]

In Adrienne Rich's poem "Cartographies of Silence" from *The Dream of a Common Language* (1978), radio figures as a "technology of silence" rather than of sound, an instrument "to drown the terror / beneath the unsaid word" of women's lives (17). In the passage quoted, the parallel syntax defers and obscures the subject who performs these repetitive, mechanized actions of "picking up the telephone," "uttering / the old script" (16), and "twisting the dials" (17) on the radio set, emphasizing her passivity and unconsciousness. As subsequent lines insist, the silence in which she lives, "in the formal network of the lie," is "not absence // of words or music or even / raw sounds" but "a plan / rigorously executed // the blueprint to a life" (17).

CHAPTER 5

At first glance, these lines, taken out of context, may read like a poetic depiction of what Betty Friedan famously called "the problem that has no name."[2] But "Cartographies of Silence" is not about the suffering of a suburban housewife in a gilded cage; rather, the eight-part lyric meditation is prompted by the poet-speaker's reflection on her and her lesbian partner's struggle to communicate with one another in "the so-called common language" of a heteropatriarchal society without replaying the broken record of a "lie" that "[i]nscribes with its unreturning stylus / the isolation it denies" (*Dream*, 16). Disillusioned, the poet expresses a desire to leave language behind to find a purity and clarity of expression that she associates with a different kind of silence: the wordless aestheticism of visual art and silent film. Even music, Rich suggests, can communicate directly in a way that poetry, as a linguistic form, cannot. "This is why the classical or the jazz music station plays?" she asks, "to give a ground of meaning to our pain?" (18). The choice of radio stations is therefore conspicuous, as only a high art station could be a "technology of silence" in this other, aesthetic sense, the instrumental radio music creating an artistic "ground of meaning" for the painful truth that the women try and fail to communicate to one another in a flawed language. Yet, in the final section of this *ars poetica*, the poet ultimately recommits to the weak signal of language, "choosing... these words, these whispers, conversations" over the transcendent silence of "the *visio beatifica*" (20) as the dialogic and noisy foundation of a feminist poetics through which "the dream of a common language" may be—at least in Rich's view—"re-visioned" as a horizon of utopian possibility.[3]

The image in Rich's poem of a lonely woman mechanically listening to a "classical music station / playing hour upon hour" also curiously recalls an old broadcast trope: that of the archetypal radio listener as an isolated housewife whose distracted listening posed a problem for radio producers and advertisers who hoped to keep her attention.[4] Across the twentieth century, the feminization of the daytime broadcast audience served to reinforce the ideology of the domestic private home as the realm of white middle-class femininity and consumerism. In the 1920s and 1930s, when the gendered trope first emerged, it also appeared in discourses that sought to promote "[r]adio's potential to bring together the isolated and lonely."[5] This idea—that radio could be a powerful tool for connecting and ending the isolation of women—resurfaced in the 1970s around the emergence of feminist radio programs, production collectives, and stations.

After a women's production collective formed at KPFA in 1971 to expand women's programming, for example, artist and activist Cathy Cade wrote to the Berkeley station to express support: "One of the particular qualities of women's oppression in much of this country is isolation. . . . It seems to me that radio is especially well suited to combat this."[6] At WBAI, the feminist radio producer Nanette Rainone explained that she purposely scheduled her groundbreaking *Consciousness Raising* call-in program for noon on Fridays so as "to reach women who, because they have small children and other female responsibilities, are often unable to join a CR group."[7] Such rhetoric may have echoed industry tropes about radio's female listenership, but the difference, of course, was that feminist radio producers sought to both awaken the (political) consciousness of their listeners and seize the microphone to amplify women's voices in protest against their silencing in the public sphere. On Pacifica Radio stations, the dream of transforming radio into a medium of communication for the liberation of women could also be heard as a feminist re-visioning of Lewis Hill's pacifist dream for how radio might be used to free listener and broadcaster alike from their "private rooms" and promote dialogue and participatory action.[8]

This chapter is about the interconnected histories of feminist poetry and feminist radio as they erupted on WBAI and other Pacifica stations in the 1970s. In some ways, it is about how women poets and radio producers worked to create—imaginatively, materially, socially—a feminist radio commons. Contesting both the exclusion of women from the public sphere and the privatizing enclosure of the airwaves as related forms of patriarchal capitalist dominance, the dream of a feminist radio commons might be conceptualized as the struggle to reclaim radio as a public resource, collectivize production, ensure women's equitable access to the airwaves, and seek justice for communities excluded, silenced, and misrepresented in media through redistribution of resources and amplification of community voices. These goals are aligned with those of community radio, and feminist radio activism, though not limited to community radio stations, was instrumental in the community radio movement that also gained momentum in the United States in the 1970s.[9] As scholars of the commons have argued, the commons is also, or first and foremost, a social practice that is neither reducible to the places, resources, and political movements in which commoning may emerge, nor outside of intersectional relations to structures of power, but one that aspires toward open, nonhierarchical, heterogeneous collectivities.[10] In the context of the feminist radio activism that emerged in the 1970s, these social practices included the formation of women's production collectives and cooperatively owned radio stations, but they also manifest in less formal, looser networks of relation among radio producers, guests, and listeners across and beyond different sectors of the women's movement.[11]

What I am characterizing, *pace* Rich, as the dream of a feminist radio commons is not therefore about codifying over the airwaves a "common language" among women—that is, if one interprets Rich's famous phrase as exemplifying the universalizing, essentializing, and separatist rhetoric associated with radical white feminist groups in the second wave. If, however, we follow Stephen Voyce in understanding the key word *common* as it appears ubiquitously in the work of Rich and other feminist poets of the era as signifying "the formation of a shared cultural and social space rather than a universal female identity," then we might see the involvement of poets in the birth of feminist radio as part of "a poetics of the common,"[12] in which "what is 'common' is not necessarily an identity, but shared social space, institutions, language, and the *work* undertaken collectively to bring about change."[13] Public radio, I argue, and Pacifica Radio in particular, was an important site for the development of this feminist practice and poetics of the commons.

Like the larger heterogeneous plurality of movements and forms of activism that get subsumed (and often erased) under the periodizing heading of second-wave feminism, however, the radio archive of feminist poetry sounds still noisier than this description might imply. Even at the local institutional level of a single radio station like WBAI, women's radio activism did not take one form, and neither did the women's poetry that came onto its airwaves, not even the form of a common "materialist-feminist . . . demand for radical equality."[14] My experience listening to some of the women's programs and poetry that broadcast on Pacifica Radio stations in the 1970s has been manifestly one of ambivalence and contradiction—of hearing efforts at inclusion paired with new forms of exclusion, of observing the work of demanding access to the cultural commons devolve into turf wars, and of marking silences and dissonances created in the absence of dialogue and by the erasures in/of the archive. This may sound like I am preparing to embark on yet another critique of the supposed failures of second-wave feminism, but that is not my aim. Instead, and ironically for a history suffused with the language of *collectives, communities, movements,* and the *common,* I am interested in what affordances might be gained by attending to the way a community radio station—and by extension its archive—creates proximities as well as solidarities, weak connections as well as strong ones.

To get a sense of the kinds of proximities I mean, and of how WBAI in the 1970s had changed since the freeform days of the 1960s, consider, by way of example, a selection of programs from the program guide for March 1978 (fig. 6). Over the course of this one month, a listener with interests in both poetry and the women's movement might have tuned in for the following:

- on International Women's Day, March 8, a full day devoted to women's music, public affairs, live radio, and literary programming, including a documentary about the poet H.D. (produced by poet Marie Ponsot and Joe Cuomo of the WBAI Drama, Literature and Art Department);
- poetry readings and interviews with Audre Lorde, Robin Morgan, Joan McNerney, Maureen Owen, and Mervyn Taylor (with Owen's program produced by the poet Susan Howe);
- an "audio-experimental theater" production of JoAnne Akalaitis's *Everything Exists Nothing Has Value,* also produced by Susan Howe;
- "A Room of One's Own," described as "[t]he second in a series of on-the-air creative writing workshops for women," hosted by Kate Ellis and Viv Sutherland as part of the regular program *Women's Studies,* and featuring submissions from WBAI listeners;
- *Live from the Nuyorican Poets Cafe,* a weekly live show featuring "music, radio drama, interviews, poetry," hosted by Miguel Algarín;
- an interview with Black feminist activists as part of a series created by African American writer and producer Donna Allegra for the Women's Department program *Everywomanspace;* and
- regular episodes of other WBAI Women's Department programs, including *More Than Half the World, Our City, Our Lives, The Real Live Lesbian Show, The Velvet Sledgehammer* ("a women's magazine of the air"), and *Women in Science.*[15]

The amount of programming related to poetry and to the feminist movement, and especially to their intersection, is striking; indeed, most of the poetry programming that aired this month featured women poets.

Figure 6. Page 10 of *WBAI Folio* (March 1978) showing program listings for March 16–19, 1978 including "A Reading by Mervyn Taylor," *Live from the Nuyorican Poets Cafe*, an *Everywomanspace* program on "The Hospus: Dying with Dignity," *Gay Rap*, a *Women's Studies* writing workshop titled "A Room of One's Own" (and a call for submissions to the series, advertising "Women Writers Wanted"), "Maureen Owen: An Interview and Reading" (produced by Susan Howe), and *The Velvet Sledgehammer*. Courtesy of the Pacifica Radio Archives.

There are various social groupings that I could map among these largely New York-based writers and producers, but what interests me most is finding poets whom one would not expect to find publishing in the same journals—Susan Howe and Robin Morgan, for example—broadcasting over the same New York FM radio frequency.[16] The radio archive thus enables an understanding of what Kim Whitehead terms "the feminist poetry movement" as a much more open structure than Whitehead or most scholars define it, one that encompasses various aesthetic traditions (neither limited to one side of, nor committed to the divide between, an accessible, expressive lyric and an avant-garde, language-oriented poetics) and that includes diverse poets engaged in a spectrum of feminist discourses.[17] Because the women's programming collectives/departments at Pacifica stations were not (contrary to the accusations of their critics) actually separatist but waged their struggle at a major public broadcasting institution alongside other racial coalitions and queer collectives at these stations, and because women worked across and outside of these collectives, a greater aesthetic and social diversity of women's poetry made it onto Pacifica's airwaves than one would find in many feminist publications of the era, and certainly than in most major male-dominated media and literary institutions.

Methodologically, my approach in this chapter therefore involves an intentional shift away from coteries and communities and toward the more diffuse, contingent, and weaker networks that can also form around a radio station and make a movement.[18] The women poets and radio producers that I discuss in this chapter are linked primarily by the fact of their having broadcast on, and brought a discourse about gender to, Pacifica Radio in the 1970s. Some of them shared strong social ties and others did not; some identified as feminists and others did not; some participated in the women's collectives at WBAI as producers or guests and others did not. They include Audre Lorde, Pat Parker, Susan Howe, and Bernadette Mayer, though I make no claims of representativeness in what turns out to be a large, not easily defined archive. Instead, I am interested in how this archive might open alternatives to the strong narrative forms, affects, and ideological critiques that have constructed the discursive objects of "1970s feminism" and "1970s poetry."[19] The recent turn in feminist, queer, and modernist studies toward more descriptive, provisional, reparative, and paratactical modes of scholarship offers perhaps a way to loosen the hold of these determinative narrative forms, not by abandoning critique for post-critique or "strong theory" for "weak theory" but by recognizing (as Heather Love does in her reading of Eve Kosofsky Sedgwick) "the impossibility of choosing between them."[20]

I am nevertheless aware of the perversity of adopting a weak-theoretical approach in the only chapter of this book to feature women poets and radio producers, especially given how heterosexist discourses often use a rhetoric of weakness to dismiss and marginalize women's sociality, political activism, and cultural production.[21] Indeed, at WBAI and other Pacifica Radio stations in the 1970s, the women's programming collectives were often blamed, along with colleagues who formed gay and lesbian and Third World collectives, for the weakening of Pacifica Radio as an institution. As with other leftist institutions, this decade in Pacifica Radio's history has often been narrated as commencing a long era of fragmentation and decline, in which the rise of identity politics at its stations is seen to have contributed to a diminishment in program quality, plummeting subscriber numbers, worsening financial precarity, and an atmosphere of fractiousness among station staff (and between individual stations and the national board).[22] It is true that struggles to diversify and democratize Pacifica stations generated intense internal conflicts about every aspect of the network's mission, audience, programming, staffing, and organizational structure. But the institution was also weakening in another, less pejorative sense, as its expansion to new stations—KPFT in Houston in 1970 and WPFW in Washington, DC, in 1977 (the latter as a Black community station)—put a decentralizing pressure on the network that created less coherence, more diversity, and greater localism in its programming (countered in turn by various efforts to unify the network).[23] Moreover, conceptualizing Pacifica as a weak institution can also be a lens for critique, in that it enables us to see the effects of the intensifying neoliberal privatization of the airwaves that was further circumscribing community access to broadcast media. As the commercial format takeover of FM radio brought about the end of the FM revolution, Pacifica increasingly saw itself as one of the few remaining independent broadcasters left to counter the new media hegemony. The sense of a loss of mission and unity at a station like WBAI thus also reflected the reality of what it means when one wavelength, so to speak, seeks to be the channel of difference and change.[24]

I am interested, then, in what it might mean, as Paul K. Saint-Amour suggests, "to leave off theorizing weakness as a failure, absence, or function of strength and instead to theorize *from* weakness as a condition endowed with traits and possibilities of its own."[25] Ephemerality, provisionality, locality: these traits are structural to community radio, and as such they may also offer ways to conceptualize the struggle for the radio commons that brought feminist voices and feminist poetry onto the airwaves. In what follows, I first recover the history of how feminist radio and poetry came to Pacifica stations before turning to a closer analysis of a few of the poets and programs that contributed to this history and its archive. And because when I refer to the radio archive of feminist poetry I mean not only a conceptual archive of the various artifacts that would document this history but a specific collection—the Pacifica Radio Archives' American Women Making History and Culture: 1963–1982 Collection (hereafter AWMHC), a digital collection of over 2,000 recordings related to Pacifica's broadcasting of the women's liberation movement that was completed and made publicly accessible in 2016—in the conclusion I reflect on how the changing digital landscape of radio preservation has the potential to bring more poets' voices out of the radio archive.

Broadcasting the Women's Liberation Movement on Pacifica Radio

In the fall of 1968, as TV and newspaper cameras fixated on the spectacle of the Miss America Pageant protest, crystallizing some of the lasting images and national myths of the U.S. women's liberation movement, radical feminist voices were beginning to find their way onto 99.5 WBAI-FM in New York. Kay Lindsey, an African American poet and activist, and Nanette Rainone, a white feminist activist, both started at WBAI in 1968 as volunteer public affairs producers. Lindsey produced programming related to both the Black liberation and women's liberation movements, including a roundtable she hosted in June titled *The Role of the Black Woman in America* with Florynce Kennedy, Eleanor Holmes Norton, and Vertamae Smart-Grosvenor.[26] In November, WBAI aired the first of a five-part series that Lindsey produced on the women's movement; simply titled *Women*, the series featured interviews and roundtable discussions with radical feminist activists on issues ranging from reproductive rights to workplace discrimination to racism.[27] While WBAI had previously aired programs on similar topics, Lindsey's programs were groundbreaking in several ways, not least because they created a platform for radical feminist activists to speak for themselves, and because they were produced by an African American woman at a station and industry dominated by white men.

Rainone, for her part, played a leading role in expanding women's programming and recruiting, training, and organizing women at the station. In 1969, Rainone started *Womankind*, the first regularly scheduled feminist radio program in the country, which featured weekly news and discussion about the women's movement.[28] By 1971, several more feminist programs had started on WBAI, including a late-night live freeform program, *Electra Rewired*, hosted by Liza Cowan; a series on women's diaries produced and read by Ann Snitow; and *Consciousness Raising*, which broadcast a taped consciousness-raising session recorded at the WBAI studios followed by a live listener call-in segment. These early feminist programs were enthusiastically received by many women listeners; according to Rainone, "[t]he first broadcast of the CR program received more mail than any other first broadcast in WBAI history."[29] But they also faced hostility and backlash, especially after Rainone decided to accept calls on *Consciousness Raising* only from women, which led to angry outcry from some listeners and many of her male colleagues.[30] In the fall of 1971, internal dissension among WBAI staff over the new feminist programming and feminist efforts to organize station staff was brought to listeners when Cowan published a letter in the November program guide charging "a male power clique" with hoarding power and perpetuating sexism, racism, and labor exploitation at the purportedly progressive station.[31] The program guide also announced Rainone's promotion to program director, the result of a contentious election. Soon after, a women's production collective formed at WBAI, and over the course of the next decade, its producers created a continuous flow of feminist programming that spanned every radio genre and included regular programs like *Everywomanspace, Lesbian Nation, Lesbian Radio Spectacular, More Than Half the World, Sojourner's Journal, The Velvet Sledgehammer*, and *Women's Studies*. In 1977, WBAI established an official women's programming department, though it was disbanded in the mid-1980s, after which the number of programs produced by women significantly declined.[32]

Feminist activism also came to KPFA and other Pacifica stations over the same period. At a NOW Bay Area Women's Rights Coalition meeting in 1969, organizers from women's groups across the region approved a plan of action that included working to increase women's programming on local FM radio station KPFA.[33] Shortly after, a Bay Area Women's Media Workshop formed to produce radio programs for various local stations and coordinate tape exchanges with other women's groups.[34] Though KPFA aired some of the workshop's programs, and devoted a day to special programming for International Women's Day on March 8, 1970, management initially resisted instituting regular women's programming. In response, a small group of activists, including the poet Susan Griffin, staged an occupation of KPFA's studios late one night under the name Radio Free Women to demand five hours a week of programming by, about, and for women.[35] By the fall of 1971, a women's production collective had formed at the station and launched the regular program *Unlearning to Not Speak*, titled after a Marge Piercy poem, which the *KPFA Folio* reported as being "on the basis of written and telephoned response, one of the most successful things KPFA has tried in a long time."[36] The collective also started airing its own *Consciousness Raising* program in 1972, and in 1973, the program *Lesbian Air* premiered alongside the gay men's program *Fruit Punch*. As at WBAI—and KPFK in Los Angeles, which by 1974 was regularly broadcasting feminist programs as well as the pathbreaking gay liberation program *IMRU*—women's programming at KPFA would continue to expand throughout the 1970s and 1980s. *Ain't I a Woman, Majority Report, Radio Free Lesbians, That Witches Rising in Ur Ear*, and *There Is a Woman in This Town* (titled after a Pat Parker poem) are just a few of the regular feminist programs that aired on KPFA in these years. In 1981, a Women's Department was finally established, with Ginny Z. Berson (co-founder of the women's record label Olivia Records) as the first director. Berson later became general program director at KPFA, and the KPFA Women's Department continued into the late 1990s.

That Pacifica Radio stations would be among the first in the U.S. to broadcast explicitly feminist programming is, in some ways, unsurprising. Women had held prominent leadership and program hosting roles at Pacifica since the beginning, when Eleanor McKinney left her NBC job to launch KPFA with Lewis Hill and serve as its first program director, and music broadcaster Gertrude Chiarito, film critic Pauline Kael, and public affairs producer Elsa Knight Thompson helped define KPFA's early sound and ethos of public intellectualism.[37] As Pacifica expanded in the 1960s and gained a national reputation as a public broadcaster committed to "free radio" and progressive politics, it would have appeared more likely than other stations to be responsive to feminist demands. But leadership roles, paid staff positions, and producing and hosting roles remained overwhelmingly dominated by white men, while women, most of whom were unpaid volunteers, typically were limited to low-level secretarial positions. And as WBAI and other Pacifica stations became more closely aligned with the counterculture and New Left in the 1960s, programs produced by, featuring, or addressed to women became rarer, even as the network was seeking to expand its audience.

These are some of the factors that made Pacifica Radio a site of feminist activism, in ways that were similar to feminist takeovers of underground periodicals and presses. Indeed, women's radio collectives at community and college stations around the country contributed to the construction of the vast feminist communications network that included the women-in-print movement as well as women's film and television collectives, record labels, theaters and festivals, and libraries and archives.[38] Periodicals like the *New York Radical Feminists Newsletter* and the Berkeley Women's Liberation newspaper *It Ain't Me Babe* regularly reported on programming and internal station politics related to the women's radio collectives at WBAI and KPFA (who in turn sourced content and participants from these periodicals). Pacifica's women's programming also circulated far beyond station signal ranges through tape exchanges and published transcripts. On the one hand, then, radio functioned as another node in what Kathryn Thoms Flannery describes as the feminist movement's "network of alternative pedagogical spaces"; on the other hand, feminist activists, steeped in a movement rhetoric that centered tropes of dialogue, speech, listening, and silence, seized on what they saw as radio's uniqueness as an audio broadcast medium to amplify women's voices.[39]

Poets were active participants in the feminist collectives that formed at Pacifica Radio stations, and the broadcasting of poetry was core to the project of feminist radio. This emphasis on poetry reflected the fact that "poetry played a central role in the radical, socialist, and lesbian feminist sectors [of the women's movement] that flourished outside the dominant culture," as Kim Whitehead observes.[40] And if "poetry was the medium of the movement," as Andrea Chesman and Polly Joan declared in their 1978 *Guide to Women's Publishing*, then radio offered an importantly auditory means of amplifying the women's poetry readings that were a significant part of the movement.[41] The oral and aural poetics of the feminist poetry movement, like that of the New American poets and other protest poetry of the sixties and seventies, found a receptive outlet on Pacifica Radio stations; in fact, the privileging of poetry by both the radical feminist movement and Pacifica Radio is what enabled a relatively diverse sounding of women's poetry on the network. A short list of some of the women poets who appeared on Pacifica in the 1970s and early 1980s (not all on women's programs) would include such names as Paula Gunn Allen, Maya Angelou, Diane di Prima, Kathleen Fraser, Judy Grahn, Marilyn Hacker, June Jordan, Joan Larkin, Janice Mirikitani, Cherríe Moraga, Muriel Rukeyser, Sonia Sanchez, Leslie Scalapino, Ntozake Shange, Anne Waldman, Alice Walker, and Nellie Wong. Poets who published in feminist and lesbian periodicals and presses were especially well represented on Pacifica stations, as were these publications themselves. But many women poets writing outside the context of feminist print cultures also appeared on Pacifica stations in this period, in part because the demand that feminist broadcasters made for greater women's representation had an impact on other programming departments.

Feminist producers also took advantage of the radio medium to replay recordings of (or dramatically perform) the voices of past women writers as a way of breaking the silence around women's histories in acts of feminist historical recovery. In 1971, for example, Nanette Rainone and Mimi Weisbord Anderson produced a WBAI documentary on Sylvia Plath, *The Blood Jet Is Poetry*, which featured archival recordings of Plath, readings from her poetry and journals, and interviews with contemporary women writers; the program was rebroadcast frequently on the network in subsequent years.[42] Pacifica's feminist producers did not only broadcast the voices of celebrated poets, however; they also believed that "the *new* writing experience, of women outside the poetry establishment was central to the feminist poetry movement."[43] This led them to promote young and unpublished writers and to encourage listeners to submit poems to be read over the air or published in the station's program guide; in so doing, they carried forward one of the Pacifica Foundation's original Articles of Incorporation, "to encourage and provide outlets for the creative skills and energies of the community."[44] To get a fuller impression of the range of women's poetry that aired on Pacifica in these years, moreover, one would have to look beyond programs explicitly designated as literary, since many of the new feminist and lesbian programs adopted a "radio magazine" format, combining talk, news, interviews, and poetry.

In fact, to recover the diversity of feminist poetry and activism at Pacifica Radio, one would also have to look beyond the women's production collectives. As we saw with Kay Lindsey, Black women were among the first to produce feminist programming at WBAI and other Pacifica stations, and women of color participated in Pacifica's women's collectives throughout the 1970s and 1980s. But women of color also often saw their position at the predominantly white network as necessitating organization along racial lines of coalition.[45] Third World radio collectives devoted to expanding Black, Native American, Latinx, and Asian American representation at Pacifica emerged roughly simultaneously to the women's collectives, and the co-emergence drove narratives among their critics about the fractiousness of identity politics, especially as these collectives were often pitted against one another in internal conflicts.[46] In reinforcing a binary between a feminism assumed to be white and racial organizing assumed to be male or unmarked by gendered concerns, however, these narratives have continued to obscure the work of women of color at the network, including those who led the formation of Third World collectives.[47] Including women's Third World organizing at Pacifica stations as part of the history of feminist radio involves recognizing what Maylei Blackwell describes as "the multiple insurgencies of women of color," which include "the tendency to work in and between movements," and which are "not likely to be registered in feminist epistemologies regulated by rigid, narrow typologies."[48]

Backlash to both the women's and Third World collectives would often accuse the groups of bad politics—of a separatism that was seen by some listeners and station staff as anathema to the spirit of public radio and the supposedly "big tent" of the left. The accusation of bad politics, however, was often accompanied by or couched in a critique of "bad sound" or "bad radio." Freeform radio DJ Larry Josephson, who served as WBAI station manager in the mid-1970s, infamously described the station as being overruled by "radical lesbian ayatollahs," positioning himself as an "outspoken defender of what he called 'good radio.'"[49] Other staff and listeners would echo this position. One listener, for example, wrote to KPFA in 1976 to complain that the station's "voice of reason and sanity" had been, in their view, "replaced with strident and harsh voices": "I could scarcely turn the dial without getting revolutionary Third-World or feminist/homosexual propaganda. It's the *tone* of the programs that bothered me, not the reasoning."[50] Discourses about sound and aesthetics have often been used to police whose voices are considered "suitable" for radio, but at Pacifica stations, these discourses also notably elided a history of encouraging its producers to depart from professionally codified radio aesthetics to communicate its commitment to authenticity, community, and experimentation. As we've seen, white male poets who came to KPFA and WBAI in the 1950s and 1960s often subverted radio standards of "good sound," and though they too had their critics, the repeated assertion by contemporaneous and later critics that the producers of the new feminist, lesbian, gay, and Third World programming "in their idealism (or dogmatism) . . . simply lacked the patience to master the skills of 'good' radio" should prompt us to interrogate what constitutes "good radio" here and according to whom.[51] An increase in the number of live call-in shows was part of what critics maligned, though this was in part a consequence of WBAI's increasingly dire financial situation, which resulted in less funding for production and greater reliance on volunteers. Still, it is apparent from the archive that these collectives created many unique and groundbreaking public affairs, commentary, and cultural programs, including poetry programs.

In the next section, I offer close listenings of just two archival programs created by the WBAI women's collective that have recently been digitized as part of the AWMHC, and that feature performances by Audre Lorde and Pat Parker, respectively. These programs—a 1972 women's poetry reading broadcast live from the WBAI studios, and a 1978 concert recording from the Varied Voices of Black Women tour—are representative of a prominent subgenre of women's radio programming from this era: the women's poetry reading or concert. Women-only events and programs were part of what brought the charge of separatism to Pacifica's women's collectives. But what does separatism mean in the context of radio, where anyone could pick up the signal? In what follows, I consider how Lorde and Parker each ambivalently navigated the exclusionary politics of radical feminist and lesbian-feminist separatisms and imagined, through their poetry and performances, heterogeneous forms of queer Black feminist subjectivities and collectivities that figuratively exceed narrow channels and wireless logics of instantaneous transmission.

"Who Said It Was Simple": Audre Lorde and Pat Parker on the Air

On October 7, 1972, broadcasting live from WBAI's studio C, the recently formed WBAI women's production collective hosted a two-hour *Women's Poetry Evening*. The program, which aired during a month specially

CHAPTER 5

devoted to women's programming on WBAI, featured music and readings by five writers: Daniela Gioseffi, Erica Jong, Audre Lorde, Jane Mayhall, and Robin Morgan. Welcoming the studio and broadcast audiences to the evening's event, the MC celebrated it as "an historic event": "not only is it the first women's poetry—live women's poetry—evening," she claimed, "but I think that it is the first live poetry reading in the history of BAI."[52] Bringing the phenomenon of the women's poetry reading to a radio audience, the program testified to the existence of a vibrant feminist literary community in New York, while the poets, in turn, spoke to the value of WBAI's new feminist programming for their own poetry.

On the recording, for example, Erica Jong introduces her poem "Alcestis on the Poetry Circuit," by noting that she "owe[s] a great debt to WBAI" for the Sylvia Plath documentary *The Blood Jet Is Poetry*. Jong had contributed to the documentary (as had Robin Morgan), and Jong recalls that "hearing the tapes that were made for that program" made her "think of all the women poets who had killed themselves, and this poem really did come out of that experience."[53] Taking up an important theme in second-wave literature and criticism, "Alcestis on the Poetry Circuit," dedicated "*In Memoriam* Marina Tsvetayeva, Anna Wickham, Sylvia Plath, Shakespeare's sister, etc., etc.," bitterly laments that women across history have been taught such extreme self-denial and self-loathing that not only are their talents wasted and possibilities limited but they are prone to self-sacrifice on the altar of male power, so that "[i]f she's an artist / ... the very fact of her gift / should cause her such pain / that she will take her own life / rather than best us."[54] The poem begins, however, by employing a trope of enslavement common in white feminist rhetoric: "The best slave / does not need to be beaten. / She beats herself" (Jong, *Half-Lives*, 25). Abstracted from the history of chattel slavery, the figure of the female slave functions as a metaphor to universalize women's oppression, and thereby implicitly racializes as white the woman who "must never go out of the house / unless veiled in paint / ... must wear tight shoes / so she always remembers her bondage" (26). Excluded from the poem's pantheon of known and unknown dead women writers, then, are all the Black women geniuses and artists who survived and died under the conditions of slavery and its afterlives (and whom Alice Walker would famously memorialize in her 1974 essay "In Search of Our Mothers' Gardens").

Lorde, who followed Jong on the program (after Jong's reading of her final poem, "On the Air," a comic poem about a man who believes his penis is a rock 'n' roll station), had also previously appeared on a WBAI women's program, but her reading was reflexive in a different sense, subtly drawing attention to the racial exclusions perpetuated in the feminist, literary, and radio communities whose convergence the event celebrated.[55] On the recording, Lorde opens with her poem "Who Said It Was Simple," which she first briefly contextualizes as written in response to a women's march that took place in New York City on August 26, 1972, just a few months earlier. She then reads, in an enunciated, assertive tone, the first lines: "There are so many roots to the tree of anger / that sometimes the branches shatter / before they bear."[56] Anger was a theme of the evening, used rhetorically by each of the white women writers as a unifying affect directed outward at a male-dominated, sexist society. The audience, at least some of whom would likely have participated in the women's march, might therefore have initially interpreted these lines as similarly directed toward the subject of the protest. But Lorde turns that anger inward, as her reading of the poem proceeds to trace the tangled "roots" of an anger that threaten the possibilities of coalition among women and the Black woman speaker's own survival, drawing attention to (and making audible for the radio audience) the fact of her presence as the only Black woman performing at the event.

"Who Said It Was Simple" also uses tropes of slavery and bondage, at first ironically, as Lorde depicts a scene in which bourgeois white women, dining at Nedick's restaurant before the march, "neither notice nor reject / the slighter pleasures of their slavery" as "[a]n almost white counterman passes / a waiting brother to serve them first" (*Collected Poems*, 92). The hyperbole of characterizing the white women's experience of patriarchy as a form of "slavery" tempered by "the slighter pleasures" of their position of dominance in a racialized class hierarchy reveals how the co-optation by white feminists of abolitionist rhetorics of slavery and liberation often served to perpetuate rather than oppose white supremacy. But Lorde's own use of this rhetoric shifts as the speaker interrogates the interlocking structures of racism, sexism, and homophobia to which she is multiply "bound":

But I who am bound by my mirror
as well as my bed
see causes in colour
as well as sex

CHAPTER 5

> and sit here wondering
> which me will survive
> all these liberations.

Lorde's more nuanced metaphor of bondage in these lines carries with it rather than obscures the ongoing histories of racial subjugation that are constitutive of (rather than distinct from) her experiences of gender and sexual oppression. However, as the final stanza suggests, the speaker's identity is "bound" not only by oppression but more complexly by an incomplete liberation. As Keith D. Leonard argues in his reading of this poem, Lorde's objectification of the poem's lyric "I" into a "me" rendered fragmented and multiple thereby challenges the expected coherence and transparency of the speaker—the subject of lyric and the subject of woman—in a way that "laments the loss of the wholeness that Lorde often claimed was her ideal" but "doesn't reside in that loss," putting into question the demand for "wholeness or homogeneity at the heart of existing and inadequate priorities of hegemony *and* of theories of liberation."[57]

After Lorde's reading of these final lines, which she delivers in an even, slightly interrogative tone, the studio audience erupts in laughter and applause.[58] Lorde's subtle pause before the final line reinforces its irony, but to my ear the laughter is strange; the poem is more searing than comic, and would be especially so if white women, who were likely the majority of the studio audience, heard themselves addressed by its critique. Regardless of its cause, the laughter serves to sonically reaffirm an atmosphere of consensus and recognition based on shared experience that redirects the critique outward rather than internalizes the poem's call to recognize difference. Since one of the traditional functions of a live studio audience is to simulate and thereby guide a broadcast's reception among its distant listeners, the audience response would also likely have affected how radio listeners interpreted the tone of the poem and subject of its address. The radio broadcast, moreover, complicates the feedback loop between the poet and her audience and creates (via the dissemination of a disembodied voice) additional layers of subject fragmentation and dispersal to the question of "which me will survive."

If Lorde's strong voicing of a multiple, fragmented subject seems figuratively to carry a weak lyric signal at the end of the poem, however, it might thereby introduce a subtle kind of interference against what Hortense

Spillers metaphorically describes as the "telegraphic coding" through which Black women are (mis)named in the American national imaginary. In the oft-cited opening to "Mama's Baby, Papa's Maybe: An American Grammar Book," Spillers lists some of the names that affix to "the 'black woman,'" "mark[ing]" her as "a locus of confounded identities." According to Spillers, these names, which include stereotypes like "Sapphire" as well as the icon of the "Black Woman at the Podium," "demonstrate a sort of telegraphic coding; they are markers so loaded with mythical prepossession that there is no easy way for the agents buried beneath them to come clean."[59] As Kimberly Lamm observes in her reading of this passage, the metaphor of the telegraph both registers as "[a]n obsolete technology" that "figures for the long histories inscribed into the icons Spillers describes" and "evokes the development of fast-moving communication technologies that transported images and words across vast spaces with an ideological efficiency capable of cohering national imaginaries."[60] While the graphemic coding of the telegraph differs from the voice transmissions of radio, both entail a wireless logic that involves the reduction of meaning and the fantasy of instantaneous transmission across time and space that Lorde's own inventive self-naming across her career ("black, lesbian, feminist, mother, poet warrior") and her acts of "biomythography" might be seen to resist and exceed.[61]

The image of Lorde as the lone Black woman at the women's poetry reading—as the righteous, isolated voice of critique and difference within a white women's movement—is not the only one of Lorde to be found in the Pacifica archives, however, nor is Lorde the only Black lesbian feminist voice to broadcast on WBAI.[62] As the decade advanced, the WBAI women's production collective began to include more Black feminist perspectives and culture in its programming, a reflection of the impact that Black feminist coalitional organizing began to have on radical feminist and lesbian feminist communities in the mid-to-late 1970s. In 1978, for example, the WBAI Women's Department produced a concert tape and interview related to the legendary Varied Voices of Black Women tour. Organized principally by Olivia Records and the Combahee River Collective, the tour of eight Northeast cities was headlined by Bay Area poet Pat Parker and musicians Gwen Avery, Linda Tillery, and Mary Watkins. "[T]he result of the work of coalitions between women of color and white women," the Varied Voices tour specifically celebrated "the building of Black Lesbian feminist culture."[63] The final concert was held

CHAPTER 5

in New York City on November 7, 1978, at the lesbian theater Medusa's Revenge, and members of the WBAI Women's Department—led by Black lesbian feminist producer, writer, and dancer Donna Allegra—recorded the performance for broadcast. Though equipment problems at the event affected the sound quality of the final tape and resulted in several minutes of Parker's performance being lost, the program aired on WBAI on December 10. Recently digitized as part of the AWMHC, the recording is, as far as I know, the only known extant audio or video recording from the Varied Voices tour; it also documents one of Parker's most celebrated performances.[64]

A major figure in Bay Area lesbian feminist poetry and activist communities (and a friend of Lorde's), Pat Parker was an accomplished performance poet. Her performances on the Varied Voices tour, and especially the debut of her long poem about African American women's history, "Movement in Black," are among her most celebrated.[65] Barbara Smith, for example, recalls that Parker "brought down the house with her poetry" at the concert in Boston, and Michelle Parkerson, who worked on production for the tour, describes how she "watched audiences of women captivated by the poem's cadence and the fearless legacy of Black women as it unfolded."[66] On the Pacifica recording, Parker begins her first set with a selection of her lesbian love poems, explaining that while she has not read these poems yet on the tour, she is inspired to do so because of the all-women's audience: "It feels good . . . knowing that there are only women in this room, and that the right people are here to hear the love poems, because they were written for women."[67] In her performance of poems like "Let me come to you naked," she makes use of a dynamic vocal range, at times speaking soft and low, almost whispering into the microphone, at other moments allowing her voice to crescendo with intensity. Her connection with her audience is palpable, as the poems elicit frequent, audible responses.

In subsequent sets, Parker channels this erotic intimacy into what she describes as consciousness-raising poems, as when she reads "There Is a Woman in This Town," a poem that, like Lorde's reading of "Who Said It Was Simple" at WBAI's studios a few years earlier, asks her auditors to critically examine intersecting forms of oppression in their lesbian-feminist communities. The poem's refrain, "Is she our sister?", employs the women's movement rhetoric of sisterhood to reveal how this sisterhood has been formed neither naturally nor through intentional coalition but through repeated acts of exclusion.[68] By centering women excluded from or on the margins of the movement—the fat woman, the butch lesbian, the formerly incarcerated woman, the drug addict, the woman who "is not a women's libber" (*Complete Works*, 160)—Parker points to a future horizon of queer feminist kinship based on indiscriminate caregiving among those "who need a sister," and who are not yet but "would be sisters" (162).

Parker's attention to the politics of exclusion in feminist communities had come up a few weeks earlier in a radio interview Donna Allegra conducted with Parker, Tillery, and Watkins for *The Lesbian Show* on WBAI. After Allegra asked about their experiences performing at both women-only and mixed-gender venues, Parker and Watkins expressed a sense of ambivalence about the former, with Parker reflecting that while "there is a certain charge, a certain feeling, that comes from performing to an all-women's audience," "there is a whole country full of, for instance, Black men and ... I don't want them not to know of the work I'm doing, because a lot of what I'm writing about is also addressed to them, is addressed to Black people."[69] While her preference, she explained, was therefore to "do both" ("I want my work to be heard. I want my work to be heard by as many people as I can reach"), as the conversation continued she reflected on how the creation of women-only spaces can also provide cover for racism and for the exclusion not only of men but of Black women, children, and (more implicitly in her remarks) trans women who are systematically excluded from the category of womanhood.[70] For regular listeners of *The Lesbian Show*, this conversation might have influenced their reception of the concert or its broadcast a few weeks later; it might also encourage us to hear in Parker's performance of "There Is a Woman in This Town" an even more ambivalent reflection about who has been excluded from "a dream of women."[71]

Parker closed her final set at the Medusa's Revenge by leading a choral reading in five voices of "Movement in Black," which extended her vision of a heterogeneous, queer feminist collectivity as emerging from Black feminist consciousness and historiography. The long poem in five parts represents a communal, continuous genealogy of African American women's resilience and resistance from the Middle Passage to the civil rights movement, and from Black nationalism to gay liberation:

CHAPTER 5

> I was a panther
> in Oakland
> in new york
> with N.O.W.
> In San Francisco
> with gay liberation
> in D.C. with
> the radical dykes
> yes, I was there
> & i'm still moving.
>
> (Parker, Complete Works, 98)

To move is to survive, and in the print version of the poem, Parker's short, enjambed lines and run-on sentences formally enact this sense of perpetual motion and continuance across difference, linking different histories and forms of activism into one long string of language, one expansive voice, one ongoing Black women's movement. In these lines in particular, the assertion via juxtaposition of Black women's participation not only in different social movements but in movements often seen as wholly distinct or even hostile to one another—for example, in both the Black Panthers and the gay rights movement—reveals the "multiple insurgencies" of Black women's activism and recovers, in turn, an insurgent queer counterhistory for Black women.[72] Listening to the choral performance adds further layers of significance to this performance of "movement." As each of the performers takes a turn voicing the poem's collective first-person speaker, the others repeat the refrain "movement in black," dramatizing the ways that movement and survival depend on the interplay between the individual and the collective, and between coalition and difference. At the end of the poem, each of the five voices individually declares, "I am a survivor," before coming together for the final "Movement in Black."[73] This assertion of survival corresponds to what Emily J. Lordi, drawing on Audre Lorde's theories of survival and eroticism, has argued about Black women soul singers like Nina Simone and Aretha Franklin, who celebrate "not only basic survival but extravagant survivorship in performance."[74] A sense of "extravagant survivorship" is also contained in the multiple valences of the title and refrain of Parker's poem, which in the context of live performance might also have signified the spectacular "movement in black" of the performers on stage.[75]

For the radio listener, though, as in my own experience listening to the archival recording, reconstructing the scene of performance would take some imaginative work. The broadcasting of the concert tape would seem to invite this kind of imaginative projection, but it might also have raised the question of whether the aura of liveness was too diminished for the performers' radical message of queer Black feminist liberation to be carried over a radio signal, especially given the technical issues that affected the recording; the fact that several minutes of the concert were unable to be recorded means that some of Parker's poetry literally did not come through. In the archive, such issues of omission and decay are compounded, generalized. But rather than idealize the recorded sound archive as a way to make the voices of the past present once again, can we imagine a mediumship, a sense of movement across time and place, that would not disavow distortion, disconnection, loss, or silence? In her introduction to the original broadcast of the Varied Voices concert tape, Donna Allegra apologized for the audio quality but explained the decision to air it anyway "in the hopes that you'll be touched by the talent and energy generated by the performers."[76] The fact that the recording is now accessible online preserves the hope that this energy might reach across time to touch us, here. Listen, then, to how these voices survive—poetically, performatively, extravagantly—not in some fiction of wholeness but in and through their movement; in and through their reproduction, disembodiment, fragmentation, dissemination; and in and through their projection toward possible common futures.

Gendering the Tape:
Susan Howe and Bernadette Mayer

My last example from the WBAI archive of 1970s feminist poetry was not produced by the women's collective and has therefore a more tangential relationship to the other programs and histories I have explored so far. In fact, the recording—a radio interview with Bernadette Mayer conducted by Susan Howe for her WBAI program *Poetry* in 1979—is not part of the AWMHC digital collection or held by the Pacifica Radio Archives but instead is available via PennSound as part of a digital collection of selected recordings from Howe's radio show. Howe, who worked as a part-time radio producer for the Drama and Literature Department at WBAI from 1975 to 1980, was never a member of the women's production collective, and her radio programs did not focus exclusively on women writers. I nevertheless see Howe as part of this history because she did contribute significantly to the broadcasting of women's poetry on WBAI; in the more than one hundred radio programs that she produced, close to half featured women writers. For her program *Poetry*, a series of half-hour readings and hour-long interviews with contemporary poets, Howe especially sought out women writers whose work was formally innovative, creating an important broadcast outlet for these poets to share their work and stage public conversations about gender and experimental writing. As Ann Vickery shows in her own study of the program, Howe thus helped to foster the emergence of contemporary avant-garde feminist poetry; she also contributed more generally to a renaissance in avant-garde literary and sound art programming on Pacifica Radio.[77] Additionally, while Howe did not identify as a feminist poet at this point in her career, she saw her radio work as an opportunity to expand her knowledge about women's writing and the feminist movement, and she occasionally featured poets whose sensibilities she considered quite different from her own, including Adrienne Rich and Audre Lorde (the latter of whom appears to have been the only woman of color to appear on one of Howe's programs).[78] As I suggested before, recovering the scope of feminist poetry broadcast on Pacifica Radio in this era requires looking beyond the women's collectives; including Howe's program in this history thus allows me to expand the archive and gesture toward some of the more proximate connections among feminist poets and across different feminist discourses that Pacifica Radio also enabled and brought into the air. Rather than attempt a full accounting of the feminist concerns of Howe's radio work, however, as Vickery offers, here I focus on her interview with Mayer to pick up a thread I have followed throughout this book about the intersections of radio and tape and to inquire how gender inflects the "tapevoice" of contemporary experimental poetry.

Over time, Howe did come to describe her radio program explicitly as a feminist intervention in male-dominated literary discourse. In a 1979 interview with Vicki Hudspith in *The Poetry Project Newsletter*, for example, Howe stated that she "made a point of interviewing women poets" on her WBAI program about their "struggles" and "role-models" (or lack thereof), and particularly about the "problem of being both a mother and a poet." "It's less a 'problem' now," she continued, "then [sic] something profoundly exciting to explore—because there are other women out there with you: Maureen Owen, Lyn Hejinian, Bernadette Mayer, to name a few."[79] Indeed, it is clear from Howe's archival correspondence that her radio show helped her to overcome feelings of isolation as a writer (including in relation to the St. Mark's Poetry Project scene) precisely because it enabled her to use the public platform of radio to initiate a dialogue with these and other writers (Helen Adam, Rae Armantrout, Kathleen Fraser, Barbara Guest, and Anne Waldman, to name a few others), and construct "a social context for her work" and "an innovative tradition of American poetry, framed specifically by Howe's concerns with an 'outsider' literary history."[80] Balancing wage, artistic, and reproductive labor was a challenge, though. As Howe noted in the same interview, both her poetry and radio work depended on her children being school-aged: "My children right now are old enough that on days when I'm not at WBAI, I work form [sic] 10 in the morning till 2 in the afternoon, but when they were small it was much harder."[81]

In the recording of her program with Mayer, which first aired on WBAI on April 22, 1979, Howe raises some of these same issues, asking Mayer about her experience of being a mother and a poet, and about their shared sense of lacking a tradition "of women who are mothers, [and] role models as poets."[82] Mayer, who was pursuing her own inquiry into these questions in the long poem *Midwinter Day*, responds candidly in reflecting on how raising young children has "fragmented" her time and transformed her relationship to writing, making her more "disciplined" and "schedule[d]," since "[y]ou can't ever figure that you're going to have a good six hours or so to do anything anymore, sometimes even to sleep." Motherhood also seems to have changed Mayer's relationship to her tape recorder, which had been (and would continue to be) an important part of Mayer's compositional practice and multimedia poetics.[83] As Mayer explains, "I do find that the tape recorder is very useful for making notes, you know, certain kind of notes, like in a situation where you're sitting around in the afternoon with babies who won't let you write things down, I can keep the recorder in the closet or something and run over and make a few notes if I want to."[84] Like any other supposedly time-saving domestic appliance, the tape recorder seems in this account to help Mayer solve the "problem" of how to be a mother and a poet by enabling her to multitask, so she can engage in artistic labor and reproductive labor at the same time. Or, if not exactly that—since, unlike Ginsberg, she finds it "impossible" to "talk poetry into the tape recorder"—tape allows her to prepare for, in order to maximize her productivity during, her second shift of late-night writing.[85]

Mayer quickly revises her assessment of the uses of tape, however, reflecting, as she continues, on the fact that new technologies also create new forms of often invisible, and therefore gendered, labor: "But I don't know what to do with it [the tape recorder] anymore, actually, because I really hate transcribing it. I find it such a chore. I think maybe if one had somebody else do the transcribing that it would be a more useful method for writing."[86] Rather than saving time in the service of a poetics of spontaneity, tape ends up creating yet another tedious "chore" for the woman poet. It is not only, as Jasper Bernes observes in reference to Mayer's earlier multimedia work *Memory*, that "recording and transmission technologies have enabled a transcription of the past beyond the capacity of the human mind to assimilate it," but that to turn tape into text, notes into a poem—even capaciously open and long poems like *Memory* or *Midwinter Day*—someone has to do the actual secretarial labor of transcription.[87] And who has the time? Not Mayer, certainly, whose disciplined schedule requires her to preserve her nighttime hours for actual writing. Indeed, while so much of the conceit and joy of Mayer's poetry from this period is the way it appears to refuse "the false choice between poetry and motherhood" by showing how a woman in a heterosexual marriage with young children might nevertheless write, as Maggie Nelson puts it, "*All day long*," it is perhaps more accurate to observe that the poems themselves often represent the time of writing as the more unsustainable *all night long*.[88] (As Mayer puts it in *Midwinter Day*, "In Yokuntown we write all night," but only one of them, I assume, will get up with the children.[89])

Earlier in the radio program, the tape recorder as a note-taking device and an ambivalent trope for a poetics of the everyday had appeared in Mayer's reading of the poem "Simplicities Are Glittering" from *The Golden Book of Words* (1978), which invites the reader into a late-night writing session:

> I hurry
> To write a sudden poem not as day is going away
> But as I'm only here in the dark
> As night is in its middle and I have no time
> For words, like sunset or dreary dawn, I see too much
> I eat and drink and smoke without pretensions each
> Note I make comes flying back on the tape recorder

> Dense and unannounced, garbled and meerschaum
> Like a pipe for smoking beer, I listen
> And breathe rapidly when I'm out to wait
> To see how suddenly a gift will alarm me
> How wasteful and quick stubbornness is, how glad
> I'll be when you lock the door and refuse to let me out[90]

If Paul Blackburn used his tape recorder as "a dimension of his material text, as immediate as pen and paper" and "a device for testing the page and its notation against the voice," then Mayer, who keeps "two pens ... open" and has "no time / [f]or words," is in too much of a hurry for this kind of attunement.[91] She finds, moreover, that the "note" she furtively spoke into her closet earlier in the day comes out "garbled" on playback, the tapevoice flooding its technological container like beer in a meerschaum pipe (or like the word "meerschaum" itself, its rich German syllables frothing like etymological sea-foam at the end of the line). The poet listens, but her listening is really a doubled or divided listening, because while she dreams of being locked in a domestic prison turned room-of-one's-own, neither she nor the "noise" of her poetic labors is so contained. As she listens, then, to the sound of her own (taped) speech, she must also keep an ear open for her sleeping daughters:

> I speak but I hear, I move each body around
> Like a piece of furniture, away from the noise
> I am making, this must be a quiet house, house of
> Experiments, quickly chosen, mercilessly followed
> Eaten so rich, so full of cream and dreamlike merriment
> The happiness of torture learned to form a wing
> I fly out easily to meet what used to come in
> No speech is filtered, garble it, effect, defect
>
> (*Eating the Colors*, 426)

Even unconscious, her children require her physical attention and strength; Mayer depicts herself comically "mov[ing] each body around / like a piece of furniture, away from the noise." The labors of the mother-poet are not only energy-sapping, though. Mayer is proud to keep—she delights in keeping—the two channels of her creative energies flowing open like her "two pens," so that hers can be both "a quiet house" and a "house of / experiments," so that she can now "fly out easily to meet what used to come in" (inspiration transformed into a mother's discipline). She has long since given up on tape transcription; the spontaneous, unfiltered speech of the poem adds new layers of "garbled" interference, yet out of them springs the "gift" she's been waiting for: the "effect" and "defect" of rhyme, the language of love and of lyric.[92] And on *this* tape, Howe's tape for radio, Mayer's voice is clear; her quick reading pace captures the speed of the lines but she reads beautifully, with skill and a sense of ease.[93]

There is, of course, another type of tape labor we might consider here, too: Howe's own. Howe edited her own tapes for broadcast and sought control over as much of the production process for her programs as she could. As she wrote in a grant application, "Apart from the taping and mixing (done by an engineer), I have handled every aspect of the production [for *Poetry*].... I feel very strongly that half of the job is in the editing. I do not believe in having others do that for me."[94] She often expressed her interest in this work, writing to Lyn Hejinian in 1978, for example, "I love the editing tapes, the archival aspect of the programs I do, the sound of the poet reading his or her own work."[95] The editing, in particular, could be laborious; when Hejinian became a co-host of the weekly live poetry program *In the American Tree* on KPFA, Howe wrote, "You can't be taping and editing as I know how much that takes, so it must be live."[96] But Howe embraced the time-consuming labor of tape editing as part of what made radio production a craft. Her program with Mayer, for example, has clearly been selectively edited and spliced from an original recording to create a narrative arc. She also insisted that she be paid for this labor and, given that WBAI was increasingly unable to pay producers, self-funded most of her radio work through grants from the New York State Council on the Arts and the National Endowment for the Arts (NEA).

As a radio producer, Howe thus differs from some of the other poet-broadcasters that I have considered in this study (Jack Spicer, Kenneth Rexroth, Paul Blackburn), whose laissez-faire approach to producing or hosting programs as unpaid volunteers for Pacifica Radio sonically "contest[ed] the nonsite of the media broadcasting studio" in part by bringing to radio what Lytle Shaw describes as the "narrowcast" tape recording practices of the New American poets.[97] While Blackburn, for instance, broadcast largely unedited tapes of coffeehouse readings on his radio show to bring WBAI audiences into the noisy sociality of the downtown poetry scene, Howe carefully edited her studio-recorded tapes to focus audience attention on the singular voice of the poet and the "audiotext" of the poems.[98] For Vickery, this approach to radio production shows Howe's engagement in Language writing's critique of oral poetics and her efforts "to challenge the cult of personality that radio encouraged" by editing her programs "to decenter and distance its effects."[99] But we might also align her literary radio aesthetic with that of David Ossman on *The Sullen Art* or even that of Pacifica founder Lewis Hill; Howe's emphasis on the autonomy of the broadcaster, the poet, the work of art, and the listener was very much in the spirit of the early Pacificans and their hopes for the kind of art and culture that noncommercial radio could foster.[100] To claim this autonomy as a woman producer, moreover, represented a feminist intervention in the male-dominated field of media production, that, importantly for Howe—whose uncle Quincy Howe was a famous broadcast journalist—was personally as well as structurally a site of patriarchal authority.[101] We might then see Howe's radio programs as loosely connected to some of the thematic concerns (if not experimental form) of her feminist poetics, which include inquiries into family genealogies, editing as an exercise of patriarchal power, sound and aurality, and a Spicerian poetics that seeks to channel the voices of the dead and the silenced voices of history.[102] Yet, it seems worth noting that the kind of individual autonomy that Howe sought as a radio producer was different than the collective autonomy sought by the WBAI Women's Department, for whom autonomous control over their own program hours, program content, resources, and staffing decisions involved collectivizing the labor of production.

Howe also produced her radio programs in part for the archive. In grant applications and correspondence, Howe often defined the purpose of her radio work as not only about cultivating an audience for contemporary poetry among radio listeners in the present but about creating "a valuable archival record of American poetry of our time" for the future.[103] This archival and documentary approach to radio, though it corresponds with Howe's archival poetics, ran counter to the increasing emphasis on live programming at WBAI as well as radio's more general association with the ephemerality and simultaneity of instantaneous transmissions. But Howe recognized the archival possibilities that the Pacifica Tape Library, established in 1972 to facilitate program sharing, made possible for the long-term preservation of poets' voices. As she wrote in a grant report, anticipating a claim I have made throughout this book, "To the public at large, the Pacifica Archives offer an invaluable oral record of American writing over the past twenty years."[104]

In 1980, though, Howe was forced to end her short career as a radio producer when her NEA funding ran out.[105] The next few years also saw the dissolution of the WBAI Women's Department and a decline in women's programming amid a severely worsening debt crisis and ongoing internal turmoil at the station. More generally, the ascendency of commercial FM radio and the NPR consolidation of public radio, combined with the Reagan administration's attack on federal arts and public media funding, would make the struggle for the radio commons more exigent. Poets and poetry continued to broadcast on WBAI and other Pacifica stations, however, extending the network's dynamic history of innovative literary broadcasting into the late twentieth and twenty-first centuries, and growing the Pacifica Radio Archives' "invaluable oral record" of contemporary poetry. In conclusion, I want to return to this (valuable, endangered, noisy) archive to reflect briefly on its significance to literary and feminist history in the digital age.

Listening to Poetry in the Digital Radio Archive

In September 2013, when I was just beginning to research the history of poetry on Pacifica Radio, I spent a few weeks at the Pacifica Radio Archives (PRA) in Los Angeles, listening to historic poetry broadcasts in the PRA offices on the top floor of radio station KPFK. It was during this visit that I first heard the voice of Lewis Hill defending *Howl* from the charge of obscenity and the rollicking voice of Kenneth Rexroth lambasting the Beats on his *Books* program; that I searched in vain for a recording of Jack Spicer's radio show; and that I listened to radio recordings of Lawrence Ferlinghetti reading poems in the KPFA studios in 1956, of Amiri Baraka giving a press conference after the 1967 Newark uprising, and of the 1977 KPFA Poetry Festival at UC Berkeley. During my visit, I was mostly limited to recordings for which there were CD listening copies available (which represent a fraction of the archives' largely undigitized tape holdings), but the PRA staff also gave me the opportunity to listen to and digitize a few recordings from the vault, generously teaching me a few basics about tape and digital preservation methods in the process, including how to treat warped and deteriorating tape, reattach splices, and set up the machine for digital transfers. Among the few tapes for which I made digital copies were Lewis Hill's *A Word by Wallace Stevens: An Essay for Radio*, from his 1954 "experiments in the broadcasting of poetry" (discussed in chapter 1), and a recording of an interview Susan Howe conducted for *Poetry* with members of the Women's Distribution Group, a small press collective based in New York.[106]

Meanwhile, the rest of the PRA staff, led at the time by director Brian DeShazor, was embarking on a large preservation project. In 2013, the PRA had recently received a major grant from the National Archives' National Historical Publications and Records Commission to preserve, catalog, digitize, and make publicly available a collection of recordings and associated program guides related to Pacifica's broadcasting of the U.S. women's liberation movement. The American Women Making History and Culture: 1963–1982 Collection (AWMHC), completed in 2016, is a digital collection of 2,024 radio recordings produced by or about women over the period from "1963, the year of publication of Betty Friedan's groundbreaking book *The Feminine Mystique*," to "1982, the year the Equal Rights Amendment failed to be ratified in Congress," and available for public streaming through the Internet Archive.[107] Like any archive, the collection has gaps and elisions, and some relevant programs from PRA's larger holdings—such as the recording of Susan Howe's interview with the Women's Distribution Group that I transferred—are not included; moreover, because the collection's selection criteria are defined according to dominant conceptions of second-wave feminism, it cannot fully capture the "multiple insurgencies" of women of color at Pacifica (compounding structural limitations of the archive around which audiotape masters would have been made or considered worth preserving). The AWMHC nevertheless preserves and makes publicly accessible an important, invaluable sonic record of feminist and queer history—and literature—that was in danger of being lost. In my own case, access to the digital collection enabled me to expand and bring new methods to bear on my research into the history of feminist poetry broadcasting on Pacifica Radio far beyond what had been or would be possible on a short-term, in-person visit.

The creation of the AWMHC is also a vivid example of how the conditions for conducting radio research, including research into literary radio histories, are changing in the digital age. In 2010, a report titled *The State of Recorded Sound Preservation in the United States*, commissioned by the National Recording Preservation Board of the Library of Congress, sounded an ominous tone, reporting that "major areas of

America's recorded sound heritage have already been destroyed or remain inaccessible to the public" and that the absence of urgent coordinated action would result in a "permanent loss of irreplaceable sound recordings in all genres."[108] In regard to radio, the report observed that "American radio broadcasting has never been documented systematically, and few archives have provided formal support of radio broadcast recordings," leading to a general lack of knowledge about "the size of the broadcast-recordings universe" for one of the most important forms of media over the last century.[109] In response, in 2014 the National Recording Preservation Board established the Radio Preservation Task Force (RPTF), a consortium of scholars, archivists, private collectors, and institutions dedicated to the preservation of radio history through the creation of an online inventory of radio collections (the Sound Collections Database), the administration of funding for endangered collections, and the support of interdisciplinary scholarship on the cultural history of radio.[110] Importantly, the RPTF's priorities extend beyond the network era to support the preservation and study of long-neglected radio histories, including early radio and late twentieth-century and twenty-first-century radio; public, educational, and community radio; and radio histories of historically marginalized communities. While this work is still only beginning, and funding resources are far from sufficient to address urgent preservation needs, it represents a turning of the tide toward a collective effort to preserve radio history and public access to the radio commons.

These recent efforts in radio preservation and scholarship have profound implications for the field of modern and contemporary poetry studies, which has also been transformed in recent decades by the creation of major digital archives of poetry audio recordings (such as PennSound) and by efforts to preserve and document histories of poetry performance, but which has tended to see the intersection of poetry and radio as largely an early twentieth-century phenomenon. The ongoing development of new digital radio collections, new scholarship in literary radio studies, and digital humanities methods and tools in the coming years will create more opportunities for scholars, students, and poets to expand our knowledge about this history and to hear—and creatively engage with—some of the diversity of poetry and poets' voices that have broadcast over the past century.

But these promising trends are countered by more worrying signs that highlight the precarity of recorded sound and radio archives—including of the Pacifica Radio Archives. In 2016, alarm bells went off in the radio preservation community after the Pacifica Foundation Board of Directors, responding to the network's debt crisis, instituted severe budget cuts and staff layoffs at the archives. The cuts led to the resignation of director Brian DeShazor and the collapse of several collaborative national partnerships and grant initiatives. In response, the leaders of the RPTF and the National Federation of Community Broadcasters called on Pacifica to transfer its major, irreplaceable archive to an educational institution.[111] As of 2022, however, the PRA collection of an estimated 100,000 original audio recordings is still housed above the KPFK studios and maintained on a shoestring budget by a small albeit dedicated staff. The loss of this archive, or even its continuation in the underresourced status quo, puts at risk one of the most significant audio collections in the U.S. of radio history, social movement history, and *literary* history. In one sense, my aim in this book has been to make a call to listen: actually listening to some of the poetry that was broadcast on Pacifica Radio stations and other public and community FM radio stations in the post-1945 era can yield rich findings and unexpected connections for literary scholars. A feminist approach to this history, however, should also attune us to the gaps, silences, and distortions of the archive as traces of not only what has been lost in the past but what is under erasure in the present—and to the ongoing, collective struggle necessary to defend our access to the cultural commons and our sonic past.

NOTES

Acknowledgments
1. Jack Spicer to Graham Mackintosh, quoted in Gizzi, "Afterword," 209.

Introduction
1. "The KPFA Poetry Festival," *KPFA Folio* 28, no. 5 (May 1977), 1, Pacifica Radio Archives Digitized Folio Collection (hereafter PF), Internet Archive, https://archive.org/details/kpfafoliomay77paci.

2. "KPFA Poetry Festival," recorded by Randy Thom and Doug Maise, May 14, 1977, part 1, Pacifica Radio Archives (hereafter PRA), AZ0079.01, CD copy of a reel-to-reel tape.

3. "KPFA Poetry Festival," *KPFA Folio*, 1.

4. Gaikowski, *Festival of Bards*.

5. "KPFA Poetry Festival," *KPFA Folio*, 1.

6. Henderson conducted a series of interviews with African American poets for KPFA in 1969; in 1977, Reed co-hosted *The Yardbird Hour* for KPFA with Al Young, which featured writers published in their multicultural little magazines *Yardbird Reader* (1972–1976) and *Y'Bird* (1977–1978). Spicer and Rexroth were both early KPFA radio hosts, as I discuss in chapter 2; Howe worked at WBAI in New York, as I discuss in chapter 5. Thomas was a producer for KPFT in Houston in the 1970s and after. Though none of the Bay Area Language poets performed at the 1977 KPFA Poetry Festival, in 1978, Lyn Hejinian and Kit Robinson began hosting the KPFA program *In the American Tree*, which would bring many of these poets to the Berkeley station for interviews and readings.

7. Allison, *Bodies on the Line*, 11–12.

8. Cantwell, *When We Were Good*, 201, 199, 201.

9. Davidson, *Ghostlier Demarcations*, 196.

10. Some of the scholarship on post-1945 poetry and electronic media includes Chasar, *Poetry Unbound*; Davidson, *Ghostlier Demarcations*; Perloff, *Radical Artifice*; Perlow, *Poem Electric*; and Shaw, *Narrowcast*.

11. I adopt the term "literary radio studies" from Ian Whittington, "Radio Studies and 20th-Century Literature." Foundational examples of modernist literary radio studies include Avery, *Radio Modernism*; Campbell, *Wireless Writing*; Cohen, Coyle, and Lewty, *Broadcasting Modernism*; Kahn and Whitehead, *Wireless Imagination*; and Morris, *Sound States*. While more recent scholarship in the field has seen a growing interest in midcentury modernisms, transnationalism, and postcolonialism

(Bloom, *Wireless Past*; Cyzewski, "Broadcasting Nature Poetry"; Keane, *Ireland and the Problem of Communication*; McEnaney, *Acoustic Properties*; Morse, *Radio Empire*), studies of later twentieth or twenty-first century literary radio histories remain rare.

12. The onetime neglect of post-1945 histories of U.S. radio by media scholars is exemplified by Erik Barnouw's influential three-volume *A History of Broadcasting in the United States*, the final volume of which, *The Image Empire: From 1953*, indicated in its title the conceptual shift from radio to television. Since the 1990s, however, the rise of radio studies as a robust field of media and cultural study has recognized the continuous significance of radio in the twentieth and twenty-first centuries.

13. Among the "big four" American broadcast networks—NBC, CBS, Mutual, and ABC—only Mutual did not make the pivot to television.

14. On the broadcasting of poetry and verse drama during the "golden age" of American network radio, see Chasar, *Everyday Reading*, 80–122, and *Poetry Unbound*, 54–78; Furr, *Recorded Poetry and Poetic Reception*, 83–113; Kaplan, *Radio and Poetry*; McCoy, "Poetry on Radio"; Selch, "Engineering Democracy"; Verma, *Theater of the Mind*; Wheeler, *Voicing American Poetry*, 39–59; and Wilson, "Gertrude Stein and the Radio."

15. Chasar, *Everyday Reading*, 84; emphasis in original.

16. Monroe, "Radio and the Poets," 32.

17. Olson, *Maximus Poems*, 14.

18. Shaw, *Narrowcast*, 2.

19. It wasn't until the mid-1970s that FM radio receivers came standard in most new cars (Sterling and Keith, *Sounds of Change*, 151).

20. Ellison, *Invisible Man*, 581.

21. Spicer, *My Vocabulary*, 374. Subsequent references are cited parenthetically as *MV*.

22. Frost, *Early FM Radio*.

23. Lessing, *Man of High Fidelity*, 171.

24. Frank O'Hara reportedly owned an FM radio set that he kept tuned exclusively to New York classical music stations WNYC and WQXR (Gooch, *City Poet*, 193). His weekend ritual of radio listening, often as an accompaniment to writing, is frequently registered in his poems—like "Radio," in which the poet apostrophizes his radio set to lament the "dreary" Saturday music programming that he supposes is better during the non-prime-time weekday hours: "All week long...you spill your miracles of Grieg / and Honegger on shut-ins. // Am I not / shut in too, and after a week / of work, don't I deserve Prokofieff?" (*Collected Poems*, 234).

25. Shepperd, "Infrastructure in the Air"; Slotten, *Radio's Hidden Voice*.

26. On the major role that the Rockefeller and Ford Foundations played in supporting the growth of educational radio and television broadcasting, see Hilmes, *Network Nations*, 106–114, 171–205. The FCC also supported public broadcasting by creating a special class of ten-watt low-power educational licenses and adopting the

Fairness Doctrine in 1949, which required broadcasters to devote airtime to debate on issues of public interest.

27. Susan Douglas titles her chapter on 1950s radio "The Kids Take Over: Transistors, DJs, and Rock 'n' Roll," in *Listening In*, 219-255.
28. Baraka [Jones], *Blues People*, 169.
29. Lott, *Love and Theft*.
30. Douglas, *Listening In*, 222.
31. "The Bleatniks," *Time*, August 11, 1961, 48.
32. Kerouac, *On the Road*, 140.
33. Kerouac, "Note," in *Mexico City Blues*; Kerouac, *On the Road*, 114.
34. McEnaney, *Acoustic Properties*, 6.
35. Barlow, *Voice Over*, 193.
36. Henderson, "Keep on Pushing," 242-243.
37. As David Grundy notes in an extended reading of this poem, Henderson attunes his readers to the fact that "what radios play is mediated through the control of scheduling and programming and, indeed, the record industry control of black music" (*Black Arts Poetry Machine*, 114).
38. Keith, *Purple Haze*, 22.
39. Keith, *Purple Haze*, 29.
40. Douglas, *Listening In*, 274-276. Underground FM radio was overwhelmingly white and male in the late 1960s and early 1970s, but a few African American men (including William "Rosko" Mercer, one of the pioneers of freeform, and Roland Young) and white women (like Raechel Donahue, Dusty Street, and Alison Steele) did make inroads as freeform DJs at underground stations. There were also a few Black-appeal stations, such as WBLS-FM (New York), whose DJs fused soul, R&B, and jazz music with Black nationalist politics, poetry, and freeform experimentation; see Barlow, *Voice Over*, 230-241.
41. Watts, Leary, Snyder, and Ginsberg, "Houseboat Summit." The transcript was originally published in *The San Francisco Oracle* 1, no. 7 (February 1967), and radio broadcast on KPFA-FM in Berkeley on June 16, 1967. Leary used similar phrasing in his published writings, such as his assertion in "Start Your Own Religion," that "[t]o turn on is to detach from the rigid addictive focus on the fake-prop TV studio set and to refocus on the natural energies within the body" (*Politics of Ecstasy*, 224).
42. Watts et al., "Houseboat Summit."
43. Leary, *Politics of Ecstasy*, 6.
44. In 1969-1970, programmer Allen Shaw also created a commercial network version of underground radio for ABC that aired as "LOVE Radio." A 1971 FCC crackdown on drug-related references in broadcast music and speech further hastened the conversion of freeform underground to AOR stations. Walker, *Rebels on the Air*, 99-100, 122-126; Sterling and Keith, *Sounds of Change*, 130, 136-137.
45. Simpson, *Early '70s Radio*; Sterling and Keith, *Sounds of Change*, 136-139, 162-168.

46. Ladd, *Radio Waves*, 162.

47. Public Broadcasting Act of 1967, 47 U.S.C. § 396(a)(1).

48. Walker, *Rebels on the Air*, 134–138, 142–145; Sterling and Keith, *Sounds of Change*, 144–147.

49. The U.S. community radio movement started to take shape in the 1970s around a few conferences, including the Alternative Media Conference at Goddard College in 1970 and the National Alternative Radio Konvention in Madison, Wisconsin, in 1974, out of which the National Federation of Community Broadcasters formed in 1975. See Barlow, "Community Radio"; Faber and Hochheimer, "Networking the Counterculture"; Walker, *Rebels*, 180–181, 233.

50. Milam, *Sex and Broadcasting*.

51. There is relatively little scholarship on U.S. college radio in this period, though historian Katherine Rye Jewell's forthcoming book on this subject, *Live from the Underground: A History of College Radio*," will hopefully begin to address the oversight. See also Schnitker, "Archives, Advocacy and Crowd-Sourcing."

52. On the history of Native American community radio, see Daley and James, *Cultural Politics*; Keith, *Signals in the Air*. On Chicano community radio history, see Casillas, *Sounds of Belonging*, 51–82; De La Torre, *Feminista Frequencies*.

53. King, "History of Struggle."

54. On Black community radio, see Barlow, *Voice Over*, 286–291. On the 1970s emergence in the U.S. of feminist radio, see Carter, "A Mic of Her Own"; on Chicana feminist broadcasting, see De La Torre, *Feminista Frequencies*.

55. An online KRAB archive is maintained by former KRAB volunteer and board member Chuck Reinsch and includes a collection of poetry-related broadcasts; http://www.krabarchive.com/krab-audio-archive-main-menu.html. An additional KRAB audio collection of lesbian feminist programming has recently been digitized by the University of Washington Libraries; see "KRAB-FM Lesbian-Feminist Radio Program Recordings," https://content.lib.washington.edu/krabfmweb/index.html.

56. Looker, *BAG*, 90–92. The Castros co-founded the *River Styx* literary magazine in 1975.

57. Mackey, "Interview by Christopher Funkhouser," 254. More recently, Kenneth Goldsmith hosted a legendary weekly experimental program on freeform station WFMU-FM in Jersey City from 1995 to 2010.

58. McCoy, "Poetry on Radio," 569–570. For a more critical view of the representation of poetry on NPR, see Spinelli, "Not Hearing Poetry."

59. Sterling and Keith, *Sounds of Change*, 155.

60. In the mid-1990s, for example, Charles Bernstein's *LINEbreak* series of interviews with poets (co-produced with Martin Spinelli) was distributed via the Public Radio Satellite System to public and college stations. More recently, podcasting has brought about a flourishing of poetry-related audio media as well as audio drama and storytelling; on the latter, see Bottomley, *Sound Streams*, 174–227.

61. In a 2015 article for *The Nation* provocatively titled "Is Pacifica Radio Worth Saving?," Pacifica historian and media scholar Matthew Lasar characterized the

once highly respected progressive network as now "widely regarded as something akin to the late Ottoman Empire of public broadcasting," a "[h]aven to conspiracy theorists, HIV skeptics and dubious health-cure infomercials." Critical dissections of Pacifica's decline since the 1990s include Dunaway, "Pacifica Radio and Community Broadcasting"; Lasar, *Uneasy Listening* and "Pacifica Radio's Crisis of Containment."

62. Bernstein, introduction, in *Close Listening*, 13. More recently, Seth Forrest has argued that the New American Poetry was also a "poetics of aurality," which he sees as informed more by "secondary orality," in Walter Ong's sense of the orality produced by electronic media technologies, than by orality per se ("Aurality and Literacy," 212).

63. Davidson, *Ghostlier Demarcations*, 199. Seth Perlow, for example, explores the tension between improvisation and recorded sound technologies in post-1945 poetry performance and its audio archives in *Poem Electric*, 179-228. Critical approaches to the intersections of literary production, recorded sound technologies, and processes of racialization have been especially developed in Black studies; see Jones, *Muse Is Music*; Moten, *In the Break*; and Reed, *Soundworks*.

64. McLuhan, *Understanding Media*. Timothy C. Campbell argues that understanding radio as a multimedia assemblage enables a fuller study of the relationship between modernist literature and wireless radio technologies not limited to what he sees as "an overemphasis on the spoken qualities of transmission" (*Wireless Writing*, xi).

65. The idea that listeners actively construct rather than passively receive what they hear, and that they do so in relation to hegemonic, historically specific aural practices that reproduce ideologies about race, gender, and sexuality, is one of the central insights that has emerged from the interdisciplinary field of sound studies; see, especially, Stoever, *Sonic Color Line*.

66. Hill quoted in Lasar, *Pacifica Radio*, 49.

Chapter 1

1. Lasar, *Pacifica Radio*, 6-7.
2. Roy Finch quoted in Lasar, *Pacifica Radio*, 6.
3. Lee Bartlett suggests that the success of Everson's application for 4-E status likely owed more to his father's position as justice of the peace in Fresno County than to his own "vaguely worded" humanist justification (*William Everson*, 33).
4. During World War I, the first conscripted war in which conscripts could not hire substitutes to serve in their place, registered COs were given the option to serve in noncombatant roles in the military; those who refused were imprisoned in military facilities. After WWII, CPS and its camps were dissolved, and new forms of alternative service remunerated by wages were made available to registered COs.
5. Taylor, *Acts of Conscience*, 22. In addition to those who served as COs, around 6,000 absolute resisters—those who resisted all forms of conscription, including registering for the draft—were imprisoned.
6. Taylor, *Acts of Conscience*, 57.
7. Everson, *Residual Years*, 15; emphasis in original.

8. In 1946, for example, after COs awaiting a protracted discharge initiated the largest strike at a CPS camp in Glendora, California, leading to the arrest of more than forty COs, Hill co-authored a public letter admonishing the strikers for overemphasizing camp conditions rather than the underlying issue of conscription itself (Lasar, *Pacifica Radio*, 19–20).

9. Muste, *World Task*, 14, 15.

10. Roy Kepler quoted in Land, *Active Radio*, 35. Kepler worked as subscriptions chief and hosted a public affairs program at KPFA in the early 1950s; in 1954, he opened the paperback bookstore Kepler's Books, which became famous for its tax resistance, and which served as the southern leg of the alternative bookstore tripod of City Lights Books, Cody's Books, and Kepler's Books (Doyle, *Radical Chapters*, 107–111).

11. Everson's emphasis on heterosexual sex and marriage as a spiritual union, sundered by war, draws on the breakup of his own first marriage and his developing Christian sacramentalism that is reflected in the larger sexual-spiritual quest of the long poem. This theme is consistent with much modernist poetry from T. S. Eliot to D. H. Lawrence to Kenneth Rexroth, but it also echoed postwar discourses about how the "excesses" of war needed to be rechanneled into heteronormativity for the sake and security of peace. "Chronicle of Division" even makes this point explicitly by asserting that heteronormativity is the primary casualty of war for both CO and soldier: "The man struck from the woman— / That is the crime. / As the armies grow, / So gathers the guilt, / So bloom the perversions" (Everson, *Residual Years*, 19). Robert Duncan, Jack Spicer, and Allen Ginsberg would offer radically different perspectives on the sexual politics of anarcho-pacifism as gay men in an oppressively homophobic society.

12. William Everson to Kermit Sheets, September 24, 1943, Untide Press Records, Box 1, Bancroft Library, University of California, Berkeley (hereafter UC).

13. William Everson to Kermit Sheets, September 26, 1943, Box 1, UC.

14. William Everson to Kemper Nomland, October 16, 1943, Box 1, UC.

15. A few other CPS specialty "schools," including a subsistence farming school at a camp in Maryland and a school to study race relations at a camp in Tennessee, had been formed prior to the Waldport Fine Arts group.

16. Wallach, "C.O. Link," 15.

17. The camp even had a small music recording room, which Coffield used to record poems and songs (McQuiddy, *Here on the Edge*, 44).

18. Lewis Hill to William Everson, June 29, 1944, Box 2, UC.

19. Hill quoted in Lasar, *Pacifica Radio*, 26.

20. Everson quoted in Metres, *Behind the Lines*, 89.

21. Hill published poems in issues 3 (summer 1944) and 4 (summer 1945) of *Illiterati*. Everson also encouraged Hill to submit a manuscript for publication by Untide, praising the "exceptional quality" of his poetry; no volume of Hill's poetry was ever published. William Everson to Lewis Hill, September 9, 1944, William Everson Papers, Box 14, folder 1, William Andrews Clark Memorial Library, University of California, Los Angeles.

22. William Everson quoted in Wallach, "C.O. Link," 18.

23. Metres, *Behind the Lines*, 19.

24. Everson to Nomland, October 16, 1943.

25. Metres, *Behind the Lines*, 76.

26. As Metres documents, the Fine Arts group even blocked the War Resisters League from publishing a proposed anthology of pacifist writing on the grounds that it would undermine their efforts to garner literary legitimacy (*Behind the Lines*, 76–77).

27. William Everson to Kenneth Patchen, August 28, 1944, Box 2, UC.

28. Later, Robert Duncan would echo these views in his correspondence with Denise Levertov criticizing her anti-Vietnam War poetry; for Duncan, as for Everson, the responsibility of the artist to protect the freedom of organic creation was itself a pacifist act that was betrayed by the coercive logic of overt political statement.

29. Kemper Nomland to Robert Duncan, July 24, 1944, Box 2, UC.

30. *Illiterati*, no. 4 (Summer 1945).

31. Hill, "Woman Screaming."

32. Patchen, "Stars Go to Sleep."

33. Tracy, *Direct Action*, 40.

34. On the elegiac tone of Everson's "Chronicle of Division," see Metres, *Behind the Lines*, 73–92; and Davidson, *San Francisco Renaissance*, 47–53.

35. Metres, *Behind the Lines*, 74.

36. Lewis Hill, "The Private Room," *Beacon: The Bulletin of the Mental Health Society of Northern California* (Fall 1952), 2, Pacifica Foundation Records, Box 8, folder 25, National Public Broadcasting Archives, University of Maryland Libraries, College Park, Maryland (hereafter PM).

37. Lasar, *Pacifica Radio*, 25. Hill, like many COs, objected to the incarceration of Japanese Americans during the war. At the peak of the war, Tule Lake incarcerated in a maximum-security facility more than 18,000 Japanese Americans—in other words, several thousand more than the total number of COs serving in CPS camps in the U.S.

38. Douglas, *Listening In*, 162.

39. Adorno, "Fetish-Character," 271.

40. Adorno, "Radio Physiognomics," 70.

41. Ibid.

42. Hill, "Theory of Listener-Sponsored Radio," 21.

43. Pacifica Radio prospectus (1946) quoted in Vera Hopkins, "Report to the Executive and Advisory Members of Pacifica Foundation on the Experience of Radio Station KPFA in Its First Five Months," 1949, in "Pacifica Radio Sampler," compiled by Hopkins, vol. 1, 1984, Bancroft Library Special Collections, University of California, Berkeley.

44. Vera Hopkins, "Some Basic History of Pacifica," 1981, in "Pacifica Radio Sampler," vol. 1.

45. Pacifica Foundation, "K-P-F-A: A Prospectus of the Pacifica Station," 1948, 18, Box 8, folder 6, PM.

46. Eleanor McKinney quoted in Lasar, *Pacifica Radio*, 62; Hill quoted in Lasar, *Pacifica Radio*, 43.

47. Lasar, *Pacifica Radio*, 64.

48. Programming highlights from KPFA's interim year are documented in Hopkins, "Report to the Executive and Advisory Members of Pacifica Foundation." The recordings of Jaime de Angulo's radio program—among the few programs to be preserved from KPFA's first year—have recently been digitized by the Pacifica Radio Archives. See Hollenbach, "Jaime de Angulo's *Indian Tales*," as well as other contributions to the *Chicago Review* special issue on *Jaime de Angulo, Gui Mayo, and West Coast Modernism*.

49. Lewis Hill, *Voluntary Listener-Sponsorship: A Report to Educational Broadcasters on the Experiment at KPFA, Berkeley, California* (Berkeley: Pacifica Foundation, 1958), Box 3, folder 4, Wisconsin Historical Society Archives, Madison, Wisconsin (hereafter PW). While Pacifica Radio is generally acknowledged to be the first and oldest listener-supported public radio network in the U.S., there are precedents. Michele Hilmes notes that "[p]ublic subscription" was considered in the 1920s by broadcasters as a possible alternative to commercial, educational, and governmental models of financing (*Radio Voices*, 9).

50. The Ford and Rockefeller Foundations were instrumental in funding the growth of public radio and television in the U.S., yet we might see KPFA's reliance on their grants as compromising Hill's intention to create a truly independent form of radio free of private and state interests—a compromise that appears even more problematic for a station with roots in the radical pacifist movement if we consider the role that these private foundations played in U.S. foreign policy and Cold War expansionism; see Parmar, *Foundations of the American Century*.

51. McKinney, "About Pacifica Radio," 12.

52. The BBC was also a major influence on (and source for) KPFA's programming in the 1950s, and some of KPFA's anti-commercial aesthetics were also borrowed from the British broadcaster's early approach to public broadcasting. As Kate Lacey describes, "the BBC of the 1920s and 1930s positively endorsed periods of silence (fifteen minutes or so) between programmes precisely to allow listeners to switch off, or to contemplate what they had just heard or were about to hear" (*Listening Publics*, 82).

53. The idea to make the *Folio* a literary supplement was floated in grant applications, correspondence, and the *Folio* itself, as in "Folio—Commercialization or Better Service?," *KPFA Program Folio* 8, no. 5 (May 26–June 8, 1957), 1, Box 3, folder 15, PW. It was never realized, but Pacifica stations have often used their program guides to publish poems, short fiction, essays, and artwork.

54. William Triest attributed most of the early *Folio* essays to Hill, as reported by Vera Hopkins, "Summary of [a] Conversation with Bill Triest," 1974, in "Pacifica Radio Sampler," vol. 1.

55. "The Man at the Microphone," *KPFA Program Folio* 2, no. 17 (October 21–November 3, 1951), 1, PF, https://archive.org/details/kpfafoliooct21nov35i1paci.

56. Lacey, *Listening Publics*, 9.

57. "Ideas and Intentions...," *KPFA Program Folio* 2, no. 25 (March 9–22, 1952), 1, Box 3, folder 10, PW.

58. Hill, *Voluntary Listener-Sponsorship*, 44.

59. Eleanor McKinney, "KPFA History," January 1960, in "Pacifica Radio Sampler," vol. 1. As Kate Lacey observes, the notion that "the default position of the [radio] listener was one of passivity out of which they had to be jolted" was a common view in twentieth-century radio discourse and was often "couched in terms of a training of the ear, or the development of a listening culture" (*Listening Publics*, 114).

60. "Briefly, on the Spoken Word...," *KPFA Program Folio* 2, no. 26 (March 23–April 5, 1952), 1, PF, https://archive.org/details/kpfafoliomar23apro552paci.

61. Spicer, *House*, 230.

62. Lewis Hill, "Report and Proposal to the Rockefeller Foundation: Summarizing a Six-Month Experiment in the Broadcasting of Poetry and Proposing Its Extension," January 20, 1955, 4, Box 28, PW.

63. I borrow this phrase from Neil Verma's *Theater of the Mind*, which traces an aesthetic history of the genre of the network radio play through the interwar, WWII, and postwar periods.

64. Lewis Hill, producer, *A Word by Wallace Stevens: An Essay for Radio*, performed by Hill and Virginia Maynard, 1954, PRA, AZ1477, reel-to-reel tape. Transcription is my own; italics are used to represent vocal emphasis.

65. It should be noted that Hill proposed this project for the NAEB while he was in self-exile from KPFA, after resigning during a period of intense leadership conflict in 1953–1954 that also saw the departure of Moore; Hill returned to head the station and the Pacifica Foundation in the fall of 1954, though he became less involved in its day-to-day operations in the years leading up to his tragic death by suicide in 1957.

66. Hill did not complete the full series as proposed and only recorded programs with the more theatrical methods (approaches four and five) for Lowell's and Stevens's poems.

67. Hill, "Report and Proposal," 3.

68. Hill, "Report and Proposal," 5, 6. There is some evidence that this "peripheral audience" for poetry did exist among the KPFA audience; after another series of poetry programs produced by Hill aired in the spring of 1957, one couple wrote to the station: "Your first program on contemporary poetry struck us as superb. We are *not* presently readers of poetry! So this was revelatory to us, and will possibly aid in opening for us the door to the art." Wally and Ginny Craig to Lewis Hill, May 30, 1957, Box 39, PW.

69. Hill solicited feedback on the programs from poets Josephine Miles and Louise Bogan, critic R. P. Blackmur, NBC executive Judith Waller, and Frederick C. Packard Jr. of *The Poet Speaks* on WGBH-FM in Boston. Miles, in her response, questioned Hill's assumption of readerly resistance: "You are now creating your own fictions of response to the poems, and they are largely ones of unease, which you believe people feel." In her view, the programs would be more successful if they

focused on dramatizing "the fiction of the poem itself" and its "creation" rather than "the hypothetical response" of the reader. Josephine Miles to Lewis Hill, January 3, 1955, Box 28, PW.

70. Lacey, *Listening Publics*, 93. See also VanCour, *Making Radio*, 45-68.

71. Stevens, "Idea of Order," 128.

72. We might see this mode of aural attention as corresponding with the one Stevens represents in "The Idea of Order at Key West," when he depicts the collective lyric speaker's self-reflexive response to hearing the singer: "Whose spirit is this? we said, because we knew / It was the spirit that we sought and knew / That we should ask this often as she sang" (129).

73. Adorno, "Radio Physiognomics," 70.

74. "The Realm of Speculation," *KPFA Program Folio* 4, no. 22 (January 24–February 6, 1954), 1, PF, https://archive.org/details/kpfafolio422paci.

75. Hill, "Report and Proposal," 11.

76. Lewis Hill, producer, *Section of a Soliloquy: On a Poem by Robert Lowell*, performed by Hill, Richard Moore, and Charles Levy, 1954, PRA, BB0962, reel-to-reel tape. Transcription is my own.

77. One of the other programs that Hill produced about "At the Indian Killer's Grave" does dramatize a conversation between two friends about the poem as they pass an evening at a local pub. The focus is again on the individual, however; as the two characters discuss their secular discomfort with the Catholic imagery in the poem, they resolve it by reinterpreting the Annunciation imagery as "call[ing] for all this to happen inside yourself," that is, a call for inner, subjective transformation. Lewis Hill, producer, *The Trouble with Being Alive: A Dialogue on a Poem by Robert Lowell*, 1954, PRA, AZ1470, reel-to-reel tape.

78. "Briefly, on the Spoken Word . . . ," 1. Jed Rasula describes Lowell's early poetry as a technically perfect and well-amplified "voice-over" in *American Poetry Wax Museum*, 40. In a 1955 letter to Hill, Rexroth strongly objected to the Lowell programs, lambasting Lowell as "a fraud both as a poet . . . and as a CO." Kenneth Rexroth to Lewis Hill, March 8, 1955, Box 1, PW.

79. Adorno, "Radio Physiognomics," 47.

80. Rexroth, "Unacknowledged Legislators," 12.

Chapter 2

1. Rexroth, *Autobiographical Novel* (rev. ed.), 518.

2. Rexroth, *Autobiographical Novel* (rev. ed.), 519. Richard Moore gives his own account of this visit by Hill to the Libertarian Circle in "Berkeley/San Francisco," 112.

3. James Tracy recounts that "Hill . . . gained a reputation as an incisive and sometimes caustic intellectual. He was known also for often speaking in cryptic terms. One C.O. recalls being asked by Bayard Rustin: 'Hey, do you happen to know Lew Hill? . . . They say that you can't understand what he's talking about'" (*Direct Action*, 49).

4. Rexroth dictated his autobiography for broadcast on KPFA and WBAI in two installments: the first beginning in 1959, and the second from 1978 to 1979. Transcripts

from the first round of tapes were revised for *An Autobiographical Novel* (1966), which covers Rexroth's early life up to his move to San Francisco in 1927. Transcripts from the later tapes, which include details about his life in San Francisco during and after WWII, became the basis for *Excerpts from a Life* (1981) and the posthumously published, expanded edition of *An Autobiographical Novel* (1991). Archival copies of the original tapes are held with Rexroth's papers at UCLA, and at the Pacifica Radio Archives.

5. Land, *Active Radio*, 99. KPFA's association with the Beats is often highlighted in radio histories. See Lasar, *Pacifica Radio*; Ledbetter, *Made Possible By*, 126; and Walker, *Rebels on the Air*, 48–49.

6. Davidson, *San Francisco Renaissance*, 1.

7. Parkinson, "Phenomenon or Generation," 283.

8. Ferlinghetti and Peters, *Literary San Francisco*, 159.

9. Spicer, *MV*, 11–12.

10. Spicer expounded on his theory of poetic dictation in a series of lectures he delivered in Vancouver in 1965, which I discuss in chapter 3.

11. Ellingham and Killian, *Poet Be Like God*, 11.

12. Moore, "Berkeley/San Francisco," 109, 112.

13. Lasar, *Pacifica Radio*, 36.

14. Spicer, *House*, 229. Subsequent references are cited parenthetically as *House*.

15. Sophie Tucker and George M. Cohan were both golden-age radio celebrities, but in 1949, they might not have seemed like the most obvious idols to choose for a new poetic movement: Cohan had died in 1942, and Tucker, though still at the height of her fame, was in her sixties.

16. Lasar, *Pacifica Radio*, 64.

17. The San Francisco poetry festivals of the late 1940s, the first of which was organized by Madeline Gleason in 1947, are generally recognized as important precedents for the large group readings associated with the San Francisco poetry community from the mid-1950s on.

18. *KPFA Interim Program Folio* 1, no. 17 (January 15–28, 1950), PF, https://archive.org/details/kpfafoliojan15jan2850paci.

19. Spicer is named in the first-ever KPFA program guide as a guest commentator for the June 11, 1949, episode of the *Folk Music Series*, and as the lead commentator for an expanded half-hour Saturday program in the subsequent issue. *KPFA Interim Program Folio* 1, no. 1 (June 5–18, 1949), 3, PF, https://archive.org/details/kpfafolio1n1paci; *KPFA Interim Program Folio* 1, no. 2 (June 19–July 2, 1949), 3, PF, https://archive.org/details/kpfafolio1n2paci. On Spicer's radio show and friendship with Herndon and Fredrickson in 1949–1950, see Ellingham and Killian, *Poet Be Like God*, 29–30.

20. Herndon, untitled, in Spicer, *Collected Books*, 375. Ellipsis, emphasis, and errors in original.

21. Ibid. Spicer's friend Sam Hardin gave a similar retrospective account of the radio show in an interview with Kevin Killian: "He'd talk about a song, tracing a line from a poem that first appears in say, 1500, and then picking it up again in 1900 and

comparing the difference. And sometimes Jack would sing—and he was the worst singer in the world. You'd be tuning into the program and you'd hear him, [imitates horrible tuneless voice]—every Saturday night. . . . He'd get Jim and Dave drunk before the program and then once the show began they'd use 'language,' and that's what Jack wanted" (quoted in Ellingham and Killian, *Poet Be Like God*, 30).

22. The last listing for Spicer's radio show in the *Folio* is for June 27, 1950, more than a year after his first named appearance in the guide. *Folio* dates should be taken with a grain of salt, though, since the schedule would not have reflected last-minute schedule changes, which were frequent in KPFA's early years. Killian and Ellingham's assertion that Spicer's radio show aired for forty weeks is plausible (*Poet Be Like God*, 30). *KPFA Program Folio* 1, no. 29 (June 18–July 1, 1950), PF, https://archive.org/details/kpfafoliojun18jul0150paci.

23. Lewis Hill, quoted in Stebbins, "Listener-Sponsored Radio," 240.

24. Ibid.

25. *KPFA Interim Program Folio*, 1, no. 2 (June 19–July 2, 1949), 3, PF, https://archive.org/details/kpfafolio1n2paci.

26. *KPFA Interim Program Folio* 1, no. 17 (January 15–28, 1950), PF, https://archive.org/details/kpfafoliojan15jan2850paci. On Spicer's adolescent interests in folk songs and musical parody, see Killian, "Jack Spicer's Secret."

27. *KPFA Interim Program Folio* 1, no. 3 (July 3–16, 1949), 4, PF, https://archive.org/details/kpfafolio1n2paci. Sam Eskin was an amateur folklorist who traveled across the U.S. and the world to record folk music and Indigenous oral literatures, which he released on LPs and broadcast on KPFA; like Spicer, he had a particular interest in bawdy songs.

28. "Report to the Executive," in Hopkins, "Pacifica Radio Sampler."

29. "Folk Music, Quid Est? . . . ," *KPFA Interim Program Folio* 1, no. 18 (January 29–February 11, 1950), 1, PF, https://archive.org/details/kpfafoliojan29feb1150paci.

30. Ibid., 12.

31. Lasar, *Pacifica Radio*, 95.

32. KPFA's first listener-subscribers had significantly more education and income than the average Bay Area resident. As Lasar reports, a 1956 station survey of subscribers revealed that 82 percent of respondents had an undergraduate degree, and more than 70 percent had some graduate education (*Pacifica Radio*, 85).

33. Lasar, *Pacifica Radio*, 85.

34. Joseph Conte interprets "Transformations II" in the context of Spicer's radio show and training in structural linguistics as "an operation on the grammar of the folk song" (*Unending Design*, 114).

35. Guthrie's "Ranger's Command," recorded in 1944, was derived from earlier cowboy ballads documented in Randolph's *Ozark Folksongs*, among other places. Guthrie's lyrics narrate the story of a cowboy who asks a "fair maiden" to accompany him to "the cold roundup"; when they are attacked in the middle of the night by a band of cattle rustlers, the woman is the first to rise, and she entreats the men to join

the fight. By some accounts, Guthrie wrote the song to inspire women to join the war effort, a context that resonates with the WWII allusions and Nazi imagery in Spicer's *The Holy Grail* (Place and Logsdon, liner notes, 12). The maiden in Guthrie's song could also be read in correspondence with Spicer's allusions in *The Holy Grail* to Gwenivere, Dorothy of the Oz series, Marilyn Monroe, and other female characters who are seen to disrupt the sanctity and seriousness of the male quest.

36. Fredman, *Contextual Practice*, 93-98.

37. Ibid., 94. See also Killian, "Jack Spicer's Secret"; and Sanders, untitled, in liner notes to *Harry Smith's Anthology of American Folk Music*, vol. 4, 9.

38. Smith, *Think of the Self Speaking*, 81; Marcus, *Old, Weird America*, 89. In a 1968 review, Rexroth described Carl Sandburg's use of folk songs in his poetry as having "transmit[ted]" to a younger generation "the old free America"—a phrase that Marcus adapted to "old, weird America" in his classic study of Bob Dylan's *Basement Tapes* (Rexroth, "From a Very Good Man").

39. Fredman, *Contextual Practice*, 94.

40. Cantwell, *When We Were Good*, 120.

41. Jack Spicer, "Jack Spicer: April 11, 1957," streaming audio file, Poetry Center Digital Archive, https://diva.sfsu.edu/collections/poetrycenter/bundles/191198.

42. On Spicer's anxiety about public poetry readings, see Ellingham and Killian, *Poet Be Like God*, 196-197.

43. Jack Spicer, "The Holy Grail, July 15, 1965," PennSound, MP3 copy, http://writing.upenn.edu/pennsound/x/Spicer.html.

44. In an interview, electronic musician Jack Dangers recounts his discovery of tapes of some of Jacobs's radio collages in Jacobs's former house in Marin County, including one with Ferlinghetti reading fake "want ads" (Dangers, "Mind of Meat Beat Manifesto"). Jacobs also released some of his tape collages as Folkways albums.

45. Lasar, *Pacifica Radio*, 65.

46. Edward Meece quoted in Lasar, *Pacifica Radio*, 65.

47. Spicer, *Tower of Babel*, 103.

48. Like his fictional counterpoint, Rexroth was never paid for his book review program; he worked for the station as a volunteer rather than a paid staff member, as have many of the cash-strapped network's program hosts over the years.

49. See Loviglio, *Radio's Intimate Public*.

50. Lasar, *Pacifica Radio*, 73.

51. Rexroth's influence at Pacifica extended beyond his *Books* program, as he operated in an unofficial advisory role, suggesting programming, facilitating partnerships with literary institutions and grants, and connecting Pacifica stations with poets, artists, musicians, and critics. Many poets who came to KPFA in its first decades did so through Rexroth's direct invitation or his indirect influence. On Moore's departure from KPFA, see Lasar, *Pacifica Radio*, 147-148; after KPFA, Moore started a career as a public television producer for KQED and in 1966 produced the documentary television series *USA: Poetry*.

52. Moore, "Berkeley/San Francisco," 113.

53. *Books* is first listed in the *Folio* schedule for November 7, 1952, and Rexroth mentioned the program in a letter to James Laughlin dated November 4 of that year; the earliest extant recordings of the program I have found date to May 1952. These do not necessarily contradict Moore's account of first approaching Rexroth in 1950. *KPFA Program Folio* 3, no. 16 (November 2–15, 1952), Box 3, folder 10, PW; Rexroth, *Rexroth and Laughlin*, 183.

54. Hill, "Private Room," 2.

55. "Ideas and Intentions," *KPFA Program Folio* 2, no. 25 (March 9–22, 1952), 1, Box 3, folder 10, PW.

56. "The Bashful Ones . . . ," *KPFA Program Folio* 3, no. 9 (July 27–August 9, 1952), 1, Box 3, folder 10, PW.

57. Kenneth Rexroth to Lewis Hill, March 8, 1955, Box 1, PW.

58. Richard Ringheim to WBAI Program Director, November 27, 1960, Box 28, PW.

59. Andre and Margaret Moreau to KPFA, n. d., Kenneth Rexroth Papers, Box 12, folder 6, Charles E. Young Research Library, University of California, Los Angeles (hereafter RC); emphasis in original.

60. Houglum, "Kenneth Rexroth and Radio Reading," 59.

61. Lasar, *Pacifica Radio*, 119, 122.

62. The accompanying profile characterizes Rexroth's *Books* as "excit[ing] considerable controversy" and "intense reactions" among the station's listeners over his opinionated reviews and "pungent criticisms of our social and civil ills." "KPFA Program Participants: Kenneth Rexroth," *KPFA Program Folio* 9, no. 5 (May 25–June 7, 1958), 1, PF, https://archive.org/details/kpfafolio95paci.

63. This does not mean that the opinions that Rexroth expressed were necessarily socially progressive or politically radical. His self-described interest in "Orientalia" involved a fetishization of East Asian culture, and his self-identification as a feminist and antiracist were frequently undermined by his expressed views and actions. By the 1960s and early 1970s, Rexroth, though still broadcasting regularly, would appear more and more out of step with the radical cultural politics being sounded by the network, which I discuss in chapters 4 and 5.

64. Hamalian, *Life*, 243.

65. See, for example, Rexroth's harsh review of Kerouac's *Mexico City Blues*, "Discordant and Cool."

66. Rexroth, "Second Post-War," 104.

67. Small collections of audio recordings of Rexroth's KPFA program can be found in the Rexroth Papers at UCLA and the Pacifica Radio Archives, though most of these recordings have not been digitized.

68. Kenneth Rexroth, "Books program, 15 May 1952," Box 98, folder 3, RC, reel-to-reel tape; "Books program, 9 July [1952]," Box 99, folder 5, RC, reel-to-reel tape.

69. Rexroth, "Books program, 15 May 1952."

70. Shaw, *Narrowcast*, 4.

71. John S. Sills to KPFA, November 30, 1960, Box 12, folder 6, RC.

72. Hamalian notes the listening parties in *Life*, 316.
73. McClure, "Seven Things."
74. Meltzer, *San Francisco Beat*, 229, 269–270.
75. David Meltzer quoted in Moore, "Berkeley/San Francisco," 113.
76. McClure, "Seven Things."
77. Rexroth quoted in Hamalian, *Life*, 221.
78. Hamalian, *Life*, 274; Jarnot, *Robert Duncan*, 169–170. Rexroth's attack on the San Francisco Catholic Archdiocese on his radio show in the context of the *Howl* case can be heard on the recording "Kenneth Rexroth on Censorship."
79. After the founding of the Poetry Center at San Francisco State College in 1954 by Ruth Witt-Diamant, KPFA regularly broadcast tapes from its events, starting with the center's inaugural reading by visiting poet Theodore Roethke.
80. Robert Duncan to Eleanor McKinney, April 18, 1957, San Francisco State College Poetry Center Records, Box 6, Bancroft Library, University of California, Berkeley.
81. Lawrence Ferlinghetti, Michael McClure, and Fred Cody, interviewees, "Rexroth, Ferlinghetti, McClure, E. B., and Fred Cody," June 1982, PRA, AZ1258, MP3 copy of a reel-to-reel tape.
82. Kenneth Rexroth, "Letter from Aix," ca. 1958–1959, PRA, BB1016.18, CD copy of a reel-to-reel tape. Beginning in the late 1950s, Rexroth expressed increasing hostility toward the sensationalized Beat phenomenon, which he believed detracted attention from the serious work being written by San Francisco poets. The hostility also stemmed from his personal dislike of Kerouac and his intensifying social paranoia, instigated by the public affair between Creeley and Rexroth's third wife, Marthe Larsen.
83. Lawrence Ferlinghetti to Kenneth Rexroth, March 14, 1959, Box 6, folder 13, RC.
84. *KPFA Program Folio* 5, no. 7 (June 27–July 10, 1954), Box 3, folder 12, PW.
85. "Exhibit 4" [transcript of broadcast recording of Ferlinghetti's 1959 *Big Table* reading], in "Response by Pacifica Foundation to FCC Letter of January 18, 1960 (Reference 8831)," 17, Box 5, PW.
86. KPFK and WBAI both canceled Rexroth's program by 1964, though he would periodically get back on their airwaves in subsequent years; writing to Rexroth about the decision to cancel the program, WBAI station manager Christopher Koch expressed his strident dislike and confusion about its appeal: "The technical quality of the tapes is absolutely atrocious. They are full of coughs, false starts, gurgles, snide comments against KPFA, etc., all of which seem to me to do you as much harm as they do the station. I don't know what your arrangement is with KPFA[.]" Christopher Koch to Kenneth Rexroth, December 22, 1964, Box 34, folder 3, RC.
87. See Chasar, *Everyday Reading*, 80–122.
88. Hamalian, *Life*, 312.
89. Kenneth Rexroth, "Autobiography (II), part 1," May 1959, Box 96, folder 1, RC, reel-to-reel tape.
90. Marie Rexroth to Harold Winkler, June 24, 1959, Box 28, PW.
91. Harold Winkler to Marie Rexroth, July 1, 1959, Box 28, PW.

92. Harold Winkler, "Pacifica Radio—Room for Dissent," *National Association of Educational Broadcasters (NAEB) Journal* 19, no. 3 (May-June 1960): 98, Box 8, folder 25, PM.

93. Listener letter to KPFA, October 17, 1955, Box 20, PW.

Chapter 3

1. Recordings were made of Ginsberg reading "Howl" prior to his appearance on KPFA, but none of these were published or broadcast until later.

2. David Lamble, quoted in Johnson and Keith, *Queer Airwaves*, 28. Pacifica Radio stations were among the first to provide an outlet for LGBTQ+ voices and perspectives; see DeShazor, "Queer Radio History."

3. Morgan and Peters, eds., *Howl on Trial*, 193.

4. Ellingham and Killian, *Poet Be Like God*, 243.

5. Spicer's untitled final poem is the last in the posthumously published *Book of Magazine Verse* (1965) and begins, "At least we both know how shitty the world is" (*MV*, 426). Though Ginsberg is never named, he is the implied addressee of Spicer's poem, which alludes to Ginsberg's poem "Kral Majales."

6. Ginsberg, *Collected Poems*, 73.

7. Ibid., 86, 83.

8. On failure as a source for "low theory" and alternative forms of queer epistemology, see Halberstam, *Queer Art of Failure*.

9. Challener, "Addressing 'Alien Worlds,'" 493.

10. Sedgwick, *Epistemology of the Closet*.

11. Ginsberg's activism in the gay rights movement is well documented. On Spicer's lesser-known and earlier activism, see Killian, "Spicer and the Mattachine."

12. D'Emilio, "Gay Politics and Community," 461-462.

13. Ginsberg, *Journals Mid-Fifties*, 61.

14. Allen Ginsberg to Kenneth Rexroth, June 15, 1955, Box 8, folder 1, RC.

15. Ginsberg, *Letters*, 118.

16. Kerouac, *Dharma Bums*, 13.

17. Tape recordings of Ginsberg reading "Howl" as well as a limited mimeograph edition of "Howl," printed by Robert Creeley and Marthe Rexroth, also circulated in the Bay Area prior to the publication of *Howl and Other Poems*.

18. Eleanor [McKinney] Moore to Allen Ginsburg [sic], October 17, 1955, Box 1, PW.

19. It is possible that Ginsberg sent KPFA one of the tapes he had recorded the previous summer at Neal Cassady's home. Recordings of Ginsberg reading and singing "Walking at Night in Key West," "The Green Automobile," and "Green Valentine Blues" attributed to this recording session appear on the first CD of *Holy Soul Jelly Roll*, though none of these correspond with McKinney's description.

20. *KPFA Program Folio* 7, no. 18 (November 25-December 8, 1956), PF, https://archive.org/details/kpfafolio718paci. It is probable that Ginsberg's reading for KPFA was taped in the station's studios on October 25, 1956, and first broadcast on December 8, 1956. The October 25 recording date is given on recordings of Ginsberg's reading

held by both the PRA (which appears to be a later edited version) and PennSound. While it is possible that KPFA broadcast the reading live or aired it soon after its recording, I think the later date of December 8, 1956, is the likely original broadcast, in part because of comments that Lewis Hill made before its later rebroadcast. "Allen Ginsberg Reads His Poetry," October 25, 1956, PRA, BB1893, CD copy of a reel-to-reel tape; "KPFA Pacifica Studio Recording," October 25, 1956, PennSound, MP3 copy, https://media.sas.upenn.edu/pennsound/authors/Ginsberg/SFSU-1956/Ginsberg-Allen_Poetry-Reading_SFSU_10-25-56.mp3.

21. The copies held by PennSound and PRA of this recording are slightly different, but the reader may assume that transcriptions and descriptions of Ginsberg's radio reading apply to both versions unless otherwise stated.

22. Ginsberg, *Howl*, 30. Subsequent references are cited parenthetically as *Howl*.

23. Ginsberg, "Notes Written," 30.

24. Despite his extensive discography, Ginsberg appears to have been especially doubtful about the value of recording "Howl" in studio conditions. For both the Evergreen record *San Francisco Poets* and the Fantasy album of *Howl and Other Poems*, Ginsberg elected to use recordings of "Howl" taped at public readings rather than in the studio.

25. Ginsberg, *Collected Poems*, 468.

26. Of course, Ginsberg was also a fan of "[t]he Super-Hit sound" of popular rock music and even aspired to be a rock musician at various points in his career, seeking out friendships and collaborations with musicians like Bob Dylan, the Beatles, Leonard Cohen, and the Clash; writing his own rock songs; and appearing in the background of album covers and documentaries like D. A. Pennebaker's *Don't Look Back* (1967).

27. For comparative analyses of Ginsberg's use of the tape recorder and radio in *Fall of America* and "Wichita Vortex Sutra" especially, see Shaw, *Narrowcast*, 35–45; Davidson, *Ghostlier Demarcations*, 203–206; Perlow, *Poem Electric*, 206–223; Hoffman, *American Poetry in Performance*, 139–142; and Yu, *Race and the Avant-Garde*, 31–36.

28. Davidson, *Ghostlier Demarcations*, 206.

29. Marit J. MacArthur describes Ginsberg's performance on the PennSound version of this recording as "somewhat monotonous," and uses digital pitch tracking tools to analyze how his pitch builds with "rising intensity" over the first minutes of his reading of part 1. MacArthur follows PennSound's original misidentification (since corrected) of this recording as having been recorded at the San Francisco Poetry Center rather than at the KPFA studios—an error only worth noting because MacArthur goes on to emphasize the importance of "audience participation" to Ginsberg's poetics; audience participation is precisely what is absent in this radio reading ("Monotony," 54).

30. Mill, "Thoughts on Poetry," 348.

31. Ginsberg, *Howl: Original Draft Facsimile*, 63.

32. Naomi Ginsberg believed that doctors had implanted antennae into her spine during insulin and electric shock therapy, through which she could receive special

broadcasts from President Roosevelt (Ginsberg, *Howl: Original Draft Facsimile*, 130n43).

33. Ginsberg, letter to the editor, reprinted in Morgan and Peters, *Howl on Trial*, 209.

34. Foucault, *History of Sexuality*, 18, 17.

35. The program first appears in the program guide scheduled for June 27, 1957, though possibly as a rebroadcast; the PRA recording is dated June 12, 1957. *KPFA Program Folio* 8, no. 7 (June 23–July 6, 1957), Box 3, folder 15, PW.

36. The other panelists, in addition to Ferlinghetti, were University of California Professor of English Mark Schorer, who would be called as witness for the defense; book critic William Hogan, who argued against the censorship of "Howl" in the *San Francisco Chronicle*; attorney George Brunn, who had participated in a legal study of customs and post office censorship; and librarian LeRoy Merritt, co-chair of the California Library Association Intellectual Freedom Committee.

37. "Panel on 'Howl,'" moderated by Lewis Hill, June 12, 1957, PRA, BB1894, CD copy of a reel-to-reel tape.

38. These comparisons are based on subtle differences between the PennSound and PRA copies of the recording. On the PennSound copy ("KPFA Pacifica Studio Recording"), you can hear Ginsberg's substitution of "blanked" and the exclusion of certain words and lines from his reading. The PRA copy ("Allen Ginsberg Reads His Poetry") appears to be the version as edited by the station for the June 1957 rebroadcast, with additional lines and words missing.

39. During the trial, the prosecution's quotation of specific lines from the poem repeatedly defied the legal precedent that had recently been set in *Roth v. United States* (1957), which defined obscenity in the context of the total work and not by way of individual words, lines, or passages.

40. Allen Ginsberg, "Why We Can't Air 'Howl,'" 1987, PRA, IZ0280, CD copy. As recently as 2014, a program about Ginsberg on *From the Vault*, a podcast and radio series created by the PRA, played only an excerpt from the 1956 recording of "Howl," prefacing it with the statement that "it is still illegal to air 'Howl' on American airwaves without language edits." "FTV443 Allen Ginsberg's 'Howl,'" *From the Vault: A Weekly Radio Program from the Pacifica Radio Archives*, November 7, 2014, MP3, https://fromthevaultradio.org/home/2014/11/07/ftv-443-allen-ginsbergs-howl/.

41. Anticipating that "Howl" would face censorship issues, Ferlinghetti and Ginsberg replaced some words with dashes in the first printings of the book; after the trial, these words were restored, with the exception of the line discussed here.

42. Ginsberg, *Howl: Original Draft Facsimile*, xii.

43. Ibid., 131n48.

44. The full line—"who were expelled from the academies for crazy & publishing obscene odes on the windows of the skull"—alludes to Ginsberg's expulsion from Columbia in 1945 for having Jack Kerouac stay over in his dorm room and for tracing lewd and antisemitic graffiti on his dirty window in protest of them not being cleaned. Ginsberg, *Howl*, 9; Schumacher, *Dharma Lion*, 54–55.

45. Ginsberg, *Howl: Original Draft Facsimile*, 126n20.
46. Morgan and Peters, eds., *Howl on Trial*, 119.
47. Ellingham and Killian, *Poet Be Like God*, 118.
48. Davidson, *Guys Like Us*, 41.
49. Duncan's publication of "The Homosexual in Society" in 1944, and the immediate negative impact that it had on his publishing opportunities, deeply affected Spicer and shaped his views on what it meant to be an openly gay writer in a hostile publishing industry.
50. James Merrill, who shared with Spicer an interest in the occult, an obsession with Cocteau's *Orphée*, and a queer poetics of dictation (though one arguably less radical and totalizing than Spicer's), also figured the spirit voices coming to his Ouija board as transmitting via "Pulse of the galactic radio / Tuned then to mortal wavelength" in his epic, *The Changing Light at Sandover*, 360.
51. Gizzi, "Afterword." Though recent scholars have reiterated the importance of the radio motif to Spicer's work, few have taken up Gizzi's radio-specific line of inquiry. Daniel Katz, for example, includes radio as part of a series of interchangeable motifs in Spicer's poetry associated with circulation and correspondence, including the letter and the post office, the telephone and the switchboard, and the computer and the network, in *Poetry of Jack Spicer*.
52. Robin Blaser's 1975 essay, "The Practice of Outside," established the importance of dictation to Spicer's poetics but made no mention of the radio metaphor. Critics who followed after Blaser in the late 1970s through the 1990s often did mention the radio motif, but rarely provided extended analysis; Joseph Conte's analysis of the radio imagery in Spicer's *Language* is an exception among this generation of critics in *Unending Design*, 105–121.
53. Davidson, *San Francisco Renaissance*, 155. See also Snediker, *Queer Optimism*, 140–146; Hlibchuk, "From Typology to Topology," 317–320.
54. Davidson, *San Francisco Renaissance*, 155.
55. Katz, *Poetry of Jack Spicer*, 8.
56. Snediker, *Queer Optimism*, 141.
57. John Emil Vincent also focuses on Spicer's lyric poems as central to his queer poetics and critiques what he sees as an overemphasis among critics on Spicer's lectures and theory of seriality in *Queer Lyrics*, 149–176.
58. Cocteau cast his former lover Jean Marais in the film's title role, and his young protégé and eventual heir Edouard Dermit in the role of Cégeste. Critics have also suggested that the character of the Princess (played by María Casares) may have been modeled after the American drag performer and aerialist Barbette (Vander Clyde Broadway), who appeared in the first of Cocteau's Orphic trilogy, *Le Sang d'un poète* (1930).
59. Katz, *Poetry of Jack Spicer*, 10.
60. On the poetry and radio imagery of the film *Orpheus*, see Gallo, "Jean Cocteau's Radio Poetry."
61. Cocteau, *Orphée*, in *Three Screenplays*, 112. The original script in French reads:

LA PRINCESSE: La radio! *Gros plan de la main de Heurtebise sur le bouton de la radio. Grésillements. Ondes courtes. On entende le télégraphe, puis une phrase:*
LA RADIO: Le silence va plus vite à reculons. Trois fois. Le silence va plus vite à reculons. Trois fois ... (*télégraphe*).
(COCTEAU, *Orphée: The Play and the Film*, 75; ellipsis in original)

62. The first book, "Homage to Creeley," was first printed as a standalone work in a mimeo edition in 1959; the complete three-book work was first published in 1962 (*MV*, 451).

63. See, for example, "Song for Bird and Myself," which also includes references to the play version of *Orpheus* (*MV*, 69-72).

64. Douglas, *Listening In*, 70.

65. Ellingham and Killian, *Poet Be Like God*, 336-341.

66. I allude here to the so-called "antisocial thesis" in queer theory. See, especially, Bersani, *Homos*; Edelman, *No Future*; and Caserio et al., "Antisocial Thesis."

67. The bracketed "goddamn" is audible in the recording but absent from Gizzi's otherwise very faithful transcription. Jack Spicer, "Lecture 2, part 1," June 15, 1965, PennSound, MP3 copy, https://media.sas.upenn.edu/pennsound/authors/Spicer/Vancouver-lecture/Spicer-Jack_Vancouver-Lecture-02-A_6-15-65.mp3.

68. Long before PennSound made digital copies of the recordings of Spicer's lecture broadly public, Pacifica Radio broadcast a recording of the first lecture (acquired from Blaser) as part of a 1966 memorial program on Spicer.

69. Nealon, *Matter of Capital*, 117.

Chapter 4

1. Ginsberg, *Collected Poems*, 209.

2. After WWII, the Lower East Side saw the arrival of Puerto Rican migrants, the departure of many Jewish and white residents, and a decline in manufacturing that, combined with urban disinvestment, resulted in an excess of empty properties that were converted into the cheaply rented flats and lofts that property developers used to attract a young, white, bohemian artist class.

3. Lasar, *Pacifica Radio*, 167-168.

4. "The Aims of WBAI," *WBAI Program Folio* 3, no. 8 (April 16-29, 1962), 3, PF, https://archive.org/details/wbaifolio38wbairich/mode/2up.

5. Land, *Active Radio*, 115. Jeff Land estimates that around 600,000 listeners tuned in weekly to WBAI in the late 1960s; in 1971, the station boasted nearly 30,000 paying subscribers (115-116). WBAI's audience declined precipitously in the 1970s and never reached these numbers again.

6. Ginsberg, "Allen Ginsberg," 194. My discussion of this interview is also informed by a partial recording in Paul Blackburn's audio archive. Though Ossman has claimed that "this historic conversation was never edited for broadcast" (Ginsberg, "Allen Ginsberg," 223), Blackburn's recording, recorded off the radio, indicates that it was.

"WBAI Interview with Allen Ginsberg. Poetry Reading by Paul Blackburn and Robert Donat," Paul Blackburn Audio Collection (hereafter BA), Archive for New Poetry, ANP Tapes SPL-155, streaming audio copy of a reel-to-reel tape, University of California, San Diego, https://library.ucsd.edu/dc/object/bb4235029j.

7. Ginsberg, "Allen Ginsberg," 194, 194–195.

8. Ginsberg, *Collected Poems*, 255.

9. Ginsberg, *Collected Poems*, 255; *WBAI Program Folio*, 2, no. 4 (February 20–March 5, 1961), 4, PF, https://archive.org/details/wbaifolio24wbairich.

10. Baraka, then LeRoi Jones, was dubbed "King of the East Village" by Isabel Eberstadt in a 1964 article in the *New York Herald Tribune*; he took the Bantuized Muslim name Imamu Ameer Baraka (later Amiri Baraka) circa 1967–1968.

11. Baraka [Jones], *Dead*, 62.

12. "Eye on New York," WCBS-TV program script for May 31, 1959, Paul Blackburn Papers, Box 19, folder 8, Archive for New Poetry, University of California, San Diego (hereafter BP). Ellipses in original.

13. Kane, *All Poets Welcome*, 2.

14. Allen, preface, in *New American Poetry*, xi.

15. Of the forty-four poets whose work appeared in *The New American Poetry*, all were white men with the exception of four white women (Helen Adam, Madeline Gleason, Barbara Guest, and Denise Levertov) and one African American writer (Baraka).

16. Ossman, "Sullen Art of David Ossman."

17. The poets who appeared on Ossman's radio shows and in *The New American Poetry* include Baraka, Blackburn, Ginsberg, Paul Carroll, Robert Creeley, Ed Dorn, Robert Duncan, Denise Levertov, Michael McClure, Kenneth Rexroth, and Gilbert Sorrentino. Many of the other poets featured on *The Sullen Art* or *The Poet in New York* were active in the downtown experimental poetry community, including George Economou, Clayton Eshleman, Robert Kelly, Jackson Mac Low, Rochelle Owens, Margaret Randall, Jerome Rothenberg, Armand Schwerner, and Diane Wakoski.

18. Nielsen, *Black Chant*, 79–80. Though Ossman did interview several women poets on his radio show, Levertov was the only woman included in the Corinth Books print edition of *The Sullen Art*.

19. The Lower East Side poetry community of the early 1960s has been the subject of several studies, anthologies, and edited collections. See Kane, *All Poets Welcome*; Bergé, *Light Years*; Clay and Phillips, *Secret Location*; De Loach, *East Side Scene*; Grundy, *Black Arts Poetry Machine*; and Thomas, "Alea's Children."

20. Kane, *All Poets Welcome*, 34.

21. Several of the women who contributed to Carol Bergé's massive retrospective *Light Years*, including Rochelle Owens, Margaret Randall, and Susan Sherman, look back critically on the sexism and homophobia of the early Lower East Side poetry community, though Bergé herself claims that "women operated under an assumptive equality" denied in almost every other avant-garde art and literary scene of the time

(Bergé, "Introduction," 17; see Owens, "Les Deux Megots"; Randall, "Poet Is Who I Am"; Sherman, "Home").

22. Ossman, *Recording the Revolution*, 13; Alan Golding offers possible reasons for why Ashbery and other New York School poets did not appear on Ossman's radio programs (Golding, introduction to *Sullen Art*, 7–8). Ossman's opinion of the New York School poets as "too 'uptown'" echoed Paul Blackburn, who, according to Kane, "viewed the poets of the New York School as perhaps a little too urbane, witty, and chatty to be welcomed fully into the relatively macho heterosexual scene that initially dominated the Lower East Side scene" (*All Poets Welcome*, 41). I would put it more starkly: for some of the male poets involved in seizing their territory in the New York poetry world, "uptown" was a homophobic signifier that they could use to distance their homosocial community from the queer associations of coterie. That it had little to do with geography is made evident by the fact that O'Hara lived from 1959 to 1963 on East Ninth Street near Avenue A on the Lower East Side. These geographic signifiers were also mutable: Baraka would later use "downtown" to signify a homosexual white bohemian coterie that must be rejected to move "uptown" to Harlem, rhetorically figured as a site for the reclaiming of a patriarchal Black masculinity.

23. Blackburn, "Paul Blackburn," 23. My analysis of this interview also draws from a recording of the broadcast that Blackburn taped off the radio; quotations are from the edited print interview unless otherwise indicated. "Interview with Paul Blackburn Conducted by David Ossman. Conversation with Paul Blackburn, LeRoi Jones and Joel Oppenheimer," recorded ca. 1960–1962, ANP Tapes SPL-161, BA, cassette copy of a reel-to-reel tape.

24. Blackburn, *Collected Poems*, 120; "Interview with Paul Blackburn Conducted by David Ossman."

25. As Marjorie Perloff wrote in a scathing review of Blackburn's *Collected Poems*, "It is not that the poet's response to this or that attractive woman, seen on a subway train, cannot be a fit occasion for poetry, but that Blackburn's language is mimetically reductive" and gives "no indication that Blackburn himself is aware that his poem is fetishizing the girl, that it is degrading to contemplate her as a piece of meat" (Perloff, "On the Other Side of the Field," 203, 205).

26. Blackburn, "Paul Blackburn," 25; "Interview with Paul Blackburn Conducted by David Ossman."

27. Blackburn, "Paul Blackburn," 25.

28. Davidson, *Guys Like Us*, 14–15.

29. Baraka [Jones], "LeRoi Jones," 80, 81. My analysis of this interview, here and later in the chapter, also draws from the archival recording in Ossman's audio collection; quotations are from the edited print interview unless otherwise indicated. "The Sullen Art with Dave Ossman and Guest—LeRoi Jones," July 20, 1960, David Ossman Tapes, Box 1, folder 9, WAV file copy of a reel-to-reel tape, University of Toledo Ward M. Canaday Center for Special Collections.

30. As Nielsen observes, "probably never before Baraka had any black poet been

so instrumental in the early careers of white poets, so integral a player in the development of the emerging poetics of his time" (*Writing between the Lines*, 216). On the importance of Baraka's early editorial work with *Yugen, The Floating Bear*, and *Kulchur*, see Lee, *Poetics of Emergence*, 41–65.

31. Nielsen, *Writing between the Lines*, 222.

32. Ossman, *Recording the Revolution*, 13. Steve Post describes WBAI's audience in the early 1960s in similarly disparaging terms: "The 'typical' WBAI listener, then, might have been described as middle-aged, well-educated, politically left (possibly a 1930s union activist and/or veteran of the Lincoln Brigade), and culturally and artistically sophisticated. I certainly would not have been a listener during those years. In fact, I knew no one who listened, or, at least, no one who would admit to it" (*Playing in the FM Band*, 67).

33. Ossman, introduction, in *Sullen Art*, 9.

34. O'Hara, *Collected Poems*, 499.

35. Kane, *All Poets Welcome*, xv.

36. Ossman directed the KPFK Drama and Literature department for a few years, and in 1966, he joined Peter Bergman, Philip Proctor, and Phil Austin as the Firesign Theatre comedy group on the late-night call-in show *Radio Free Oz*. Firesign Theatre went on to create surreal, improvisatory works of audio theater that aired on KPFK and other FM freeform stations and were released as LP records that became cult favorites in the 1970s; later, Ossman created experimental arts programming for NPR.

37. Herntonand Henderson's meeting is recounted in Hernton, "Les Deux Megots Mon Amour," 293; and Kane, *All Poets Welcome*, 80–81. On the Umbra workshop, see Grundy, *Black Arts Poetry Machine*; Kane, *All Poets Welcome*, 79–90; Nielsen, *Black Chant*, 109–160; Thomas, "Shadow World."

38. Kane, *All Poets Welcome*, 48–54.

39. *WBAI Program Folio* 4, no. 17 (August 19–September 1, 1963), 10, PF, https://archive.org/details/wbaifolio417wbairich/mode/2up/.

40. Smethurst, *Black Arts Movement*, 148.

41. Baraka also appeared on WBAI around this time in his role as a jazz critic; in 1962, for example, he moderated a WBAI roundtable titled *Jazz of a Minority* with Ornette Coleman, Cecil Taylor, George Russell, and Gunther Schuller. *WBAI Program Folio* 3, no. 19 (September 17–30, 1962), 4, PF, https://archive.org/details/fowbai19620917ia/mode/2up; see also Nielsen, "'Now Is the Time,'" 35.

42. Bergé, "Remembrance of Things," 82.

43. "A Real Vision: Paul Blackburn Memorial Reading on Radio Station WBAI," 1972, ANP Tapes SPL-423, BA, streaming audio copy of a reel-to-reel tape, https://library.ucsd.edu/dc/object/bb54983946.

44. Holman, "Just a Moment."

45. Ong, *Orality and Literacy*.

46. Davidson, *Ghostlier Demarcations*, 196–223; Shaw, *Narrowcast*, 40.

47. Shaw argues that poets fixated on "radio because they had *access* to it as producers (not merely consumers), and they were often linked up (made aware of

one another) by radio in ways that were largely impossible with television," though his primary example is Cid Corman's WMEX-AM show from the early 1950s rather than FM "radio stations like KPFA" (noted in passing) (*Narrowcast*, 23, 26).

48. The term *narrowcasting* did not come into common usage until the invention of cable television, and, strictly speaking, the kind of radio stations I discuss in this book did not narrowcast but broadcast freely to anyone in the signal range with a receiver. My usage aligns with more figurative senses that describe targeted rhetorical appeals to narrowly defined markets or audiences. Narrowcasting in the form of market segmentation is also what propelled the commercial takeover of FM radio in the 1970s and 1980s. After the invention of album-oriented rock (AOR) formats successfully capitalized on freeform underground radio, commercial stations sought to maximize profitability by adopting new music and talk formats market-tested to appeal to specific audiences narrowed by region, race, gender, age, and other characteristics.

49. "WBAI Interview with Allen Ginsberg."

50. On Blackburn's tape exchange with Cortázar, see Feinsod, *Poetry of the Americas*, 216–217.

51. "Radio Broadcast of Gemini 7 Space Flight, Dec. 4, 1965," ANP Tapes SPL-244, BA, cassette copy of a reel-to-reel tape.

52. Blackburn, *Collected Poems*, 383, 384.

53. Kenneth Goldsmith's *The Weather* (2005) and *Traffic* (2007) take this kind of radio transcription to its conceptual endpoint by dedicating entire books to transcriptions of weather and traffic reports from New York AM radio station 1010 WINS.

54. "[Robert] Kelly Discusses Paul Blackburn on The Lipstick of Noise," recorded by Steve Evans, 2007, PennSound, MP3, https://media.sas.upenn.edu/pennsound/authors/Kelly/Kelly-Robert_Remembering-Blackburn_The-Lipstick-of-Noise_4-07.mp3.

55. Blackburn, "Paul Blackburn," 23.

56. Bob Fass quoted in Fisher, *Something in the Air*, 130.

57. See Fisher, *Something in the Air*, 127–157, and the 2014 film documentary *Radio Unnameable*, directed by Jessica Wolfson and Paul Lovelace.

58. Steve Post, "Thon Alice: A Semi-Accurate Recollection," *WBAI Folio* 13, no. 1 (January 1972), 8, PF, https://archive.org/details/wbaifolio131wbairich/mode/2up.

59. Poets from the Lower East Side poetry community who appeared on Blackburn's radio show (either in person or via prerecorded tapes of their performances) include Carol Bergé, Paul Carroll, Clayton Eshleman, Robert Kelly, John Keys, Joel Oppenheimer, and Diane Wakoski. Most of the other poets featured on the program had either also been invited by Blackburn to read at the coffeehouse series or were otherwise part of Blackburn's social and tape exchange networks; these include Robert Creeley, Robert Duncan, Ed Dorn, Ted Enslin, Charles Olson, and John Wieners.

60. "John Keys Reads His Work on Paul Blackburn's Contemporary Poetry Radio Program, December 2, 1964," ANP Tapes SPL-329, BA, streaming audio copy of a reel-to-reel tape, https://library.ucsd.edu/dc/object/bb0856167w.

61. Davidson, "'By Ear, He Sd.,'" 107.
62. Kane, *All Poets Welcome*, 54–55.
63. Jarolim, "Paul Blackburn," 28–29.
64. Nielsen, *Writing between the Lines*, 233.
65. Paul Blackburn, "Plain Song," ca. 1965–1966, Box 5, folder 12, BP. Spellman left New York soon after leaving WBAI, moving to Atlanta, where he helped establish several Black Arts cultural institutions; see Smethurst, *Black Arts Movement*, 336–338.
66. Michael Silverton, for example, featured many of the writers associated with the Poetry Project on his WBAI program *New York Poets* (1967–1968); Susan Howe occasionally broadcast edited recordings of Poetry Project workshops on her program *Poetry* (1975–1980); and beginning in the 1980s, WBAI began to regularly broadcast Poetry Project readings under the direction of John Fisk. The first iteration of the Nuyorican Poets Cafe grew out of a salon Miguel Algarín started in 1973 for Puerto Rican, Latinx, and African American writers; in 1977, Algarín started hosting *Live from the Nuyorican Poets Cafe* on WBAI, a regular monthly program that continued until the end of the reading series and then resumed when the venue began its second life in the 1990s on East Third Street.
67. This taping session was recorded on two reels, each of which also contains other content. The beginning of their conversation appears on the recording "Interview with Paul Blackburn Conducted by David Ossman," discussed earlier in this chapter; the rest is recorded on "A Saturday Night Taping: Poetry Reading and Discussion. Poetry Reading, July 11, 1962," ANP Tapes SPL-175, BA, streaming audio copy of a reel-to-reel tape, https://library.ucsd.edu/dc/object/bb51229627. The 1962 date is an estimated one given by the archive and is based contextually on other datable material on the second reel.
68. "Interview with Paul Blackburn Conducted by David Ossman."
69. Ibid.
70. "Saturday Night Taping."
71. Baraka [Jones], *Dead*, 63. For a revisionary queer reading of the rhetoric of homosexuality and rape in Baraka's work of this period, see Scott, *Extravagant Abjection*, 172–203.
72. "Saturday Night Taping."
73. Baraka [Jones], *Dead*, 64; "Saturday Night Taping."
74. Baraka (with Harris), "Interview," 174. Baraka's 1959 trip to Cuba, and subsequent activism with Fair Play for Cuba, On Guard for Freedom, the Organization of Young Men, and the 1961 UN protests, were instrumental to his developing political consciousness.
75. Baraka (with Benston), "Amiri Baraka: An Interview," 108; Baraka, *Fiction*, 176.
76. Baraka [Jones], "LeRoi Jones Talking." Daniel Matlin tracks the nuances of Baraka's shifting modes of address and reception in these years in *On the Corner*, 123–194.
77. Phillip Brian Harper complicates the claim that Black Arts poets rhetorically shifted their address to Black audiences in "Nationalism and Social Division."

78. On the cultural politics of Baraka's institution-building during his Black nationalist period, see Woodard, *Nation within a Nation*.

79. Smethurst, *Brick City Vanguard*, 117. Smethurst argues that even Allen Ginsberg "did not receive the same sort of attention to the implications of alterations in his actual performing voice (e.g., as a register of a changing sense of his Jewishness, his Jerseyness, his queerness, and so on) as Baraka did" (118).

80. Baraka [Jones], "How You Sound??"; Harris, "'How You Sound??,'" 313.

81. "The Sullen Art with David Ossman and Guest—LeRoi Jones." The other poems that Baraka read on the program were "For Hettie," "One Night Stand," and "The Turncoat."

82. On the radio as a trope in Baraka's early work, see Harrison, "LeRoi Jones's Radio."

83. Baraka [Jones], *Preface*, 12.

84. On Baraka's and Kerouac's shared love for *The Shadow* and American pop culture of the 1930s-1940s, see Harris, *Poetry and Poetics*, 51.

85. As Werner Sollors writes of the radio allusions in Baraka's poem "Look for You Yesterday, Here You Come Today": "What was once culture for the millions is now, in an ironically elitist turn, become a secret password, a code understood only by those few visionaries who are 'dumb' enough 'to be sentimental about anything'" (*Amiri Baraka/LeRoi Jones*, 54).

86. Daniel Punday asserts that the "evol" pun is "a purely typographical one and just the sort of link that a speech by The Shadow could not invoke" ("Black Arts Movement," 786), but as radio scholar Jason Loviglio observes, Cranston/The Shadow was a master of transduction as well as hypnosis, with many of the radio plots hinging on his expert use of electronic communication media to send coded messages, disrupt nefarious plots, and sway public opinion (*Radio's Intimate Public*, 102-122). In my view, Baraka's "evol" pun is very much in the spirit of the radio hero, though transmuted to different ends.

87. Morrison, *Playing in the Dark*, 46.

88. "The Sullen Art with Dave Ossman and Guest—LeRoi Jones."

89. On Baraka's early recordings and reading style, see Smethurst, *Brick City Vanguard*, 128-139.

90. Baraka, *Autobiography*, 27.

91. Ibid., 61-62.

92. Ellison, *Invisible Man*, 581.

93. Baraka [Jones], *Preface*, 12.

94. Matlin, *On the Corner*, 132.

95. Thomas, *Extraordinary Measures*, 201.

96. Ibid., 201-202.

97. "Gwendolyn Brooks and LeRoi Jones Poetry Reading," 2 parts, recorded August 1964, PRA, BB1910A and BB1910B, streaming audio copies of reel-to-reel tapes; https://archive.org/details/pacifica_radio_archives-BB1910A (part 1); https://archive.org/details/pacifica_radio_archives-BB1910B. (part 2). The Negro Writers Conference at

Asilomar was covered by *Newsweek*, *Negro Digest*, *Ebony*, the *San Francisco Chronicle*, and other national and local press outlets. Baraka's own brief account appears in his *Autobiography*, 280-281; Kenneth Rexroth, who participated in the conference, also provided a bombastic account for the *San Francisco Examiner*, "Descendants of a Heroic Negro Past."

98. Baraka's lectures at Asilomar were titled "Tell It Like It Is: The Young Negro Writer" and "Philistinism and the Negro Writer," the latter of which excerpted from his essay "LeRoi Jones Talking."

99. In addition to the PRA digital recordings cited, PennSound has a digital copy of Baraka's reading only. Brooks's reading has not received the same scholarly attention as Baraka's; Raphael Allison's analysis is an exception in *Bodies on the Line*, 128-133.

100. *WBAI Program Folio*, 5, no. 21 (November 9-22, 1964), Box 11, folder 7, PW.

101. New York Art Quartet with Baraka [Jones], *New York Art Quartet*.

102. There is some debate about whether the NYAQ's ESP-Disk sessions at Bell Sound Studios were recorded on November 2 or 26, 1964; Ben Young convincingly argues in favor of the November 2 date based on contemporaneous press reports in the liner notes to *Call It Art*, 78.

103. On these recently rediscovered recordings, see Nielsen, *Inside Songs*, 28-31.

104. "Poetry Reading, December 26, 1963," ANP Tapes, SPL-193, BA, cassette copy of a reel-to-reel tape.

105. Nielsen, *Black Chant*, 191.

106. Vera Hopkins, "Background for Directors of Pacifica Foundation," March 5-7, 1965, Box 1, folder 1, PW.

107. Vera Hopkins, Minutes of the meeting of the Pacifica Foundation Board, March 5-7, 1965, Box 1, folder 1, PW.

108. Harris, "How You Sound??," 314; see also Smethurst, *Brick City Vanguard*, 141-148; Nielsen, *Black Chant*, 190-195; Reed, *Soundworks*, 119-125; and Benston, *Performing Blackness*, 220.

109. "Gwendolyn Brooks and LeRoi Jones Poetry Reading," part 2 (BB1910B).

110. Baraka [Jones], *Dead*, 62-63.

111. Moten, *In the Break*, 97.

112. Nielsen, *Black Chant*, 195.

113. Reed, *Soundworks*, 124, 125.

114. Baraka [Jones], *Dead*, 62.

115. Baraka [Jones], *Black Magic*, 192.

116. Ibid., 115.

117. Ibid., 225.

Chapter 5

1. Rich, *Dream*, 16-17.
2. Friedan, *Feminine Mystique*.
3. Rich, "When We Dead Awaken."
4. Goodman, "Distracted Listening," 24-28.

5. Lacey, *Feminine Frequencies*, 45.
6. Cathy Cade to KPFA, March 14, 1971, Box 12, PW.
7. Rainone, "Men and Violence," 63.
8. Hill, "Private Room."
9. Community radio stations were important sites of feminist media activism, and feminist broadcasters were active in the formation of the National Federation of Community Broadcasters in 1975. Women's advocacy also led the Corporation for Public Broadcasting to form a Task Force on Women in Public Broadcasting, whose 1975 report found that women were significantly discriminated against in employment and underrepresented in public media and made recommendations for addressing the inequity. Isber and Cantor, *Report of the Task Force*.
10. See, e.g., Federici, *Re-enchanting the World*; Hardt and Negri, *Commonwealth*; Harney and Moten, *Undercommons*.
11. On U.S. feminist radio of the 1970s and 1980s, see Carter, "A Mic of Her Own"; De La Torre, *Feminista Frequencies*. On feminist radio and women's community radio activism beyond the U.S. (and especially in the context of Western feminist movements), see Arthurs and Zacharias, "Women and Radio"; O'Brien, "Women in Community Radio"; Copeland, "Broadcasting Queer Feminisms"; Mitchell, "Re-Sounding Feminist Radio"; and Mitchell, *Women and Radio*.
12. Voyce, *Poetic Community*, 170.
13. Ibid., 185.
14. Ibid., 200.
15. *WBAI Folio* (March 1978), PF, https://archive.org/details/wbaifoliomar78 wbairich/mode/2up. This program guide also reports on Pacifica's upcoming Supreme Court case, which concerned the FCC's censure of Pacifica for indecency after a daytime WBAI freeform program broadcast George Carlin's "Filthy Words" comedy routine in 1973. Oral arguments for *FCC v. Pacifica Foundation* took place on April 18–19, 1978; the consequential Supreme Court decision, which ruled against Pacifica and affirmed that the government agency could regulate indecency and not only obscenity in broadcasting, was handed down on July 13.
16. As for mapping stronger social ties: Susan Howe's friendship with Maureen Owen stands out, and we could use the connection each had to the St. Mark's Poetry Project to create further East Village links with JoAnne Akalaitis and Miguel Algarín. Similarly, we could connect Audre Lorde and Donna Allegra through their involvement in a network of East Coast Black lesbian feminist writers, or Lorde, Robin Morgan, Kate Ellis, and some of the other producers in the WBAI Women's Department through their publications in the same second-wave feminist periodicals.
17. Whitehead seeks an inclusive definition of the feminist poetry movement, but her characterization of the movement's dominant poetics as defined by an effort "to strip language and form of excess flourish and meaning and make it accessible to ordinary women" would exclude poets interested in formal experimentalism (*Feminist Poetry Movement*, xix). The sense among experimental women writers of being doubly marginalized in the feminist poetry movement and a male-dominated

avant-garde is what spurred the emergence of a discourse on feminist avant-garde poetry. On the feminist poetry movement, see also Clausen, *Movement of Poets*; Flannery, *Feminist Literacies*, 97–131; Garber, *Identity Poetics*; and Ostriker, *Stealing the Language*. On avant-garde feminist poetry, see DuPlessis, *Pink Guitar*; Evans, *After Patriarchal Poetry*; Fraser, "Tradition of Marginality"; Hinton and Hogue, *We Who Love to Be Astonished*; Seita, *Provisional Avant-Gardes*, 129–159; and Vickery, *Leaving Lines of Gender*.

18. Paul K. Saint-Amour makes a similar point about how radio creates weak-tied literary networks, though his reference is the BBC, a very different institution than Pacifica, especially in terms of its relation to empire and state power ("Weak Theory, Weak Modernism," 450).

19. On "the 1970s" as it signifies discursively in contemporary feminist historiography as the essentializing feminist "past" that must be left behind or to which we must return (and the need to tell feminist histories differently), see Hemmings, *Why Stories Matter*; and Hemmings and Brain, "Imagining the Feminist Seventies." In the discourse of contemporary poetry studies, "the 1970s" signifies the beginning of a widening divide between, on the one hand, a multiethnic flourishing of "identity"-based poetry and, on the other, a white avant-garde most closely associated with Language writing; for scholarship that works to deconstruct this identity/experimental binary, see Keller and Miller, *Feminist Measures*; Kinnahan, *Lyric Interventions*; Leonard, "'Which Me Will Survive'"; Nielsen, *Black Chant*; and Yu, *Race and the Avant-Garde*.

20. Love, "Truth and Consequences," 239. See also, among others, Felski, *Limits of Critique*; Halberstam, *Queer Art of Failure*; Saint-Amour, *Weak Theory*; Sedgwick, *Touching Feeling*; Dimock, "Weak Theory."

21. Susan Stanford Friedman, for example, objects to "weak theory" on exactly these grounds, tracing the genealogy of her own career to 1970s feminist criticism that she "want[s] to see linked with the non-normative, persistent strength of the outsiders" rather than with "weakness" ("Provisionally Persistent"). Voyce, citing Jo Freeman's warnings about the "tyranny of structurelessness," also warns against romanticizing the decentralized networks of the women's movement (*Poetic Community*, 165).

22. See Dunaway, "Pacifica Radio"; Land, *Active Radio*, 113–132; Lasar, *Uneasy Listening*. These critics also see Pacifica's internal dissension in this period as related to structural problems with the network's management structure and external pressures, including its battles with the FCC and a changing media, political, and economic climate.

23. Pacifica Radio's expansion also met with resistance: KPFT was bombed twice in its first year of broadcasting by the Ku Klux Klan.

24. As KPFK program director Clare Spark put it, "A major question we had to deal with was whether one medium can serve as both an instrument for social change ... and a community-access open forum. A system of communications more rational than the commercial American one, which leaves room for neither alternative, would allow for both in separate media" (Spark, "Pacifica Radio," 578).

25. Saint-Amour, "Weak Theory, Weak Modernism," 439.

26. Kay Lindsey, producer, "The Role of the Black Woman in America," 1968, AWMHC, streaming audio copy of a reel-to-reel tape, https://archive.org/details/pacifica_radio_archives-BB3193.

27. Archival recordings of all five parts of Kay Lindsey's *Women* series are digitally available to stream as part of the AWMHC (BB3866.01-05).

28. Hole and Levine, *Rebirth of Feminism*, 275.

29. Rainone, "Men and Violence," 63.

30. As Lasar points out, Rainone's critics rarely acknowledged that "the majority of call-ins to WBAI's free-form segments came from men" (*Uneasy Listening*, 156). One of these freeform DJs, Steve Post, admitted that "Rainone took a good deal of abuse from the largely male-dominated staff (myself included)" but that "[l]istener reaction, on the other hand, was decisively affirmative.... *CR* [*Consciousness Raising*] ran for two years, and along the way probably touched and helped transform more lives than all of WBAI's broadcasting of the previous decades" (Post, *Playing in the FM Band*, 104).

31. Liza Cowan, "A Letter to the Staff and Listeners—," *WBAI Folio* 12, no. 11 (November 1971), PF, https://archive.org/details/wbaifolio1211wbairich. See also Lasar, *Uneasy Listening*, 154.

32. Judy Pasternak, "A Short History of Women's Programming at WBAI," *WBAI Folio* (July/August 1993), 3–4, PF, https://archive.org/details/wbaifoliojulaug93wbairich/mode/2up; and, in the same issue, Sharon Griffiths, "Reflections from the Last Head of WBAI's Women's Department," 4.

33. Gilmore, *Groundswell*, 101.

34. Berkeley Women's Liberation, "Announcements."

35. Rosen, *World Split Open*, 207; Berkeley Women's Liberation, "Struggle."

36. Larry Lee, "Program Notes," *KPFA Folio* 23, no. 15 (March 1972), 5, PF, https://archive.org/details/kpfafoliomar72paci.

37. Vera Hopkins, who served as the institutional archivist for Pacifica Radio from the 1950s to the 1980s, is another important name to mention here. Indeed, my study is deeply indebted to Hopkins, who originally collected many of the institutional records now in the PW and PM. Her curatorial hand, however, has at times also presented challenges, most notably for this chapter; as Lasar puts it, Hopkins was "no friend to Third World departments anywhere" (nor to women's departments, for that matter), and consequently network records from this period provide a clear example of how gendered and racialized erasures get produced in archive creation (*Uneasy Listening*, 125).

38. The longest-running feminist radio collective in the United States is the Sophie's Parlor Media Collective, which originally formed at Georgetown University station WGTB-FM in 1972; the collective and its program, *Sophie's Parlor*, moved to Pacifica station WPFW-FM in Washington, DC, where it still broadcasts today. For other examples, see Carter, "Mic of Her Own," 172–180.

39. Flannery, *Feminist Literacies*, 13.

40. Whitehead, *Feminist Poetry Movement*, xix.

41. Chesman and Joan, *Guide to Women's Publishing*, 3. On the importance of women's poetry readings, especially, to feminist and lesbian feminist communities, see Garber, *Identity Poetics*; Grahn, "Women's Poetry Readings (Part 1)" and "Women's Poetry Readings (Part 2)"; and Jaffer, "For Women Poets."

42. Nanette Rainone and Mimi Weisbord Anderson, producers, "The Blood Jet Is Poetry: The Life and Work of Sylvia Plath," [1971], 2 parts, AWMHC, streaming audio copies of reel-to-reel tapes, https://archive.org/details/pacifica_radio_archives-BC0636A (part 1); https://archive.org/details/pacifica_radio_archives-BC0636B (part 2). Rainone, notably, was not as invested in women's poetry as some of the other feminist producers at WBAI; in "An Abridged History of Women's Programming," which she wrote for the *Folio* in 1972, she stated that she was "disappointed" when *Womankind* "began to rely on 'cultural' programming" including "poetry readings" instead of "new groups, takeovers, demonstrations, conferences." *WBAI Folio* 13, no. 9 (October 1972), 4, PF, https://archive.org/details/wbaifolio139wbairich/mode/2up.

43. Whitehead, *Feminist Poetry Movement*, 31.

44. Pacifica Foundation, "Articles of Incorporation of Pacifica Foundation (a Non-profit Corporation) as Amended," 1948, Box 1, PW.

45. Lindsey described her own sense of struggle against the erasure of Black women in the women's liberation movement in an essay titled "The Black Woman as a Woman," published in Toni Cade Bambara's landmark anthology *The Black Woman* (1970).

46. At WBAI, for example, these conflicts reached a crisis level in 1976–1977 when a new program director, Pablo Yoruba Guzman, announced his intention to overhaul WBAI's programming around popular music and a "nuevo barrio" sound, aiming to appeal to Latinx and Black audiences. In protest, a contingent of the station's programmers, including freeform DJ Bob Fass, occupied the station and its transmitter control room at the Empire State Building; Pacifica took the station off the air, and the lockout lasted over a month, after which the station largely reverted to its earlier piecemeal approach to programming (with dysfunction as a norm). The women's collective seized the moment and successfully petitioned to become an official department, while the Third World Department was disbanded. Land, *Active Radio*, 129–132; Lasar, *Uneasy Listening*, 157–158.

47. A few examples: Deloris Costello started the program *Black Awareness* at WBAI in 1970 and founded and directed WBAI's Third World Communications Vanguard collective from 1972 to 1977. Yolande de Freitas, a young multiracial woman, spent a short, contentious tenure at KPFA from 1971 to 1972 as one of only two women in paid (half-time) staff positions, during which time she produced Black, Chicana, and transnational feminist programs for *Unlearning to Not Speak* and led demands for the establishment of the Third World department. Peggy Berryhill (Muscogee) also started working at KPFA in 1973 as a student journalist for the *Native American Student's Hour*, which she transformed into the celebrated and long-running weekly program *Living on Indian Time*.

48. Blackwell, ¡Chicana Power!, 27.
49. Larry Josephson quoted in Land, *Active Radio*, 126; Lasar, *Uneasy Listening*, 155.
50. Listener letter to KPFA, October 10, 1976, Box 17, PW; emphasis in original.
51. Land, *Active Radio*, 125.
52. Poetry had certainly been broadcast live on WBAI before on freeform programs and fundraising marathons, but it may be true that this was the first poetry event with a live studio audience that WBAI hosted. Daniela Gioseffi et al., performers, "Women's Poetry Evening," produced by Mimi Anderson and Brett Vuolo, October 7, 1972, 2 parts, AWMHC, streaming audio copies of reel-to-reel tapes, https://archive.org/details/pacifica_radio_archives-BC1223A (part 1); https://archive.org/details/pacifica_radio_archives-BC1223B (part 2).
53. Gioseffi et al., "Women's Poetry Evening" (part 1). Robin Morgan also performed at this reading her poem about Plath, "Arraignment," which accuses Ted Hughes of being responsible for Plath's death.
54. Jong, *Half-Lives*, 25, 26.
55. Lorde had previously appeared on WBAI in July 1972 as one of the featured poets on the series *Women Poets Reading*. "Audre Lorde (Episode 4 of 4)," produced by Mimi Anderson, July 7, 1972, AWMHC, streaming audio copy of a reel-to-reel tape, https://archive.org/details/pacifica_radio_archives-BC0949.04.
56. Lorde, *Collected Poems*, 92; Gioseffi et al., "Women's Poetry Evening" (part 1).
57. Leonard, "'Which Me Will Survive,'" 766.
58. Gioseffi et al., "Women's Poetry Evening" (part 1).
59. Spillers, "Mama's Baby," 65. Leonard also cites Spillers's article as part of his analysis of the significance of the name "girls" in Lorde's "Who Said It Was Simple" ("'Which Me Will Survive,'" 765).
60. Lamm, *Addressing the Other Woman*, 51.
61. Lorde quoted in De Veaux, *Warrior Poet*, xiv; Lorde, *Zami*.
62. A 1979 recording of Lorde on a late-night WBAI live call-in show hosted by the Black feminist poet Judy Dothard Simmons, for example, offers a vibrant counterportrait of Lorde in a relaxed, flirtatious, loquacious performance. "Aude Lorde Interviewed by Judy Simmons (Part 1 of 4)," 1979, AWMHC, streaming audio copy of a reel-to-reel tape, https://archive.org/details/pacifica_radio_archives-IZ1339A.
63. Bessie Smith Memorial Production Collective, letter to the editor; Smith and Smith, "Varied Voices." The Bessie Smith Memorial Production Collective was formed by members of the Combahee River Collective to organize these concerts.
64. Pat Parker, Gwen Avery, Linda Tillery, and Mary Watkins, performers, "The Varied Voices of Black Women: An Olivia Records Concert," produced by Donna Allegra, Adrienne Gantt, Judie Pasternak, and Viv Sutherland, recorded November 7, 1978, AWMHC, streaming audio copy of a reel-to-reel tape, https://archive.org/details/pacifica_radio_archives-IZ1427.
65. Parker was invited to headline the Varied Voices tour as the only poet because of her connection to Olivia Records; in 1976, she had released a spoken word album

with Judy Grahn, *Where Would I Be without You*, and she had also collaborated as a lyricist on one of Mary Watkins's albums.

66. Smith, untitled essay, 39; Parkerson, untitled essay, 30.

67. Parker et al., "Varied Voices."

68. Parker, *Complete Works*, 160.

69. Donna Allegra, host, "The Lesbian Show—October 23, 1978: Varied Voices of Black Women," interview with Pat Parker, Linda Tillery, and Mary Watkins, AWMHC, streaming audio copy of a reel-to-reel tape, https://archive.org/details/pacifica_radio_archives-IZ1060.

70. Parker does not directly address the issue of transphobia in lesbian-feminist communities in this interview, but her account of being run out of both women's restrooms and lesbian bars as a Black butch woman points to the intersection of anti-Black racism and cisheterosexism. Also of potential relevance here are the transphobic attacks on Sandy Stone, a white trans woman who worked as Olivia Records' sound engineer (including for Parker's album) until she was forced to resign the women's collective in 1977 after receiving death threats and after a group of lesbian feminists threatened to boycott the label.

71. Parker, *Complete Works*, 162.

72. Blackwell, *¡Chicana Power!*, 27.

73. Parker, *Complete Works*, 101; Parker et al., "Varied Voices."

74. Lordi, "Souls Intact," 67.

75. In their interview with Allegra, Parker and Tillery both discussed the importance of their sartorial style as part of their performance aesthetic.

76. Parker et al., "Varied Voices."

77. Vickery, *Leaving Lines*, 77–87. In the 1970s and 1980s, program directors Charles Ruas at WBAI, Charles Amirkhanian at KPFA, and Paul Vangelisti at KPFK brought a renewed emphasis on innovative poetry, drama, music, and sound art to the network's cultural programming. Howe's *Poetry* and the KPFA program *In the American Tree* (1978–1981), which was initially hosted by Lyn Hejinian and Kit Robinson (and later by Alan Bernheimer and then Erica Hunt), were especially instrumental in bringing writers associated with Language writing to Pacifica. Language writers' engagements with radio as producers and in their own "counterpunching" poetry is beyond my scope, but merits further study, especially in relation to their critique of voice in poetry and commercial broadcast media.

78. In addition to Lorde, a few male poets of color (Ishmael Reed, Simon J. Ortiz, Tom Weatherly) appeared as featured readers on *Poetry*, but in general the whiteness of Howe's radio program, while not surprising, is nevertheless striking when considered in the broadcast context of WBAI in the late 1970s. Race is not only a question of representation, though, and it would be worth considering when a discourse on race, including as intersected with gender, becomes audible on Howe's radio programs, especially in the context of what Timothy Yu identifies as "the 'ethnicization' of the avant-garde" in this period among white male Language writers (*Race and the Avant-Garde*, 17).

NOTES TO PAGES 179–183

79. Howe (with Hudspith), "Interview with Susan Howe."

80. Vickery, *Leaving Lines*, 79.

81. Howe (with Hudspith), "Interview with Susan Howe."

82. Mayer, "Bernadette Mayer with Susan Howe." The audio can be accessed via PennSound; Susan Howe and Bernadette Mayer, "Bernadette Mayer, April 22, 1979," PennSound, MP3 copy, https://writing.upenn.edu/pennsound/x/Howe-Pacifica.php.

83. Tape recordings and transcripts, for example, are central to *Memory*, which Mayer first exhibited as a multimedia installation in 1972; see Kilbane, "Sounding Memory."

84. Mayer, "Bernadette Mayer with Susan Howe."

85. Jasper Bernes reads Mayer's 1970s poetry and its motif of speed in relation to the multitasking that increasingly comes to define the "double day" of feminized labor in the late twentieth century (*Work of Art*, 120–148).

86. Mayer, "Bernadette Mayer with Susan Howe."

87. Bernes, *Work of Art*, 137. The labor of audio transcription was a constant chore for me in the research for this book, so I am grateful here to Michael Nardone for publishing the interview transcript (Mayer, "Bernadette Mayer with Susan Howe").

88. Nelson, *Women, the New York School*, 110.

89. Mayer, *Midwinter Day*, 99.

90. Mayer, *Eating the Colors*, 426.

91. Davidson, *Ghostlier Demarcations*, 207; Mayer, *Eating the Colors*, 426. In this poem, the sense of hurry also arises from a classic lyric theme: the poet's meditation on mortality.

92. On Mayer's turn toward lyricism and a speech-based poetics in the late 1970s against the tide of Language poetry's critique of both, see White, *Lyric Shame*, 154–209.

93. Mayer, "Bernadette Mayer, April 22, 1979."

94. Susan Howe, Letter of support for grant application to the National Endowment for the Humanities for "The World Viewed," November 1, 1979, Susan Howe Papers, Box 70, folder 6, Archive for New Poetry, University of California, San Diego.

95. Susan Howe to Lyn Hejinian, December 26, 1978, Lyn Hejinian Papers, Box 4, folder 18, Archive for New Poetry, University of California, San Diego.

96. Susan Howe to Lyn Hejinian, December 7, 1978, Hejinian Papers, Box 4, folder 18.

97. Shaw, *Narrowcast*, 3.

98. Charles Bernstein uses the term "audiotext" (over *recorded, performed,* or *oral poem*) for "the audible acoustic text of the poem," which puts emphasis on the sounding(s) of the poem over the expressive performance of the poet (*Close Listening*, 12).

99. Vickery, *Leaving Lines*, 80.

100. Like Spicer's and Baraka's, Howe's radio aesthetic was also shaped by her nostalgic attachment to network-era radio; as she reflected in a 1995 interview with Lynn Keller, "I am a product of radio days. My childhood imagination was shaped by

listening to *The Lone Ranger, The Shadow, Grand Central Station* ... not just music as on FM radio now, but drama, news, all popular culture" (Howe [with Keller], "Interview with Susan Howe," 14).

101. As a CBS news commentator in the 1940s, Quincy Howe "was one of the first radio journalists to bring the news of World War II into American homes"; his biography, as a former director of the ACLU and staunch isolationist turned influential war supporter, also intersects (and departs) in interesting ways with that of Lewis Hill (Applegate, "Howe, Quincy," 182). He died in 1977, but before his death, Susan Howe interviewed him for a radio documentary she produced on the Boston poet John Wheelwright, which brought her uncle's voice posthumously back onto radio when WBAI aired the program in 1980.

102. Drawing a speculative connection between Howe's radio program and her poetry, Vickery likewise observes that "[t]he role of the editor ... is strongly apparent in her work," including in *The Liberties* (1980), Howe's major poetic work of this period (*Leaving Lines*, 81).

103. Susan Howe to Brian O'Doherty, January 12, 1979, Howe Papers, Box 70, folder 3.

104. Susan Howe, "Final Report for Grant Period from 1 September 1978 to 30 June 1979," Howe Papers, Box 70, folder 5. Ironically, only around twenty of Howe's radio programs from her five years at WBAI appear in Pacifica Radio Archives catalog, and only five are included in the AWMHC; her own larger collection of radio tapes is housed at the Archive for New Poetry at the University of California, San Diego.

105. In 1979, the NEA denied Howe's grant renewal application for her radio programs on the grounds, according to Howe, that the Media Arts division had "decided not to fund *any* poetry projects." Though Howe was able to secure a smaller grant from the NEA Literature division, the fact that it could only be used to pay poets' honoraria and not to pay for her own labor forced Howe to reluctantly discontinue her radio work. Susan Howe to Lyn Hejinian, January 17, [1979], Hejinian Papers, Box 4, folder 18; additional correspondence and draft applications related to these grants are in Howe Papers, Box 70, folder 3.

106. For her program on the Women's Distribution Group, Howe interviewed members Barbara Barracks, Roberta Gould, Maureen Owen, Marty Potlinger, and Fran Winant. Pacifica's copy of the program has not been made publicly accessible for online streaming; Howe's own copy of the interview is held with her tape collection at the Archive for New Poetry. On the Women's Distribution Group and with reference to this radio interview, see Vickery, *Leaving Lines*, 65. Susan Howe, producer and interviewer, "The Women's Distribution Group," September 14, 1977, PRA, IZ0085, reel-to-reel tape; Susan Howe, "Interview, Sept. 14, 1977; Women's Distribution Group," Archive for New Poetry, ANP Tapes SPL-1128, cassette copy of a reel-to-reel tape.

107. Beiser and McGee, "Listening and Learning," 262.

108. Bamberger and Brylawski, *State of Recorded Sound Preservation*, vii.

109. Ibid., 20.

110. "About," Library of Congress Radio Preservation Task Force, https://radiopreservation.org/about/. The Sound Collections Database can be accessed at https://database.radiopreservation.org/; a keyword search of this still-growing database retrieves several radio collections with poetry recordings. See also Goodman et al., "Building the National Radio Recordings Database." Beyond the RPTF, other major digital preservation projects of relevance to the study of poetry and U.S. public radio are the American Archive of Public Broadcasting from the Library of Congress and GBH Archives, accessible at https://americanarchive.org/; and Unlocking the Airwaves, an online collection of recordings and print materials from the NAEB, accessible at https://www.unlockingtheairwaves.org/.

111. Aguilar, "NFCB Calls for Responsible Action"; Shepperd, "Endangered Sounds."

BIBLIOGRAPHY

Archival Sources

American Women Making History and Culture: 1963–1982 Collection, Pacifica Radio Archives, Internet Archive, https://archive.org/details/Pacifica_radio_archives_NHPRC1_American (AWMHC).
David Ossman Tapes, University of Toledo Ward M. Canaday Center for Special Collections, Toledo, Ohio.
Kenneth Rexroth Papers, Charles E. Young Research Library, University of California, Los Angeles (RC).
Little Magazine Collection, Department of Special Collections, University of Wisconsin–Madison.
Lyn Hejinian Papers, Archive for New Poetry, University of California, San Diego.
Pacifica Foundation Records, National Public Broadcasting Archives, University of Maryland Libraries, College Park, Maryland (PM).
Pacifica Foundation Records, Wisconsin Historical Society Archives, Madison, Wisconsin (PW).
Pacifica Radio Archives, North Hollywood, California (PRA).
Pacifica Radio Archives Digitized Folio Collection, Internet Archive, https://archive.org/details/pacifica (PF).
Pacifica Radio Sampler, Bancroft Library, University of California, Berkeley.
Paul Blackburn Audio Collection, Archive for New Poetry, University of California, San Diego (BA).
Paul Blackburn Papers, Archive for New Poetry, University of California, San Diego (BP).
PennSound, Center for Programs in Contemporary Writing, University of Pennsylvania, https://writing.upenn.edu/pennsound/.
The Poetry Center Digital Archive, San Francisco State University, https://diva.sfsu.edu/collections/poetrycenter.
The Poetry Center Records, Bancroft Library, University of California, Berkeley.
Susan Howe Papers, Archive for New Poetry, University of California, San Diego.
Untide Press Records, Bancroft Library, University of California, Berkeley (UC).
William Everson Papers, William Andrews Clark Memorial Library, University of California, Los Angeles.

BIBLIOGRAPHY

Published Sources

Adorno, Theodor W. "On the Fetish-Character in Music and the Regression of Listening." In *The Essential Frankfurt School Reader*, edited by Andrew Arato and Eike Gebhardt, 270–299. New York: Urizen, 1978.

Adorno, Theodor W. "Radio Physiognomics." In *Current of Music: Elements of a Radio Theory*, edited by Robert Hullot-Kentor, 41–132. Cambridge, UK: Polity, 2009.

Aguilar, Ernesto. "NFCB Calls for Responsible Action to Preserve and Protect the Pacifica Radio Archives." National Federation of Community Broadcasters, August 29, 2016. https://nfcb.org/nfcb-calls-to-save-the-pacifica-radio-archives/.

Allen, Donald, ed. *The New American Poetry, 1945–1960*. New York: Grove Press, 1960.

Allison, Raphael. *Bodies on the Line: Performance and the Sixties Poetry Reading*. Iowa City: University of Iowa Press, 2014.

Applegate, Edd. "Howe, Quincy 1900–1977." In *Biographical Encyclopedia of American Radio*, edited by Christopher H. Sterling and Cary O'Dell, concise and revised edition, 182–183. New York: Routledge, 2011.

Arthurs, Jane, and Usha Zacharias, eds. "Introduction: Women and Radio." *Feminist Media Studies* 7, no. 3 (2007): 333–348.

Avery, Todd. *Radio Modernism: Literature, Ethics, and the BBC, 1922–1938*. Aldershot, UK: Ashgate, 2006.

Bamberger, Rob, and Sam Brylawski, on behalf of the National Recording Preservation Board. *The State of Recorded Sound Preservation in the United States: A National Legacy at Risk in the Digital Age*. Washington, DC: Council on Library and Information Resources and Library of Congress, 2010.

Baraka, Amiri. "Amiri Baraka: An Interview." Interview by Kimberly W. Benston. In *Conversations with Amiri Baraka*, edited by Charlie Reilly, 105–117. Jackson: University Press of Mississippi, 1994.

Baraka, Amiri. *The Autobiography of LeRoi Jones*. Chicago: Chicago Review Press, 2012.

Baraka, Amiri [LeRoi Jones]. *Black Magic: Poetry 1961–1967*. Indianapolis: Bobbs-Merrill, 1969.

Baraka, Amiri [LeRoi Jones]. *Blues People: Negro Music in White America*. 1963. New York: Harper Perennial, 1999.

Baraka, Amiri [LeRoi Jones]. *The Dead Lecturer*. New York: Grove Press, 1964.

Baraka, Amiri [Imamu Amiri Baraka]. *The Fiction of LeRoi Jones/Amiri Baraka*. Chicago: Lawrence Hill Books, 2000.

Baraka, Amiri [LeRoi Jones]. "How You Sound??" In *The New American Poetry*, edited by Donald Allen, 424–425. New York: Grove Press, 1960.

Baraka, Amiri. "An Interview with Amiri Baraka." Interview by William J. Harris. 1980. In *Conversations with Amiri Baraka*, edited by Charlie Reilly, 168–180. Jackson: University Press of Mississippi, 1994.

Baraka, Amiri [LeRoi Jones]. "LeRoi Jones." Interview by David Ossman. In *Sullen Art: Interviews*, by Ossman, 77–81.

Baraka, Amiri [LeRoi Jones]. "LeRoi Jones Talking." In *Home: Social Essays*, 179–188. New York: William Morrow, 1966.

Baraka, Amiri [LeRoi Jones]. *Preface to a Twenty Volume Suicide Note . . . .* New York: Totem Press/Corinth Books, 1961.

Barlow, William. "Community Radio in the US: The Struggle for a Democratic Medium." *Media, Culture and Society* 10, no. 1 (1988): 81–105.

Barlow, William. *Voice Over: The Making of Black Radio*. Philadelphia: Temple University Press, 1999.

Barnouw, Erik. *A History of Broadcasting in the United States*. 3 vols. New York: Oxford University Press, 1966–1970.

Bartlett, Lee. *William Everson: The Life of Brother Antoninus*. New York: New Directions, 1988.

Beiser, Jolene M., and Holly Rose McGee. "Listening and Learning: Pacifica Radio Archives' 'American Women: 1963-1982' Digitization and Access Project." *Collections* 14, no. 3 (2018): 257–276.

Benston, Kimberly W. *Performing Blackness: Enactments of African-American Modernism*. London: Routledge, 2000.

Bergé, Carol. "Introduction (a Sociocultural Study)." In *Light Years*, edited by Bergé, 1–42.

Bergé, Carol, ed. *Light Years: An Anthology on Sociocultural Happenings (Multimedia in the East Village, 1960-1966)*. New York/Santa Fe: Spuyten Duyvil/AWAREing Press, 2010.

Bergé, Carol. "Remembrance of Things to Come." In *Light Years*, edited by Bergé, 77–103.

Berkeley Women's Liberation. "Announcements." *It Ain't Me Babe* 1, no. 13 (September 4–17, 1970): 19.

Berkeley Women's Liberation. "Struggle." *It Ain't Me Babe* 1, no. 11 (August 6–20, 1970): 5.

Bernes, Jasper. *The Work of Art in the Age of Deindustrialization*. Stanford, CA: Stanford University Press, 2017.

Bernstein, Charles, ed. *Close Listening: Poetry and the Performed Word*. New York: Oxford University Press, 1998.

Bersani, Leo. *Homos*. Cambridge, MA: Harvard University Press, 1995.

The Bessie Smith Memorial Production Collective. Letter to the editor. *Sojourner* 4, no. 5 (1979): 4.

Blackburn, Paul. *The Collected Poems of Paul Blackburn*. Edited by Edith Jarolim. New York: Persea Books, 1985.

Blackburn, Paul. "Paul Blackburn." Interview by David Ossman. In *Sullen Art: Interviews*, by Ossman, 22–26.

Blackwell, Maylei. *¡Chicana Power! Contested Histories of Feminism in the Chicano Movement*. Austin: University of Texas Press, 2011.

Blaser, Robin. "The Practice of Outside." 1975. In *The Collected Books of Jack Spicer*, by Jack Spicer, edited by Blaser, 271-329. Santa Rosa, CA: Black Sparrow Press, 1996.

"The Bleatniks." *Time*, August 11, 1961, sec. Leisure.

Bloom, Emily C. *The Wireless Past: Anglo-Irish Writers and the BBC, 1931-1968*. Oxford: Oxford University Press, 2016.

Bottomley, Andrew J. *Sound Streams: A Cultural History of Radio-Internet Convergence*. Ann Arbor: University of Michigan Press, 2020.

Campbell, Timothy C. *Wireless Writing in the Age of Marconi*. Minneapolis: University of Minnesota Press, 2006.

Cantwell, Robert. *When We Were Good: The Folk Revival*. Cambridge, MA: Harvard University Press, 1996.

Carter, Susan. "A Mic of Her Own: Stations, Collectives, and Women's Access to Radio." *Journal of Radio Studies* 11, no. 2 (2004): 169-183.

Caserio, Robert L., et al., contributors. "Forum: The Antisocial Thesis in Queer Theory." *PMLA* 121, no. 3 (2006): 819-828.

Casillas, Dolores Inés. *Sounds of Belonging: U.S. Spanish-Language Radio and Public Advocacy*. New York: NYU Press, 2014.

Challener, Scott. "Addressing 'Alien Worlds': Publics and Persons in the Poetry of Jack Spicer." *Contemporary Literature* 58, no. 4 (2017): 492-525.

Chasar, Mike. *Everyday Reading: Poetry and Popular Culture in Modern America*. New York: Columbia University Press, 2012.

Chasar, Mike. *Poetry Unbound: Poems and New Media from the Magic Lantern to Instagram*. New York: Columbia University Press, 2020.

Chesman, Andrea, and Polly Joan. *Guide to Women's Publishing*. Paradise, CA: Dustbooks, 1978.

Clausen, Jan. *A Movement of Poets: Thoughts on Poetry and Feminism*. New York: Long Haul Press, 1982.

Clay, Steven, and Rodney Phillips. *A Secret Location on the Lower East Side: Adventures in Writing, 1960-1980: A Sourcebook of Information*. New York: New York Public Library and Granary Books, 1998.

Cocteau, Jean. *Orphée*. In *Three Screenplays: L'Eternel Retour, Orphée, La Belle et la bête*, translated by Carol Martin-Sperry, 101-192. New York: Grossman Publishers, 1972.

Cocteau, Jean. *Orphée: The Play and the Film*. Edited by E. Freeman. London: Bristol Classical Press, 1992.

Cocteau, Jean, director. *Orpheus*. 1950. Criterion Collection, 2011. DVD.

Cohen, Debra Rae, Michael Coyle, and Jane Lewty, eds. *Broadcasting Modernism*. Gainesville: University Press of Florida, 2009.

Conte, Joseph M. *Unending Design: The Forms of Postmodern Poetry*. Ithaca, NY: Cornell University Press, 1991.

Copeland, Stacey. "Broadcasting Queer Feminisms: Lesbian and Queer Women Programming in Transnational, Local, and Community Radio." *Journal of Radio & Audio Media* 25, no. 2 (2018): 209-223.

Cyzewski, Julie. "Broadcasting Nature Poetry: Una Marson and the BBC's Overseas Service." *PMLA* 133, no. 3 (2018): 575–593.

Daley, Patrick, and Beverly A. James. *Cultural Politics and the Mass Media: Alaska Native Voices*. Urbana: University of Illinois Press, 2004.

Dangers, Jack. "Jack Dangers: The Mind of Meat Beat Manifesto." Interview by Paul Olson. *All About Jazz*, October 24, 2005. http://www.allaboutjazz.com11/jack-dangers-the-mind-of-meat-beat-manifesto-by-paul-olson.php.

Davidson, Michael. "'By Ear, He Sd.': Audio Tapes and Contemporary Criticism." *Credences* 1, no. 1 (1981): 105–120.

Davidson, Michael. *Ghostlier Demarcations: Modern Poetry and the Material Word*. Berkeley: University of California Press, 1997.

Davidson, Michael. *Guys Like Us: Citing Masculinity in Cold War Poetics*. Chicago: University of Chicago Press, 2004.

Davidson, Michael. *The San Francisco Renaissance: Poetics and Community at Mid-century*. Cambridge: Cambridge University Press, 1989.

De La Torre, Monica. *Feminista Frequencies: Community Building through Radio in the Yakima Valley*. Seattle: University of Washington Press, 2022.

De Loach, Allen, ed. *The East Side Scene: American Poetry, 1960–1965*. New York: Doubleday, 1972.

De Veaux, Alexis. *Warrior Poet: A Biography of Audre Lorde*. New York: Norton, 2004.

D'Emilio, John. "Gay Politics and Community in San Francisco since World War II." In *Hidden from History: Reclaiming the Gay and Lesbian Past*, edited by Martin B. Duberman, Martha Vicinus, and George Chauncey, 456–473. New York: Penguin, 1990.

DeShazor, Brian. "Queer Radio History: Pacifica Radio." *Journal of Radio & Audio Media* 25, no. 2 (2018): 253–265.

Dimock, Wai Chee. "Weak Theory: Henry James, Colm Tóibín, and W. B. Yeats." *Critical Inquiry* 39, no. 4 (2013): 732–753.

Douglas, Susan J. *Listening In: Radio and the American Imagination*. Minneapolis: University of Minnesota Press, 2004.

Doyle, Michael. *Radical Chapters: Pacifist Bookseller Roy Kepler and the Paperback Revolution*. Syracuse, NY: Syracuse University Press, 2012.

Dunaway, David K. "Pacifica Radio and Community Broadcasting." *Journal of Radio Studies* 12, no. 2 (2005): 240–255.

DuPlessis, Rachel Blau. *The Pink Guitar: Writing as Feminist Practice*. Tuscaloosa: University of Alabama Press, 2006.

Eberstadt, Isabel. "King of the East Village." *New York Herald Tribune*, December 13, 1964.

Edelman, Lee. *No Future: Queer Theory and the Death Drive*. Durham, NC: Duke University Press, 2004.

Ellingham, Lewis, and Kevin Killian. *Poet Be Like God: Jack Spicer and the San Francisco Renaissance*. Hanover, NH: Wesleyan University Press, 1998.

Ellison, Ralph. *Invisible Man*. 1952. New York: Vintage, 1995.
Evans, Steve, ed. *After Patriarchal Poetry: Feminism and the Contemporary Avant-Garde*. Special Issue of *differences: A Journal of Feminist Cultural Studies* 12, no. 2 (2001).
Everson, William. *The Residual Years*. New York: New Directions, 1948.
Everson, William. *The Waldport Poems*. Waldport, OR: Untide Press, 1944.
Everson, William. *X War Elegies*. Waldport, OR: Untide Press, 1943.
Faber, Liz W., and John L. Hochheimer. "Networking the Counterculture: The 1970 Alternative Media Conference at Goddard College." *Journal of Radio & Audio Media* 23, no. 2 (2016): 200–212.
Federici, Silvia. *Re-enchanting the World: Feminism and the Politics of the Commons*. Oakland, CA: PM Press, 2019.
Feinsod, Harris. *The Poetry of the Americas: From Good Neighbors to Countercultures*. New York: Oxford University Press, 2017.
Felski, Rita. *The Limits of Critique*. Chicago: University of Chicago Press, 2015.
Ferlinghetti, Lawrence. "Introduction: 'Howl' at the Frontiers." In *Howl on Trial*, edited by Morgan and Peters, xi–xiv.
Ferlinghetti, Lawrence, and Nancy J. Peters. *Literary San Francisco: A Pictorial History from Its Beginnings to the Present Day*. San Francisco: City Lights/Harper & Row, 1980.
Fisher, Marc. *Something in the Air: Radio, Rock, and the Revolution That Shaped a Generation*. New York: Random House, 2007.
Flannery, Kathryn Thoms. *Feminist Literacies, 1968–75*. Urbana: University of Illinois Press, 2005.
Forrest, Seth. "Aurality and Literacy: The New American Poets and the Age of Technological Reproduction." In *The New American Poetry: Fifty Years Later*, edited by John R. Woznicki, 199–220. Bethlehem, PA: Lehigh University Press, 2013.
Foucault, Michel. *The History of Sexuality*. Translated by Robert Hurley. 3 vols. New York: Vintage Books, 1990.
Fraser, Kathleen. "The Tradition of Marginality." *Frontiers: A Journal of Women Studies* 10, no. 3 (1989): 22–27.
Fredman, Stephen. *Contextual Practice: Assemblage and the Erotic in Postwar Poetry and Art*. Stanford, CA: Stanford University Press, 2010.
Friedan, Betty. *The Feminine Mystique*. 1963. New York: Norton, 2001.
Friedman, Susan Stanford. "Provisionally Persistent." In "Responses to the Special Issue on Weak Theory, Part III," edited by Debra Rae Cohen. *Modernism/Modernity Print Plus*, April 2, 2019. https://modernismmodernity.org/forums/posts/responses-special-issue-weak-theory-part-iii.
Frost, Gary L. *Early FM Radio: Incremental Technology in Twentieth-Century America*. Baltimore: Johns Hopkins University Press, 2010.
Furr, Derek. *Recorded Poetry and Poetic Reception from Edna Millay to the Circle of Robert Lowell*. Basingstoke, UK: Palgrave Macmillan, 2010.

BIBLIOGRAPHY

Gaikowski, Richard, director. *Festival of Bards*. Canyon Cinema Co-op, 1977. VHS.

Gallo, Rubén. "Jean Cocteau's Radio Poetry." In *The Sound of Poetry / The Poetry of Sound*, edited by Marjorie Perloff and Craig Douglas Dworkin, 205-218. Chicago: University of Chicago Press, 2009.

Garber, Linda. *Identity Poetics: Race, Class, and the Lesbian-Feminist Roots of Queer Theory*. New York: Columbia University Press, 2001.

Garcia, Edgar, ed. *Jaime de Angulo, Gui Mayo, and West Coast Modernism*. Special issue of *Chicago Review* 64, no. 1/2/3 (Summer 2021).

Gilmore, Stephanie. *Groundswell: Grassroots Feminist Activism in Postwar America*. New York: Routledge, 2013.

Ginsberg, Allen. "Allen Ginsberg." Interview by David Ossman. In *Sullen Art: Recording the Revolution in American Poetry*, by Ossman, 191-224.

Ginsberg, Allen. *Collected Poems: 1947-1980*. New York: Harper Perennial, 1988.

Ginsberg, Allen. *The Fall of America: Poems of These States, 1965-1971*. San Francisco: City Lights Books, 1972.

Ginsberg, Allen. *Holy Soul Jelly Roll: Poems & Songs, 1949-1993*. Audio CD. 4 vols. Rhino, 1994.

Ginsberg, Allen. *Howl: Original Draft Facsimile, Transcript and Variant Versions, Fully Annotated by Author, with Contemporaneous Correspondence, Account of First Public Reading, Legal Skirmishes, Precursor Texts and Bibliography*. Edited by Barry Miles. New York: Harper Perennial, 2006.

Ginsberg, Allen. *Howl and Other Poems*. San Francisco: City Lights Books, 1996.

Ginsberg, Allen. *Journals Mid-Fifties, 1954-1958*. Edited by Gordon Ball. New York: HarperCollins, 1995.

Ginsberg, Allen. Letter to the editor. *San Francisco Chronicle*, July 26, 1959. Reprinted in *Howl on Trial*, edited by Morgan and Peters, 209-211.

Ginsberg, Allen. *The Letters of Allen Ginsberg*. Edited by Bill Morgan. Philadelphia: Da Capo Press, 2008.

Ginsberg, Allen. "Notes Written on Finally Recording 'Howl.'" In *A Casebook on the Beat*, edited by Thomas Parkinson, 27-30. New York: Crowell, 1961.

Gizzi, Peter. "Afterword: Jack Spicer and the Practice of Reading." In *The House That Jack Built: The Collected Lectures of Jack Spicer*, by Spicer, edited by Peter Gizzi, 173-225. Hanover, NH: Wesleyan University Press, 1998.

Golding, Alan C. Introduction. In *Sullen Art: Recording the Revolution in American Poetry*, by Ossman, 1-9.

Goldsmith, Kenneth. *Traffic*. Los Angeles: Make Now Press, 2007.

Goldsmith, Kenneth. *The Weather*. Los Angeles: Make Now Press, 2005.

Gooch, Brad. *City Poet: The Life and Times of Frank O'Hara*. New York: Harper Perennial, 2014.

Goodman, David. "Distracted Listening: On Not Making Sound Choices in the 1930s." In *Sound in the Age of Mechanical Reproduction*, edited by David Suisman and Susan Strasser, 15-46. Philadelphia: University of Pennsylvania Press, 2010.

Goodmann, Emily, Mark A. Matienzo, Shawn VanCour, and William Vanden Dries. "Building the National Radio Recordings Database: A Big Data Approach to Documenting Audio Heritage." *2019 IEEE International Conference on Big Data (Big Data)*, December 2019, 3080-3086.

Grahn, Judy. "Katharyn Machan Aal Interviews Judy Grahn on Women's Poetry Readings: History and Performance (Part 1)." 1982. *Sinister Wisdom* 25 (Winter 1984): 67-76.

Grahn, Judy. "Katharyn Machan Aal Interviews Judy Grahn on Women's Poetry Readings: History and Performance (Part 2)." 1982. *Sinister Wisdom* 27 (Fall 1984): 54-61.

Grundy, David. *A Black Arts Poetry Machine: Amiri Baraka and the Umbra Poets*. London: Bloomsbury, 2019.

Guthrie, Woody. "Ranger's Command." *Buffalo Skinners*, vol. 4 of *The Asch Recordings*, compact disc, track 1. Smithsonian Folkways Records, 1999.

Halberstam, Jack. *The Queer Art of Failure*. Durham, NC: Duke University Press, 2011.

Hamalian, Linda. *A Life of Kenneth Rexroth*. New York: Norton, 1991.

Hardt, Michael, and Antonio Negri. *Commonwealth*. Cambridge, MA: Belknap Press, 2009.

Harney, Stefano, and Fred Moten. *The Undercommons: Fugitive Planning & Black Study*. Wivenhoe, UK: Minor Compositions, 2013.

Harper, Phillip Brian. "Nationalism and Social Division in Black Arts Poetry of the 1960s." *Critical Inquiry* 19, no. 2 (1993): 234-255.

Harris, William J. "'How You Sound??' Amiri Baraka Writes Free Jazz." In *Uptown Conversation: The New Jazz Studies*, edited by Robert O'Meally, Brent Hayes Edwards, and Farah Jasmine Griffin, 312-325. New York: Columbia University Press, 2004.

Harris, William J. *The Poetry and Poetics of Amiri Baraka: The Jazz Aesthetic*. Columbia: University of Missouri Press, 1985.

Harrison, K. C. "LeRoi Jones's Radio and the Literary 'Break' from Ellison to Burroughs." *African American Review* 47, no. 2/3 (Summer/Fall 2014): 357-374.

Hemmings, Clare. *Why Stories Matter: The Political Grammar of Feminist Theory*. Durham, NC: Duke University Press, 2011.

Hemmings, Clare, and Josephine Brain. "Imagining the Feminist Seventies." In *The Feminist Seventies*, edited by Helen Graham, 11-24. York, UK: Raw Nerve Books, 2003.

Henderson, David. "Keep on Pushing (Harlem Riots / Summer / 1964)." In *Black Fire: An Anthology of Afro-American Writing*, edited by Amiri Baraka and Larry Neal, 239-244. Baltimore: Black Classic Press, 1968.

Herndon, Jim. Letter to Robin Blaser. In *The Collected Books of Jack Spicer*, by Jack Spicer, edited by Robin Blaser, 375-378. Santa Rosa, CA: Black Sparrow Press, 1996.

Hernton, Calvin. "Les Deux Megots Mon Amour." In *Light Years*, edited by Bergé, 291–306.

Hill, Lewis. "Of a Woman Screaming in the Street." *Illiterati* 4 (Summer 1945). Little Magazine Collection, Department of Special Collections, University of Wisconsin–Madison.

Hill, Lewis. "The Private Room." *Beacon: The Bulletin of the Mental Health Society of Northern California*, Fall 1952, 1–6. Box 8, folder 25, PM.

Hill, Lewis. "The Theory of Listener-Sponsored Radio." In *The Exacting Ear: The Story of Listener-Sponsored Radio, and an Anthology of Programs from KPFA, KPFK, and WBAI*, edited by Eleanor McKinney, 19–26. New York: Pantheon, 1966.

Hill, Lewis. *Voluntary Listener-Sponsorship: A Report to Educational Broadcasters on the Experiment at KPFA, Berkeley, California*. Berkeley, CA: Pacifica Foundation, 1958. Box 3, folder 4, PW.

Hilmes, Michele. *Network Nations: A Transnational History of British and American Broadcasting*. New York: Routledge, 2012.

Hilmes, Michele. *Radio Voices: American Broadcasting, 1922–1952*. Minneapolis: University of Minnesota Press, 1997.

Hinton, Laura, and Cynthia Hogue, eds. *We Who Love to Be Astonished: Experimental Women's Writing and Performance Poetics*. Tuscaloosa: University of Alabama Press, 2002.

Hlibchuk, Geoffrey. "From Typology to Topology: On Jack Spicer." *Contemporary Literature* 51, no. 2 (2010): 310–340.

Hoffman, Tyler. *American Poetry in Performance: From Walt Whitman to Hip Hop*. Ann Arbor: University of Michigan Press, 2011.

Hole, Judith, and Ellen Levine. *Rebirth of Feminism*. New York: Quadrangle Books, 1971.

Hollenbach, Lisa. "Jaime de Angulo's *Indian Tales* and KPFA-FM." *Chicago Review* 64, no. 1/2/3 (Summer 2021): 86–94.

Holman, Bob. "Just a Moment: Paul Blackburn and the Fragmentation of the New American Poetry." *Jacket*, no. 12 (July 2000). http://jacketmagazine.com/12/blac-hol.html.

Houglum, Brook. "Kenneth Rexroth and Radio Reading." *ESC: English Studies in Canada* 33, no. 4 (2007): 55–66.

Howe, Susan. "Interview with Susan Howe." Interview by Vicki Hudspith. *The Poetry Project Newsletter* 68 (October 1979): 7.

Howe, Susan. "An Interview with Susan Howe." Interview by Lynn Keller. *Contemporary Literature* 36, no. 1 (1995): 1–34.

Illiterati 4 (Summer 1945). Little Magazine Collection, Department of Special Collections, University of Wisconsin–Madison.

Isber, Caroline, and Muriel G. Cantor. *Report of the Task Force on Women in Public Broadcasting*. Washington, DC: Corporation for Public Broadcasting, 1975.

Jaffer, Frances. "For Women Poets, For Poetry: A Journal Entry." In *The Poetry Reading: A Contemporary Compendium on Language & Performance*, edited by Stephen Vincent and Ellen Zweig, 58-63. San Francisco: Momo's Press, 1981.

Jarnot, Lisa. *Robert Duncan, The Ambassador from Venus: A Biography*. Berkeley: University of California Press, 2012.

Jarolim, Edith. "Paul Blackburn." In *The Beats: Literary Bohemians in Postwar America*, edited by Ann Charters, vol. 1, 24-32. Dictionary of Literary Biography 16. Detroit: Gale, 1983.

Johnson, Phylis, and Michael C. Keith. *Queer Airwaves: The Story of Gay and Lesbian Broadcasting*. Armonk, NY: M.E. Sharpe, 2001.

Jones, Meta DuEwa. *The Muse Is Music: Jazz Poetry from the Harlem Renaissance to Spoken Word*. Urbana: University of Illinois Press, 2011.

Jong, Erica. *Half-Lives*. New York: Holt, Rinehart and Winston, 1973.

Kahn, Douglas, and Gregory Whitehead, eds. *Wireless Imagination: Sound, Radio, and the Avant-Garde*. Cambridge, MA: MIT Press, 1992.

Kane, Daniel. *All Poets Welcome: The Lower East Side Poetry Scene in the 1960s*. Berkeley: University of California Press, 2003.

Kaplan, Milton Allen. *Radio and Poetry*. New York: Columbia University Press, 1949.

Katz, Daniel. *The Poetry of Jack Spicer*. Edinburgh: Edinburgh University Press, 2013.

Keane, Damien. *Ireland and the Problem of Information: Irish Writing, Radio, Late Modernist Communication*. University Park: Pennsylvania State University Press, 2014.

Keith, Michael C. *Signals in the Air: Native Broadcasting in America*. Westport, CT: Praeger, 1995.

Keith, Michael C. *Voices in the Purple Haze: Underground Radio and the Sixties*. Westport, CT: Praeger, 1997.

Keller, Lynn, and Cristanne Miller. *Feminist Measures: Soundings in Poetry and Theory*. Ann Arbor: University of Michigan Press, 1994.

Kerouac, Jack. *The Dharma Bums*. New York: Penguin, 1958.

Kerouac, Jack. *Mexico City Blues: 242 Choruses*. 1959. New York: Grove/Atlantic, 2007.

Kerouac, Jack. *On the Road*. New York: Penguin, 1957.

Kilbane, Matthew. "Sounding Memory." In *Bernadette Mayer*, edited by Kristin Grogan and David B. Hobbs. *Post45*, July 27, 2021. https://post45.org/2021/07/sounding-memory/.

Killian, Kevin. "Jack Spicer's Secret." *Jacket*, no. 37 (2009). http://jacketmagazine.com/37/killian-spicer.shtml.

Killian, Kevin. "Spicer and the Mattachine." In *After Spicer: Critical Essays*, edited by John Emil Vincent, 16-35. Middletown, CT: Wesleyan University Press, 2011.

King, Gretchen. "History of Struggle: The Global Story of Community Broadcasting Practices, or a Brief History of Community Radio." *Westminster Papers in Communication and Culture* 12, no. 2 (2017): 18-36.

Kinnahan, Linda A. *Lyric Interventions: Feminism, Experimental Poetry, and Contemporary Discourse.* Iowa City: University of Iowa Press, 2004.

Lacey, Kate. *Feminine Frequencies: Gender, German Radio, and the Public Sphere, 1923-1945.* Ann Arbor: University of Michigan Press, 1999.

Lacey, Kate. *Listening Publics: The Politics and Experience of Listening in the Media Age.* Cambridge, UK: Polity Press, 2013.

Ladd, Jim. *Radio Waves: Life and Revolution on the FM Dial.* New York: St. Martin's Press, 1991.

Lamm, Kimberly. *Addressing the Other Woman: Textual Correspondences in Feminist Art and Writing.* Manchester: Manchester University Press, 2018.

Land, Jeff. *Active Radio: Pacifica's Brash Experiment.* Minneapolis: University of Minnesota Press, 1999.

Lasar, Matthew. "Is Pacifica Radio Worth Saving?" *The Nation,* February 11, 2015. http://www.thenation.com/article/197825/pacifica-radio-worth-saving.

Lasar, Matthew. *Pacifica Radio: The Rise of an Alternative Network.* Updated ed. Philadelphia: Temple University Press, 2000.

Lasar, Matthew. "Pacifica Radio's Crisis of Containment." In *Public Broadcasting and the Public Interest,* edited by Michael P. McCauley et al., 62-68. Armonk, NY: M.E. Sharpe, 2003.

Lasar, Matthew. *Uneasy Listening: Pacifica Radio's Civil War.* Cambridge, UK: Black Apollo Press, 2006.

Leary, Timothy. *The Politics of Ecstasy.* 4th ed. Berkeley, CA: Ronin, 1990.

Ledbetter, James. *Made Possible By . . . : The Death of Public Broadcasting in the United States.* London: Verso, 1998.

Lee, Benjamin. *Poetics of Emergence: Affect and History in Postwar Experimental Poetry.* Iowa City: University of Iowa Press, 2020.

Leonard, Keith D. "'Which Me Will Survive': Rethinking Identity, Reclaiming Audre Lorde." *Callaloo* 35, no. 3 (2012): 758-777.

Lessing, Lawrence. *Man of High Fidelity: Edwin Howard Armstrong.* New York: Bantam Books, 1969.

Lindsey, Kay. "The Black Woman as a Woman." In *The Black Woman: An Anthology,* 1970, edited by Toni Cade Bambara, 103-108. New York: Washington Square Press, 2005.

Looker, Benjamin. *BAG: "Point from Which Creation Begins": The Black Artists' Group of St. Louis.* St. Louis: Missouri Historical Society Press, 2004.

Lorde, Audre. *The Collected Poems of Audre Lorde.* New York: Norton, 1997.

Lorde, Audre. *Zami: A New Spelling of My Name: A Biomythography.* Trumansburg, NY: Crossing Press, 1982.

Lordi, Emily J. "Souls Intact: The Soul Performances of Audre Lorde, Aretha Franklin, and Nina Simone." *Women & Performance: A Journal of Feminist Theory* 26, no. 1 (2016): 55-71.

Lott, Eric. *Love and Theft: Blackface Minstrelsy and the American Working Class.* New York: Oxford University Press, 1993.

Love, Heather. "Truth and Consequences: On Paranoid Reading and Reparative Reading." *Criticism* 52, no. 2 (2010): 235–241.

Loviglio, Jason. *Radio's Intimate Public: Network Broadcasting and Mass-Mediated Democracy*. Minneapolis: University of Minnesota Press, 2005.

MacArthur, Marit J. "Monotony, the Churches of Poetry Reading, and Sound Studies." *PMLA* 131, no. 1 (2016): 38–63.

Mackey, Nathaniel. "Interview by Christopher Funkhouser." 1991. In *Paracritical Hinge: Essays, Talks, Notes, Interviews*, 251–267. Iowa City: University of Iowa Press, 2018.

Marcus, Greil. *The Old, Weird America: The World of Bob Dylan's Basement Tapes*. New York: Picador, 2001.

Matlin, Daniel. *On the Corner: African American Intellectuals and the Urban Crisis*. Cambridge, MA: Harvard University Press, 2013.

Mayer, Bernadette. "Bernadette Mayer with Susan Howe in 1979." Interview by Howe. Transcribed and edited by Michael Nardone. *Jacket2*, May 8, 2015. https://jacket2.org/interviews/bernadette-mayer-susan-howe-1979.

Mayer, Bernadette. *Eating the Colors of a Lineup of Words: The Early Books of Bernadette Mayer*. Barrytown, NY: Station Hill, 2015.

Mayer, Bernadette. *Midwinter Day*. 1982. New York: New Directions, 1999.

McClure, Michael. "Seven Things About Kenneth Rexroth." *Big Bridge* 10 (n.d.). http://www.bigbridge.org/issue10/elegymmcclure.htm.

McCoy, Brad. "Poetry on Radio." In *The Concise Encyclopedia of American Radio*, edited by Christopher H. Sterling and Cary O'Dell, 565–571. New York: Routledge, 2010.

McEnaney, Tom. *Acoustic Properties: Radio, Narrative, and the New Neighborhood of the Americas*. Evanston, IL: Northwestern University Press, 2017.

McKinney, Eleanor. "About Pacifica Radio Broadcast, 1962." In *The Exacting Ear: The Story of Listener-Sponsored Radio, and an Anthology of Programs from KPFA, KPFK, and WBAI*, edited by Eleanor McKinney, 9–17. New York: Pantheon, 1966.

McLuhan, Marshall. *Understanding Media: The Extensions of Man*. 2nd ed. New York: New American Library, 1964.

McQuiddy, Steve. *Here on the Edge: How a Small Group of World War II Conscientious Objectors Took Art and Peace from the Margins to the Mainstream*. Corvallis: Oregon State University Press, 2013.

Meltzer, David, ed. *San Francisco Beat: Talking with the Poets*. San Francisco: City Lights Books, 2001.

Merrill, James. *The Changing Light at Sandover*. Edited by J. D. McClatchy and Stephen Yenser. New York: Knopf, 2011.

Metres, Philip. *Behind the Lines: War Resistance Poetry on the American Homefront since 1941*. Iowa City: University of Iowa Press, 2007.

BIBLIOGRAPHY

Milam, Lorenzo W. *Sex and Broadcasting: A Handbook on Starting a Radio Station for the Community.* 3rd ed. Los Gatos, CA: Dildo Press, 1975.

Mill, John Stuart. "Thoughts on Poetry and Its Varieties." In *Autobiography and Literary Essays*, vol. 1 of *The Collected Works of John Stuart Mill*, edited by John M. Robson and Jack Stillinger, 341–366. Abingdon, UK: Routledge, 1981.

Mitchell, Caroline. "Re-Sounding Feminist Radio: A Journey through Women's Community Radio Archives." *Feminist Media Histories* 1, no. 4 (2015): 126–143.

Mitchell, Caroline, ed. *Women and Radio: Airing Differences.* London: Routledge, 2000.

Monroe, Harriet. "The Radio and the Poets." *Poetry* 36, no. 1 (April 1930): 32–35.

Moore, Richard O. "Berkeley/San Francisco Poetry Communities in the Early 1940s." *Talisman*, no. 10 (1993): 108–114.

Morgan, Bill, and Nancy J. Peters, eds. *Howl on Trial: The Battle for Free Expression.* San Francisco: City Lights Books, 2006.

Morris, Adalaide, ed. *Sound States: Innovative Poetics and Acoustical Technologies.* Chapel Hill: University of North Carolina Press, 1997.

Morrison, Toni. *Playing in the Dark: Whiteness and the Literary Imagination.* Cambridge, MA: Harvard University Press, 1992.

Morse, Daniel Ryan. *Radio Empire: The BBC's Eastern Service and the Emergence of the Global Anglophone Novel.* New York: Columbia University Press, 2020.

Moten, Fred. *In the Break: The Aesthetics of the Black Radical Tradition.* Minneapolis: University of Minnesota Press, 2003.

Muste, A. J. *The World Task of Pacifism.* Wallingford, PA: Pendle Hill, 1941.

Nealon, Christopher S. *The Matter of Capital: Poetry and Crisis in the American Century.* Cambridge, MA: Harvard University Press, 2011.

Nelson, Maggie. *Women, the New York School, and Other True Abstractions.* Iowa City: University of Iowa Press, 2007.

New York Art Quartet with Amiri Baraka [Leroi Jones]. *New York Art Quartet.* LP. New York: ESP Disk, 1965.

Nielsen, Aldon Lynn. *Black Chant: Languages of African-American Postmodernism.* Cambridge: Cambridge University Press, 1997.

Nielsen, Aldon Lynn. *The Inside Songs of Amiri Baraka.* Cham, Switzerland: Palgrave Macmillan, 2021.

Nielsen, Aldon Lynn. "'Now Is the Time': Voicing against the Grain of Orality." In *People Get Ready: The Future of Jazz Is Now!*, edited by Ajay Heble and Rob Wallace, 31–43. Durham, NC: Duke University Press, 2013.

Nielsen, Aldon Lynn. *Writing between the Lines: Race and Intertextuality.* Athens: University of Georgia Press, 1994.

O'Brien, Anne. "Women in Community Radio: A Framework of Gendered Participation." *Feminist Media Studies* 19, no. 6 (2019): 787–802.

O'Hara, Frank. *The Collected Poems of Frank O'Hara.* Edited by Donald Allen. Berkeley: University of California Press, 1995.

Olson, Charles. *The Maximus Poems*. Edited by George F. Butterick. Berkeley: University of California Press, 1983.

Ong, Walter J. *Orality and Literacy: The Technologizing of the Word*. New York: Routledge, 1988.

Ossman, David. *The Sullen Art: Interviews by David Ossman with Modern American Poets*. New York: Corinth Books, 1963.

Ossman, David. *The Sullen Art: Recording the Revolution in American Poetry*. Toledo, OH: University of Toledo Press, 2016.

Ossman, David. "The Sullen Art of David Ossman." *Firezine*, no. 2 (Winter 1996/1997). http://www.firezine.net/issue2/fz2_05.htm.

Ostriker, Alicia. *Stealing the Language: The Emergence of Women's Poetry in America*. Boston: Beacon Press, 1986.

Owens, Rochelle. "Les Deux Megots." In *Light Years*, edited by Bergé, 439–450.

Parker, Pat. *The Complete Works of Pat Parker*. Edited by Julie R. Enszer. Brookville, NY: A Midsummer Night's Press; Dover, FL: Sinister Wisdom, 2016.

Parker, Pat. *Movement in Black: The Collected Poetry of Pat Parker, 1961–1978*. Expanded ed. Ithaca, NY: Firebrand Books, 1999.

Parker, Pat, and Judy Grahn. *Where Would I Be without You: The Poetry of Pat Parker and Judy Grahn*. LP. Olivia Records, 1976.

Parkerson, Michelle. Untitled essay. In *Movement in Black*, by Parker, 34–36.

Parkinson, Thomas. "Phenomenon or Generation." In *A Casebook on the Beat*, edited by Thomas Parkinson, 276–290. New York: Crowell, 1961.

Parmar, Inderjeet. *Foundations of the American Century: The Ford, Carnegie, and Rockefeller Foundations in the Rise of American Power*. New York: Columbia University Press, 2012.

Patchen, Kenneth. *An Astonished Eye Looks Out of the Air*. Waldport, OR: Untide Press, 1945.

Patchen, Kenneth. "The Stars Go to Sleep So Peacefully." *Illiterati* 4 (Summer 1945). Little Magazine Collection, Department of Special Collections, University of Wisconsin–Madison.

Perloff, Marjorie. "On the Other Side of the Field." *Parnassus: Poetry in Review* 14, no. 2 (1988): 197–214.

Perloff, Marjorie. *Radical Artifice: Writing Poetry in the Age of Media*. Chicago: University of Chicago Press, 1991.

Perlow, Seth. *The Poem Electric: Technology and the American Lyric*. Minneapolis: University of Minnesota Press, 2018.

Place, Jeff, and Guy Logsdon. Liner notes. *Buffalo Skinners*, vol. 4 of *The Asch Recordings*, by Woody Guthrie, compact disc. Smithsonian Folkways Records, 1999.

Post, Steve. *Playing in the FM Band: A Personal Account of Free Radio*. New York: Viking Press, 1974.

Punday, Daniel. "The Black Arts Movement and the Genealogy of Multimedia." *New Literary History* 37, no. 4 (2006): 777–794.

Rainone, Nanette. "Men and Violence: WBAI Consciousness Raising." In *Radical Feminism*, edited by Anne Koedt, Ellen Levine, and Anita Rapone, 63–71. New York: Quadrangle Books, 1973.

Randall, Margaret. "Poet Is Who I Am: Les Deux Megots." In *Light Years*, edited by Bergé, 453–470.

Randolph, Vance. *Ozark Folksongs*. Edited by Norm Cohen. Abridged. Urbana: University of Illinois Press, 1982.

Rasula, Jed. *The American Poetry Wax Museum: Reality Effects, 1940–1990*. Urbana, IL: National Council of Teachers of English, 1996.

Reed, Anthony. *Soundworks: Race, Sound, and Poetry in Production*. Durham, NC: Duke University Press, 2021.

Rexroth, Kenneth. *An Autobiographical Novel*. New York: New Directions, 1966.

Rexroth, Kenneth. *An Autobiographical Novel*. Rev. and expanded ed. Edited by Linda Hamalian. New York: New Directions, 1991.

Rexroth, Kenneth. "Descendants of a Heroic Negro Past." *San Francisco Examiner*, August 16, 1964.

Rexroth, Kenneth. "Discordant and Cool." Review of *Mexico City Blues*, by Jack Kerouac. *New York Times Book Review*, November 29, 1959.

Rexroth, Kenneth. *Excerpts from a Life*. Edited by Bradford Morrow. Santa Barbara, CA: Conjunctions, 1981.

Rexroth, Kenneth. "From a Very Good Man." Review of *The Letters of Carl Sandburg*, edited by Herbert Mitgang. *New York Times Book Review*, September 29, 1968.

Rexroth, Kenneth. *Kenneth Rexroth and James Laughlin: Selected Letters*. Edited by Lee Bartlett. New York: W.W. Norton, 1991.

Rexroth, Kenneth. "Kenneth Rexroth on Censorship." In *Pacifica Radio: Sixty Years, Sixty Voices Collection*, compact disc 3, track 2. North Hollywood, CA: Pacifica Radio Archives, 2009.

Rexroth, Kenneth. "The Second Post-War, the Second Interbellum, the Permanent War Generation." In *The Alternative Society: Essays from the Other World*, 97–124. New York: Herder and Herder, 1970.

Rexroth, Kenneth. "Unacknowledged Legislators and Art Pour Art." In *Bird in the Bush: Obvious Essays*, 3–18. New York: New Directions, 1959.

Rich, Adrienne. *The Dream of a Common Language*. New York: Norton, 1978.

Rich, Adrienne. "When We Dead Awaken: Writing as Re-Vision." *College English* 34, no. 1 (1972): 18–30.

Rosen, Ruth. *The World Split Open: How the Modern Women's Movement Changed America*. New York: Penguin Books, 2000.

Saint-Amour, Paul K., ed. *Weak Theory*. Special issue of *Modernism/Modernity* 25, no. 3 (2018).

Saint-Amour, Paul K. "Weak Theory, Weak Modernism." *Modernism/Modernity* 25, no. 3 (2018): 437–459.

Sanders, Ed. Untitled essay. In liner notes, *Harry Smith's Anthology of American Folk Music*, by Harry Smith, 2 compact discs with 96-page liner notes book, vol. 4, 4–30. Austin: Revenant / Harry Smith Archives, 2000.

Schnitker, Laura. "Archives, Advocacy and Crowd-Sourcing: Towards a More Complete Historiography of College Radio." *Journal of Radio & Audio Media* 23, no. 2 (2016): 341–348.

Schumacher, Michael. *Dharma Lion: A Biography of Allen Ginsberg*. Expanded edition. Minneapolis: University of Minnesota Press, 2016.

Scott, Darieck. *Extravagant Abjection: Blackness, Power, and Sexuality in the African American Literary Imagination*. New York: NYU Press, 2010.

Sedgwick, Eve Kosofsky. *Epistemology of the Closet*. Berkeley: University of California Press, 1990.

Sedgwick, Eve Kosofsky. *Touching Feeling: Affect, Pedagogy, Performativity*. Durham, NC: Duke University Press, 2003.

Seita, Sophie. *Provisional Avant-Gardes: Little Magazine Communities from Dada to Digital*. Stanford, CA: Stanford University Press, 2019.

Selch, Andrea Helen. "Engineering Democracy: Commercial Radio's Use of Poetry, 1920–1946." PhD diss., Duke University, 1999.

Shaw, Lytle. *Narrowcast: Poetry and Audio Research*. Stanford, CA: Stanford University Press, 2018.

Shepperd, Josh. "The Endangered Sounds of Community Activism's Largest U.S. Archive." *Issues & Advocacy: A Roundtable of the Society of American Archivists* (blog), August 17, 2016. https://issuesandadvocacy.wordpress.com/2016/08/17/the-endangered-sounds-of-community-activisms-largest-u-s-archive/.

Shepperd, Josh. "Infrastructure in the Air: The Office of Education and the Development of Public Broadcasting in the United States, 1934–1944." *Critical Studies in Media Communication* 31, no. 3 (2014): 230–243.

Sherman, Susan. "Home: The Deux Megots, The Hardware Poets Playhouse, the Metro Café." In *Light Years*, edited by Bergé, 519–538.

Simpson, Kim. *Early '70s Radio: The American Format Revolution*. New York: Continuum, 2011.

Slotten, Richard Hugh. *Radio's Hidden Voice: The Origins of Public Broadcasting in the United States*. Urbana: University of Illinois Press, 2009.

Smethurst, James Edward. *The Black Arts Movement: Literary Nationalism in the 1960s and 1970s*. Chapel Hill: University of North Carolina Press, 2005.

Smethurst, James Edward. *Brick City Vanguard: Amiri Baraka, Black Music, Black Modernity*. Amherst: University of Massachusetts Press, 2020.

Smith, Barbara. Untitled essay. In *Movement in Black*, by Parker, 39–40.

Smith, Barbara, and Beverly Smith. "The Varied Voices of Black Women." *Sojourner* 4, no. 2 (October 1978): 5+.

Smith, Harry. *Think of the Self Speaking: Harry Smith, Selected Interviews*. Edited by Rani Singh. Seattle: Elbow / Cityful Press, 1999.

Snediker, Michael D. *Queer Optimism: Lyric Personhood and Other Felicitous Persuasions*. Minneapolis: University of Minnesota Press, 2009.

Sollors, Werner. *Amiri Baraka/LeRoi Jones: The Quest for a "Populist Modernism."* New York: Columbia University Press, 1978.

Spark, Clare. "Pacifica Radio and the Politics of Culture." In *American Media and Mass Culture: Left Perspectives*, edited by Donald Lazere, 577–590. Berkeley: University of California Press, 1987.

Spellman, A. B. *Four Lives in the Bebop Business*. New York: Pantheon Books, 1966.

Spicer, Jack. *The Collected Books of Jack Spicer*. Edited by Robin Blaser. 1975. Santa Rosa, CA: Black Sparrow Press, 1996.

Spicer, Jack. *The House That Jack Built: The Collected Lectures of Jack Spicer*. Edited by Peter Gizzi. Hanover, NH: Wesleyan University Press, 1998.

Spicer, Jack. *My Vocabulary Did This to Me: The Collected Poetry of Jack Spicer*. Edited by Peter Gizzi and Kevin Killian. Middletown, CT: Wesleyan University Press, 2008.

Spicer, Jack. *The Tower of Babel*. Hoboken, NJ: Talisman House, 1994.

Spillers, Hortense J. "Mama's Baby, Papa's Maybe: An American Grammar Book." *Diacritics* 17, no. 2 (1987): 65–81.

Spinelli, Martin. "Not Hearing Poetry on Public Radio." In *Communities of the Air: Radio Century, Radio Culture*, edited by Susan Merrill Squier, 195–214. Durham, NC: Duke University Press, 2003.

Stebbins, Gene R. "Listener-Sponsored Radio: The Pacifica Stations." PhD diss., The Ohio State University, 1969.

Sterling, Christopher H., and Michael C. Keith. *Sounds of Change: A History of FM Broadcasting in America*. Chapel Hill: University of North Carolina Press, 2008.

Stevens, Wallace. "The Idea of Order at Key West." In *The Collected Poems of Wallace Stevens*, 128–130. New York: Vintage, 1990.

Stoever, Jennifer Lynn. *The Sonic Color Line: Race and the Cultural Politics of Listening*. New York: NYU Press, 2016.

Taylor, Steven J. *Acts of Conscience: World War II, Mental Institutions, and Religious Objectors*. Syracuse, NY: Syracuse University Press, 2009.

Thomas, Lorenzo. "Alea's Children: The Avant-Garde on the Lower East Side, 1960–1970." *African American Review* 27, no. 4 (1993): 573–578.

Thomas, Lorenzo. *Extraordinary Measures: Afrocentric Modernism and Twentieth-Century American Poetry*. Tuscaloosa: University of Alabama Press, 2000.

Thomas, Lorenzo. "The Shadow World: New York's Umbra Workshop & Origins of the Black Arts Movement." *Callaloo*, no. 4 (1978): 53–72.

Tracy, James. *Direct Action: Radical Pacifism from the Union Eight to the Chicago Seven*. Chicago: University of Chicago Press, 1996.

VanCour, Shawn. *Making Radio: Early Radio Production and the Rise of Modern Sound Culture*. New York: Oxford University Press, 2018.

Verma, Neil. *Theater of the Mind: Imagination, Aesthetics, and American Radio Drama*. Chicago: University of Chicago Press, 2012.

Vickery, Ann. *Leaving Lines of Gender: A Feminist Genealogy of Language Writing*. Hanover, NH: Wesleyan University Press, 2000.

Vincent, John Emil. *Queer Lyrics: Difficulty and Closure in American Poetry*. New York: Palgrave Macmillan, 2002.

Voyce, Stephen. *Poetic Community: Avant-Garde Activism and Cold War Culture*. Toronto: University of Toronto Press, 2013.

Walker, Alice. "In Search of Our Mothers' Gardens." 1974. In *In Search of Our Mothers' Gardens: Womanist Prose*, 231–243. Orlando, FL: Houghton Mifflin Harcourt, 1983.

Walker, Jesse. *Rebels on the Air: An Alternative History of Radio in America*. New York: NYU Press, 2001.

Wallach, Glenn. "The C.O. Link: Conscientious Objection to World War II and the San Francisco Renaissance." *Brethren Life and Thought* 27, no. 1 (1982): 15–34.

Watts, Alan, Timothy Leary, Gary Snyder, and Allen Ginsberg. "The Houseboat Summit." February 1967. *The Library*. https://www.organism.earth/library/document/houseboat-summit.

Wheeler, Lesley. *Voicing American Poetry: Sound and Performance from the 1920s to the Present*. Ithaca, NY: Cornell University Press, 2008.

White, Gillian. *Lyric Shame: The "Lyric" Subject of Contemporary American Poetry*. Cambridge, MA: Harvard University Press, 2014.

Whitehead, Kim. *The Feminist Poetry Movement*. Jackson: University Press of Mississippi, 1996.

Whittington, Ian. "Radio Studies and 20th-Century Literature: Ethics, Aesthetics, and Remediation." *Literature Compass* 11, no. 9 (2014): 634–648.

Wilson, Sarah. "Gertrude Stein and the Radio." *Modernism/Modernity* 11, no. 2 (2004): 261–278.

Winkler, Harold. "Pacifica Radio—Room for Dissent." *National Association of Educational Broadcasters (NAEB) Journal* 19, no. 3 (May-June 1960): 95–103. Box 8, folder 25, PM.

Wolfson, Jessica, and Paul Lovelace, directors. *Radio Unnameable*. Kino International, 2014. DVD.

Woodard, Komozi. *A Nation within a Nation: Amiri Baraka (LeRoi Jones) and Black Power Politics*. Chapel Hill: University of North Carolina Press, 1999.

Young, Ben. Liner notes. *Call It Art*, by the New York Art Quartet. Triple Point Records, 2013. LP.

Yu, Timothy. *Race and the Avant-Garde: Experimental and Asian American Poetry since 1965*. Stanford, CA: Stanford University Press, 2009.

INDEX

Abrams, Lee, 16
activism, 11, 17, 213n74; Black women's, 176; feminist, 157–158, 162, 164–165, 166–168, 216n9; free speech, 126; gay and lesbian, 122, 204n11
Adam, Helen, 23, 107, 179, 209n15
Adorno, Theodor W., 40–41, 52, 56,
aesthetics, 3, 27, 122, 146, 156, 168–169; anti-commercial, 44, 196n52; of authenticity, 100, 169; Beat, 58; Black, 134, 152; Black Arts, 141, 154; broadcast, 60; collage, 72; depoliticized, 34; feminist, 25, 161, 222n100; folk, 65; hi-fi, 78; "hybrid highbrow," 69, 88; low-fi, 79; pacifist, 32, 36
Albee, Edward, 104
alienation, 39–40, 50, 149, 152–153
Allegra, Donna, 159, 174–175, 177, 216n16
Allen, Donald, 107, 128, 167
Allison, Raphael, 4, 215n99
Alta, 1–2
alternative media, 2, 4, 15, 22, 27, 38, 126, 151
anarchism, 31, 57, 62
Angulo, Jaime de, 43
Armstrong, Edwin Howard, 9
archives, 159, 166, 184–187; audio, 21, 25, 151; digital audio, 184–187; feminist, 158–159, 161, 163, 166, 169, 177–178; gaps within, 158, 177, 185–187; Pacifica Radio, 3, 20, 48, 96, 150, 163, 173, 177, 184, 187; precarity of, 186–187; public radio, 20
audience: broadcast, 43, 45, 60, 77, 85, 141, 156; coterie, 22, 39–47, 49, 52, 56, 60–61, 71, 74, 83, 87, 89, 126; feminization of, 156; narrowcast, 45, 136, 142; peripheral, 49; -poet relation, 14, 20–21, 47, 98, 172, 174, 183; and race, 145. *See also* listenership
authenticity, 4, 64–65, 67, 78, 100, 141, 169
authoritarianism, 37–38, 41, 52, 105–106
avant-garde, the, 3–4, 7, 18, 23, 59, 73–75, 83, 85, 122, 126, 128–129, 141–142, 149, 151, 161, 178, 209n21, 217n17, 217n19, 221n78
Avery, Gwen, 173

Baraka, Amiri, 8, 11, 21, 24, 80, 126–129, 131–132, 135, 142–150, 152–154, 184; "Bad Mouth," 150; "Black Dada Nihilismus," 144–146, 149–153; *Black Magic*, 150; *Blues People*, 11; *The Dead Lecturer*, 144–145, 149–150; *Dutchman*, 145, 149; "Heroes are Gang Leaders," 143; "In Memory of Radio," 146–148; "In One Battle," 150; *Preface to a Twenty Volume Suicide Note . . . .*, 146, 149; radio appearances of, 131–132, 143–146, 149–153, 221n41; *The System of Dante's Hell*, 149; *The Toilet*, 149; "Western Front," 150
Barlow, William, 131
Beat movement, the, 3, 11–12, 15, 23, 38, 58–59, 74–75, 77, 80, 82, 85–87, 90–94, 109, 123, 125, 127–128, 133, 147, 149–150, 184
Bergé, Carol, 109, 129n21

(243)

INDEX

Berger, Art, 135
Berkeley Poetry Conference (1965), 59, 72–73
Berkeley Renaissance, 59, 62, 66, 107–108
Bernes, Jasper, 180, 222n85
Bernstein, Charles, 20, 222n98
Berrigan, Ted, 134, 149
Berson, Ginny Z., 165
Black Artists' Group (BAG), 18
Black Arts movement, 24, 126, 141–142, 148
Black Mountain poetry, 128, 132
Black nationalism, 144–146, 175
Blackburn, Paul, 8, 24, 126–132, 134–135, 137–144, 151, 181–182, 210n22, 212n52; "The Franklin Avenue Line," 130–131; "Newsclips 2. (Dec/ 6–7).," 138–139; "The Once-Over," 131; "Pre-Lenten Gestures," 139; radio broadcasts of, 126, 130–131, 134–138, 141–142
Blackwell, Maylei, 168
Blaser, Robin, 62, 64, 91, 107
Bly, Robert, 1
Boucher, Anthony, 125
British Broadcasting Corporation (BBC), 5, 44, 47, 125, 137
broadcasting: and AM radio, 9–10, 11–13; FCC regulation of, 66, 85, 104; and FM radio, 14, 97; industry, 3, 5–7, 101, 125, 137; in poetry, 61, 77; of poetry, 21, 23, 26–27, 34, 45, 47–49, 56, 59, 178, 185; and propaganda, 40; and protest, 30; public, 10, 18, 122, 161, 190n26, 196n52; of women's liberation movement, 163–169. *See also* narrowcasting; radio; television
Brooks, Gwendolyn, 150, 215n99
Burroughs, William S., 100, 123, 134

Campbell, Timothy C., 193n64
Canadian Broadcasting Corporation (CBC), 5
Cantwell, Robert, 4, 72
Carlin, George, 104, 216n15
Cassady, Neal, 12, 92, 100, 204n19
censorship, 80, 108; of *Howl*, 59, 84, 88–105, 121, 125; self-, 102–103, 116; and sexuality, 23, 59, 84, 88–105, 108; vocalization of, 103, 105. *See also* Ginsberg, Allen; Federal Communications Commission (FCC)
Chasar, Mike, 5
civil rights movement, 11, 24, 30, 87, 124, 134, 175
Civilian Public Service camps, 26, 28–29, 31, 33, 35, 38, 193n4, 194n8, 194n15
Cocteau, Jean: *Orpheus*, 111–113, 115–116, 207n58
Cody, Fred, 1
coffeehouse reading scenes, 24, 127, 129–130, 133–134, 141, 182, 212n59
Coffield, Glenn, 31, 194n17
Cohan, George M., 63, 199n15
Cold War, the, 6, 10, 27, 47, 49, 53, 55, 69, 87, 93, 100
collectivity, 1, 4, 22, 32, 135, 164–165, 169, 173, 176–177, 183, 186–187, 198n72, 218n38
Combahee River Collective, 173
communication: crisis, 22, 27, 38–40, 100, 125; forms of, 83, 87; negation of, 120; theory, 40–41
Communications Act (1934), 10
The Compass, 32, 34
conformity, 36, 39, 50, 79
consumer culture, 6, 15, 92, 156
Corman, Cid, 6
Corporation for Public Broadcasting (CPB), 16, 216n9
Corwin, Norman, 5
coteries, 23, 107, 140, 147, 161; avant-garde, 85; of listeners, 74, 94; literary, 60, 62, 66, 94, 110; poetics,

INDEX

47, 58, 60, 74, 88, 93–94, 100, 132–133, 136–137, 147; of poets, 62, 90, 93, 108; queer, 66, 74, 94, 118, 132, 210n22
counterculture, 4, 15, 23, 27, 56, 90–91, 94, 124, 166
Creeley, Robert, 80, 84–85, 104, 113, 120, 138, 143

Davidson, Michael, 98, 107–109, 136, 141
Dellinger, Dave, 30
Dent, Tom, 134–135, 142
di Prima, Diane, 80, 129, 167
dictation: poetic, 23–24, 61, 72–73, 75, 108–110, 117, 119–121, 207n50; representation of, 111, 114; theory of, 103, 109, 111, 116
disembodiment, 52–53, 172, 177
distortion, 9, 11, 83, 187
Dorn, Ed, 1, 143
Douglas, Susan J., 11, 40, 114
Duncan, Robert, 2, 45, 53, 58, 62, 74, 80, 84, 88, 94, 106–107, 143, 194n11, 195n28
Dylan, Bob, 73, 133 140, 205n26

East Village, 123, 126, 140. *See also* Lower East Side
Eberhart, Richard, 48
Eliot, T. S., 3, 54, 70, 85, 194n11; *The Waste Land*, 70–71
Elliott, Malinké, 18
Ellison, Ralph, 7
embodiment, 21, 98, 114, 116, 136, 152
ephemerality, 17, 59, 138, 151, 163, 183
Everson, William, 8, 22–23, 26–40, 53, 58, 80; "Chronicle of Division," 29, 31, 37–38, 40, 194n11; "Now in These Days," 31; *X War Elegies*, 31, 33, 35

Fass, Bob, 14, 73, 140, 219n46
FCC v. Pacifica Foundation, 104, 216n15
Federal Communications Commission (FCC), 9–10, 14, 40, 42, 66, 85–86, 104, 151, 190n26, 191n44, 216n15
feminisms, 2, 17, 25, 155–189, 216n9, 216n16–17, 218n38; queer Black, 169, 177; second-wave, 25, 185, 216n16. *See also* poetics: feminist; poetry: feminist; poetry: women's; radio: feminist
Feminist Radio Network, 18
Ferlinghetti, Lawrence, 23, 58, 68, 73, 80, 85–86, 88, 90, 95, 102–103, 184; "The Great Chinese Dragon," 86; "The Insoluble Problem," 86; radio appearances of, 85–86, 102; "Tentative Description of a Dinner Given to Promote the Impeachment of President Eisenhower," 86
Festival of Bards (dir. Gaikowski), 2
FitzGerald, Russell, 106
Flannery, Kathryn Thoms, 166
FM radio: college, 17–19, 76, 166, 192n51; and counterculture, 9, 23, 56, 91, 125, 166; early, 2, 6–7, 10, 67; expansion of, 9–10, 137, 162; independent, 2, 10, 14, 24, 28, 33, 42, 74, 162; invention of, 9; non-commercial, 2, 7, 10, 14, 16–17, 21–22, 27, 42–43, 57, 78–79, 86, 90, 98, 102, 122, 153–154, 183; privatization of, 5, 10, 162; revolution, 6–7, 14, 16–17, 35, 37, 59, 124, 126, 162
folk music, 4, 23, 43–44, 60–74, 91, 122
Foucault, Michel, 101
Fraser, Kathleen, 134, 167, 179
Fredman, Stephen, 71–72
Fredrickson, Dave, 63–64
Freed, Alan, 11, 13
Friedan, Betty, 156, 185

García Camarillo, Cecilio, 18
gay rights movement, 94, 176, 204n11
Ginsberg, Allen, 1, 6–8, 15, 21, 23, 58, 80, 85, 88–106, 122–123, 125, 129, 137, 140, 143, 154, 179, 204n1,

(245)

INDEX

204n5, 204n19, 205n24, 205n26, 209n17; "345 W. 15th St.," 92; "In Back of the Real," 96–97; "Bayonne Turnpike to Tuscarora," 98; "Dream Record: June 8, 1955," 95; *The Fall of America: Poems of these States, 1965–1971*, 6, 92, 98, 121; "The Green Automobile," 92; *Howl*, 23, 59, 84, 88–90, 91, 96–106, 108, 121, 123, 125, 137, 184, 205n24, 206n36, 206n40–41; censorship and obscenity trial of, 59, 88, 90, 102–106, 125, 206n36, 206n40–41; composition of, 95; radio broadcast of, 88–90, 95–100, 102–105; "Kaddish," 123; "Magic Psalm," 125; radio appearances of, 1, 7–8, 15, 23, 80, 88–91, 96–100, 102–105, 123, 125, 137, 140; "A Supermarket in California," 96–97, 99; "Wichita Vortex Sutra," 92
Gioseffi, Daniela, 170
Gizzi, Peter, 108, 207n51
Goldsmith, Kenneth, 192n57, 212n53
Grahn, Judy, 18, 167, 221n65
Griffin, Susan, 165
Gross, Terry, 19
Guthrie, Woody, 71–72, 201n35

Hacker, Marilyn, 18, 167
Hagedorn, Jessica, 1–2, 80
Harris, Jana, 1–2
Harris, William J., 145–146
Hawkins, Bobbie Louise, 1
Hejinian, Lyn, 178, 182, 189n6
Henderson, David, 1, 3, 134–135, 140, 189n6, 191n37; "Keep on Pushing (Harlem Riots / Summer / 1964)," 13; radio performances of, 3, 140, 189n6
Henderson, Douglas "Jocko," 13
Hernández Cruz, Victor, 1
Herndon, James, 63–67, 69
Hernton, Calvin, 134–135
Hill, Lewis, 2, 8, 21–22, 26–55, 57–58, 60, 62, 66, 77–79, 90, 99, 102–104, 136, 165, 183–184, 194n8, 194n21, 195n37, 197n65–66, 197n68–69, 198n77, 198n3; "Experiment in the Broadcasting of Poetry," 47–48, 56; founding of Pacifica Radio, 21–22, 26, 38–43; "Of a Woman Screaming in the Street," 36, 39; pacifism of, 12, 26–30, 33–34, 36, 45, 53, 56, 79, 157, 195n37; "The Private Room," 39, 47, 50, 100; radio productions of, 47–56, 197n65–66, 197n68–69, 198n77; *Voluntary Listener Sponsorship*, 43
hippies, 15, 114, 140
Hoffman, Abbie, 140
homophobia, 93, 107, 117, 171, 194n11, 209n21, 210n22
homosexuality, 75, 93–94, 104, 106, 113. *See also* queerness
Hopkins, Vera, 218n37
Houglum, Brook, 79
Howe, Susan, 3, 8, 21, 25, 159–161, 177–185, 189n6, 213n66, 223n105–106; radio broadcasts of, 159–161, 177–185, 189n6, 213n66, 223n105–106
Hughes, Langston, 3
Hunt, Erica, 135, 221n77

identity politics, 162, 168
Illiterati, 31–38, 44
impersonality, 108–109

jazz music, 11–12, 16, 18, 24, 44, 58–59, 80, 102, 108, 118, 127, 129–130, 133–136, 138, 140–141, 150–156, 191n40
Johnson, Joseph, 134
Jong, Erica, 170–171; "Alcestis on the Poetry Circuit," 170; "On the Air," 170–171; radio appearances of, 170–171
Joyce, James: *Finnegans Wake*, 107, 117–118

(246)

INDEX

Kane, Daniel, 128, 130, 133, 201n22
Kantorowicz, Ernst, 62
Katz, Daniel, 111, 116, 207n51
Keillor, Garrison, 19
Kepler, Roy, 30, 194n10
Kerouac, Jack, 12, 80, 82, 85, 95, 100, 127, 147, 203n82, 206n44; *The Dharma Bums*, 95; *On the Road*, 12, 59, 80, 127
Keys, John, 141–142, 212n59
Kinnell, Galway, 127
KPFA-FM, 14–19, 21–23, 27, 30, 39, 42–49, 53, 56–93, 95–102, 105, 124–125, 136–137, 157, 165–169, 182, 184, 189n6, 191n41, 194n10, 196n48, 196n50, 196n52, 198n4, 199n19, 200n22, 200n32, 201n51, 203n79, 205n20, 219n47; anti-commercialism of, 44; early programming of, 44–56, 200n22; founding of, 41–43; *KPFA Program Folio*, 44–46, 53, 63, 67–68, 80–81, 96, 165; Poetry Festival, 1, 3, 184, 189n6; and the San Francisco Renaissance, 57–93
KPFK-FM, 2, 86, 124, 133, 165, 184, 187, 203n86, 211n36, 221n77
KPFT-FM, 2, 162
KRAB-FM, 17–18, 192n55
Kyger, Joanne, 1, 107

labor: in Civilian Public Service camps, 29–32, 37; feminized, 179–182, 222n85; of radio production, 164, 182–183, 223n105; unionism, 57, 80
Lacey, Kate, 49, 196n52, 197n59
Lamantia, Philip, 23, 58, 80, 95
Lamble, David, 89
Lamm, Kimberly, 173
Lasar, Matthew, 42, 69, 77, 80, 192n61, 200n32, 218n30, 218n37
Leary, Timothy, 15, 191n41
Leite, George, 43

Leonard, John, 14
Leonard, Keith D., 172, 220n59
Levertov, Denise, 80, 127, 195n28, 209n15, 209n18
Libertarian Circle, 57–58, 62, 83
Lindsey, Kay, 163, 168, 219n45
listenership: coterie, 60, 94, 161; diffuse, 59, 161
listening: close, 20–21, 52, 83, 169; and coteries, 94; counter-, 148; as feminist practice, 25; individualized, 10, 22, 27, 45; and pacifism, 37–38; as participatory, 4, 27, 52, 56; performance of, 153; poetics of, 20, 127; as rebellion, 12
literary radio studies, 4, 186, 189n11
little magazines, 31, 44, 86, 90, 124, 128–129, 132, 189n6. *See also* small press publishing
liveness, 177
localism, 17, 162–163
Lorca, Federico García, 65, 108
Lorde, Audre, 8, 25, 159, 161, 169–174, 176, 178, 216n16, 220n55, 220n62, 221n78; radio appearances of, 159, 170–173, 178, 220n62; "Who Said It Was Simple," 169, 171–172, 174
Lordi, Emily J., 176
loss, 101, 121, 162, 172, 177, 186–187
love, 11, 36, 70–71, 79, 87, 95, 97, 102, 146–147, 174, 182
Lowell, Robert, 48, 53–54, 56, 198n77–78; "At the Indian Killer's Grave," 53–54, 198n77
Lower East Side, 24, 122–154, 208n2, 209n21, 210n22, 212n59
lyric, the, 70, 74, 100, 107, 113, 156, 161, 172, 182, 198n72, 207n57, 222n91

MacAdams, Lewis, 1
MacArthur, Marit J., 205n29
Mackey, Nathaniel, 18, 135
MacLeish, Archibald, 5

(247)

INDEX

Malone, Ted, 5
Marcus, Greil, 72, 201n38
materiality: phonic, 21, 82, 120; somatic, 110
Mayer, Bernadette, 8, 25, 161, 177–182, 222n83, 222n85; *Memory*, 180, 222n83; *Midwinter Day*, 179–180; radio appearances of, 177–182; "Simplicities are Glittering," 180
Mayhall, Jane, 170
McCarthyism, 47
McClure, Michael, 84, 95, 209n17
McEnaney, Tom, 12
McKinney, Eleanor, 42, 45, 62, 84, 96, 124, 165
McLuhan, Marshall, 21, 83
Meltzer, David, 84
Mercer, William "Rosko," 14, 191n40
Merrill, James, 207n50
Metres, Philip, 34–35, 38, 195n26
Milam, Lorenzo, 17
Miles, Josephine, 23, 197n69
Mill, John Stuart, 100
Millay, Edna St. Vincent, 5
Miller, Henry, 36
modernism, 3
modernist studies, 5, 161
Monroe, Harriet, 5–6
Moore, Marianne, 48
Moore, Richard, 22, 42–44, 53–55, 58, 62–63, 65, 69, 78
Morgan, Robin, 159, 161, 170, 216n16, 220n53
Moten, Fred, 152
Muste, A. J., 30

narrowcasting, 126, 134, 136–137, 142, 182, 212n48
National Committee on Conscientious Objectors (NCCO), 28
National Public Radio (NPR), 16–19, 184, 211n86

New American Poetry, 3, 8, 24, 87, 91, 127–131, 136, 143, 146, 193n62, 209n17
New Criticism, 3, 22, 35, 48, 50, 52–53, 63, 85
New Left, the, 4, 69, 166
New York School, 128, 130, 210n22
Nielsen, Aldon Lynn, 129, 142, 151, 153, 210n30
Nomland, Kemper, 31–32, 34–36
nostalgia, 87, 127, 138, 147, 154, 222n100

obscenity, 24, 66, 85, 88, 90, 102–108, 117–119, 151, 184, 206n39, 216n15
O'Hara, Frank, 132–133, 147, 149, 190n24, 210n22; "Personal Poem," 132–133, 147; "Personism: A Manifesto," 133; "Radio," 190n24
Olson, Charles, 143, 212n59
orality, 20–21, 63, 98, 135, 193n62
Orlovsky, Peter, 1, 95, 123
Ortiz, Simon J., 1, 221n78
Ossman, David, 123, 125, 128–133, 137, 141, 143, 146–147, 183, 208n6, 209n17, 211n36; radio broadcasts of, 125, 128–133, 137, 141, 143, 146–147, 183, 209n17

Pacifica Foundation, 10, 26, 41–42, 67, 104, 187, 197n85
Pacifica Radio, 2–3, 7–8, 10, 14, 16–17, 19–20, 21–27, 30, 34, 38–58, 62, 73–74, 86–91, 93, 96–98, 104, 122–125, 128, 133, 136–137, 146, 149–151, 157–158, 161–163, 165–167, 177–178, 182, 184–187, 192–193n61, 196n49, 218n37
pacifism, 12, 26–38, 45, 53, 56, 79, 157, 194n11, 195n37; World War II conscientious objection, 21, 26–30
Parker, Pat, 8, 25, 161, 165, 169, 173–177, 220n65, 221n70; "Let Me Come to You Naked," 174; "Movement in Black," 174–176; radio appearances

of, 174–177; "There is a Woman in this Town," 174–175
Parkerson, Michelle, 174
Parkinson, Thomas, 58–59
Patchen, Kenneth, 31, 35–36, 80, 94; "The Stars Go to Sleep So Peacefully," 36
Patterson, Charles, 135
performance, 2–3, 7, 20, 122, 143, 186; of Baraka, 146–153; of Dylan, 72; embodied, 3, 98; of Ginsberg, 95–99, 106, 205n29; of Keys, 141; of Lorde, 220n62; of Parker, 174–177; public, 2, 59; of Rexroth, 80; of Spicer, 73; spoken word, 2
Perloff, Marjorie, 210n25
Piercy, Marge, 165
Plath, Sylvia, 167, 170, 220n53
poetics: aural, 20, 24, 126, 135, 141; of the common, 158; coterie, 47, 58, 74, 88, 94, 108, 132–133, 136–137; as "counterpunching," 23, 73; of dictation, 72–73, 108, 111, 207n50; feminist, 156, 183; impersonal, 110, 115, 119; of interference, 24; modernist, 52; oral, 3, 8, 20, 24–25, 60, 87, 98, 128, 138, 183; projective, 146, 152; queer, 23, 93, 122, 207n50, 207n57; radiophonic, 20–25; telepathic, 23
poetry: apolitical, 35; experimental, 22, 27, 126, 128, 178, 209n17; feminist, 157–158, 161, 163, 166–167, 174, 177–178, 185, 216n17; and new media, 4, 63; oral, 7–8, 23, 136; pacifist, 27; and protest, 2, 104, 166; queer, 22, 93, 122, 207n50, 207n57; women's, 158, 161, 166–170, 173, 178, 219n42
Poetry Project, the, 24, 124, 126, 142–143
Pound, Ezra, 43, 84
programming: Black, 135; feminist, 17, 25, 157, 159, 161–170; folk music, 69, 73; gay, 169; lesbian, 17, 169; Third World, 25, 169
protest, 1–2, 4, 7, 30, 32–33, 104, 157, 163, 166, 171. *See also* activism; poetry: protest
Public Broadcasting Act (1967), 16
public poet, 77, 87, 93. *See also* poetry
Punday, Daniel, 214n86

queerness, 8, 23–24, 66, 71, 74, 89, 92–94, 97, 106, 118, 120–122, 125, 132, 161, 169, 175–177, 185; and desire, 26, 106, 111, 121; and listening, 97; and obscenity, 104, 106; and poetics, 23, 93, 122, 207n50, 207n57; and sociality, 66, 74, 94, 118, 132, 161; as static, 106–122

race, 11, 72, 129, 131, 145, 221n78
racism, 11, 13, 80, 163–164, 171, 175, 221n70
radio: alternative, 19, 62, 91; anti-commercialism of, 44, 79; Black-appeal, 11, 13, 191n40; commercial, 2, 5–9, 11, 17, 27, 38–39, 44–45, 78, 89, 92, 98, 124, 136; community, 17–19, 154, 157, 159, 163, 186, 192n49, 216n9; as "counterpunching," 89–122; drama, 5, 48–51, 53, 159; feminist, 155–188; freeform, 7, 14, 16–17, 24, 73, 140, 168; and free speech, 23, 66, 91, 102–104, 124, 126, 142; as poetic motif, 2–3, 23–24, 75, 91–93, 98–102, 108–122, 126–127, 139, 155, 207n51, 207n52; preservation, 163, 186–187; progressive rock, 6, 14, 154; and queer connection, 93, 121; and regionalism, 74–75; transistor, 11–12, 59, 106, 109, 114, 116, 138; and war propaganda, 92. *See also* broadcasting; FM radio; Pacifica Radio

(249)

Rainone, Nanette, 157, 163–164, 167, 218n30, 219n42
Reed, Anthony, 153
Reed, Ishmael, 1, 3, 134, 221n78
Rexroth, Kenneth, 3, 8, 23, 56–60, 62, 72–90, 94–95, 125, 136, 182, 184, 189n6, 194n11, 198n78, 198n4, 201n38, 201n48, 202n62, 203n82; radio broadcasts of, 75–76, 78–87, 202n62, 203n86
Rich, Adrienne, 25, 155–158, 178; "Cartographies of Silence," 155–156
rock 'n' roll, 6, 11, 13, 44, 171
Rukeyser, Muriel, 43, 167
Rustin, Bayard, 30, 43, 198n3
Rutlin, Ajulé, 18

Saint-Amour, Paul K., 162–163, 217n18
San Francisco Renaissance, 1, 3, 21–23, 26–27, 29, 35, 42 57–88, 91, 124, 128
Sanchez, Sonia, 18, 167
Sandburg, Carl, 3, 201n38
Sedgwick, Eve Kosofsky, 94, 162
Seeger, Pete, 72–73
separatism, 158, 161, 168–169; lesbian-feminist, 158
sexism, 80, 164, 171, 209n21
sexuality, 23, 103, 108, 117, 145, 193n65. *See also* homosexuality; queerness
Shaw, Lytle, 6, 82, 136, 182, 211n47
Sheets, Kermit, 31–32, 34, 38
silence, 9, 23, 41, 44, 112, 144, 149, 155–156, 166–167, 177, 196n52
Six Gallery reading (1955), 59, 95–96
small press publishing, 26, 31–32, 34–35, 44, 90, 124, 129, 133, 185. *See also* little magazines
Smethurst, James, 146, 214n79
Smith, Barbara, 174
Smith, Harry, 71–73
Snediker, Michael, 109, 116
Snyder, Gary, 15, 80, 95
Soldofsky, Alan, 1

Spellman, A. B., 8, 135, 140, 142
Spicer, Jack, 3, 8, 23–24, 43, 47, 58, 60–77, 84, 87–91, 93–95, 106–112, 114–119, 121–122, 182, 189n6, 194n11, 199n10, 199n19, 200n27, 207n49; *Admonitions*, 107, 118–119; *After Lorca*, 65, 106–108; "An Apocalypse for Three Voices," 60–61; "The Book of Galahad," 70; and "counterpunching," 8, 23, 62, 73, 89, 94, 105, 109, 114, 117, 122; dictation in, 23–24, 61, 72–75, 108–111, 114, 116–117, 119–121, 207n50, 207n52; *The Heads of the Town Up to the Aether*, 92, 112, 119; *The Holy Grail*, 70, 72, 117, 201n35; "Homage to Creeley," 113, 120; *Language*, 8, 70, 92, 109, 114, 119, 121; *Letters to James Alexander*, 110, 113; "The Poet and Poetry: A Symposium," 63; radio broadcasts of, 61–69, 72, 74, 189n6, 199n19, 199–200n21, 200n22; "A Textbook of Poetry," 119–120; *The Tower of Babel*, 75–78; "Transformations II," 70, 200n34
Spillers, Hortense, 173
spoken word performance. *See* performance: spoken word
spontaneity, 3, 13, 67, 79, 92, 98, 148, 180
Stevens, Wallace, 48, 51, 53; "The Idea of Order at Key West," 48, 51, 198n72
surveillance, 23, 37, 94, 100, 134

tape recorder, 4, 6, 15, 78, 83, 98, 134–140, 179–181
"tapevoice," 4, 98, 136–137, 178, 181
Telecommunications Act (1996), 19
television, 3–6, 9–10, 15–16, 43, 101, 127, 136, 166, 190n12, 190n13, 190n26, 196n48, 212n48
Thomas, Lorenzo, 3, 135, 149
Tillery, Linda, 173, 175
Touré, Askia M., 134

INDEX

Tracy, James, 36, 198n3
Tucker, Sophie, 63, 199n15

Umbra poets, 134–135
Untide Press, 28–29, 31, 33–35, 37
U.S. broadcasting industry, 3, 5–6, 8, 125

Varied Voices of Black Women, 169, 173–177
ventriloquy, 11, 13, 138
Vickery, Ann, 178, 183, 223n102
Vietnam War, 1, 25, 35, 92, 195n28
virtuality, 59, 83, 121
voice: disembodied, 52–53, 172; embodied, 2, 52–53. *See also* "tapevoice"
Voyce, Stephen, 158, 217n17

Wakoski, Diane, 134, 209n17, 212n59
Waldman, Anne, 167, 179
Waldport Fine Arts group, 27, 33, 56, 194n15

Walker, Alice, 167, 170
Wallace, Jo Anne, 1
War Resisters League, 28, 195n26
Warhol, Andy, 134
Watkins, Mary, 173, 175, 221n65
Watts, Alan, 15
WBAI-FM, 2, 17, 14, 21, 24–25, 73, 84, 104, 122–154, 157–171, 173–174, 178–179, 182–184
weak theory, 162–163, 217n21
Whitehead, Kim, 161, 166, 216n17
Winters, Yvor, 28
Witt-Diamant, Ruth, 94, 203n79
Woodcock, George 31, 36
World War II, 26, 29, 36, 40. *See also* pacifism: World War II conscientious objection
WPFW-FM, 2, 162, 218n38

Yu, Timothy, 221n78

CONTEMPORARY NORTH AMERICAN POETRY SERIES

Bodies on the Line: Performance and the Sixties Poetry Reading
by Raphael Allison

Industrial Poetics: Demo Tracks for a Mobile Culture
by Joe Amato

What Are Poets For? An Anthropology of Contemporary Poetry and Poetics
by Gerald L. Bruns

Reading Duncan Reading: Robert Duncan and the Poetics of Derivation
edited by Stephen Collis and Graham Lyons

Postliterary America: From Bagel Shop Jazz to Micropoetries
by Maria Damon

Among Friends: Engendering the Social Site of Poetry
edited by Anne Dewey and Libbie Rifkin

Translingual Poetics: Writing Personhood Under Settler Colonialism
by Sarah Dowling

Purple Passages: Pound, Eliot, Zukofsky, Olson, Creeley, and the Ends of Patriarchal Poetry
by Rachel Blau DuPlessis

On Mount Vision: Forms of the Sacred in Contemporary American Poetry
by Norman Finkelstein

Writing Not Writing: Poetry, Crisis, and Responsibility
by Tom Fisher

Form, Power, and Person in Robert Creeley's Life and Work
edited by Stephen Fredman and Steve McCaffery

Redstart: An Ecological Poetics
by Forrest Gander and John Kinsella

Jorie Graham: Essays on the Poetry
edited by Thomas Gardner
University of Wisconsin Press, 2005

Gary Snyder and the Pacific Rim: Creating Countercultural Community
by Timothy Gray

Urban Pastoral: Natural Currents in the New York School
by Timothy Gray

Nathaniel Mackey, Destination Out: Essays on His Work
edited by Jeanne Heuving

Poetry FM: American Poetry and Radio Counterculture
by Lisa Hollenbach

Poetics and Praxis 'After' Objectivism
edited by W. Scott Howard and Broc Rossell

Ecopoetics: Essays in the Field
edited by Angela Hume and Gillian Osborne

Racial Things, Racial Forms: Objecthood in Avant-Garde Asian American Poetry
by Joseph Jonghyun Jeon

We Saw the Light: Conversations between the New American Cinema and Poetry
by Daniel Kane

Ghostly Figures: Memory and Belatedness in Postwar American Poetry
by Ann Keniston

Poetics of Emergence: Affect and History in Postwar Experimental Poetry
by Benjamin Lee

Contested Records: The Turn to Documents in Contemporary North American Poetry
by Michael Leong

History, Memory, and the Literary Left: Modern American Poetry, 1935–1968
by John Lowney

Paracritical Hinge: Essays, Talks, Notes, Interviews
by Nathaniel Mackey

Behind the Lines: War Resistance Poetry on the American Homefront since 1941
by Philip Metres

Poetry Matters: Neoliberalism, Affect, and the Posthuman in Twenty-First Century North American Feminist Poetics
by Heather Milne

Hold-Outs: The Los Angeles Poetry Renaissance, 1948–1992
by Bill Mohr

In Visible Movement: Nuyorican Poetry from the Sixties to Slam
by Urayoán Noel

Reading Project: *A Collaborative Analysis of William Poundstone's* Project for Tachistoscope {Bottomless Pit}
by Jessica Pressman, Mark C. Marino, and Jeremy Douglass

Frank O'Hara: The Poetics of Coterie
by Lytle Shaw

Renegade Poetics: Black Aesthetics and Formal Innovation in African American Poetry
by Evie Shockley

Questions of Poetics: Language Writing and Consequences
by Barrett Watten

Radical Vernacular: Lorine Niedecker and the Poetics of Place
edited by Elizabeth Willis